66-28106 (10-20-66)

TWENTIETH CENTURY VIEWS

The aim of this series is to present the best in
contemporary critical opinion on major authors,
providing a twentieth century perspective on
their changing status in an era of profound
revaluation.

Maynard Mack, *Series Editor*
Yale University

VIRGIL

A COLLECTION OF CRITICAL ESSAYS

Edited by

Steele Commager

Prentice-Hall, Inc.  *Englewood Cliffs, N. J.*
A SPECTRUM BOOK

Current printing (last number):

10 9 8 7 6 5 4 3 2 1

Contents

Introduction

by Steele Commager

Mantua me genuit, Calabri rapuere, tenet nunc
Parthenope: cecini pascua, rura, duces.

These lines constitute the epitaph on Virgil's supposed tomb
at Naples. *Cecini pascua, rura, duces:* "I sang of pastures, of culti-
vated fields, and of rulers." So summarized, the progression from
Eclogues (37 B.C.) to *Georgics* (29 B.C.) to *Aeneid* (19 B.C.) seems
eminently logical. In terms of subject, Virgil's work proposes a miniature of the evolution of civilization, from shepherds to farmers to
warriors. In terms of style, he advances from the lesser genre to the
greater: from pastoral to didactic to epic. So compelling did the
logic of such a transition seem, that the sixteenth century Italian
humanists generalized it into the prescribed pattern of development
for an epic poet. One may doubt that Virgil had any thoughts of an
Aeneid at the time of the *Eclogues;* yet certain themes persist in all
three genres. One of the most obvious, as it is one of the most important, is that of death and rebirth, of a flawed past and a redeemed future.

The fourth, or Messianic, Eclogue has received an elegant suffi-
ciency of scholarly discussion, and there is no need to rehearse the
poem's description of a mysterious child during whose lifetime the
Golden Age will return: wars shall cease, the sin (*scelus*) of the
Roman people be redeemed, and a superabundant fertility possess
the fields. We might, however, notice its closeness, though in inverted form, to the first Eclogue, a dialogue between Tityrus and
Meliboeus. Meliboeus, dispossessed as a result of the civil wars, is
compelled to leave his fields in search of a new home: "such disorder is there throughout the land" (*E.* 1.12). One of the goats he
leads with him has just lost her kids, after being forced to bear them
upon the bare rocks, where they died. War, disorder, and frustrated
fertility are the heritage of the past. Tityrus, almost certainly a
mask for Virgil himself, survives to sing and pasture his oxen as

1

before only through the intervention of the god-like Octavian: "O Meliboeus, it was a god who bestowed this peace upon us" (*E.* 1.6). Similarly, in the ninth Eclogue, it is the star representing the deified soul of Octavian's adoptive father, Julius Caesar, that makes the fields fertile and gives a promise of continuity: "Graft your pears, Daphnis, your granchildren shall gather fruits of your planting" (*E.* 9.50).

The benevolent aspect assigned to Julius Caesar and to Octavian, as well as the apparently specific details of the child savior in the fourth Eclogue, might be taken to indicate that Virgil actually believed a transformation for the better to be imminent in Rome's political future. Yet it is difficult not to wonder whether, in the turbulent period of the early thirties, Virgil may not have felt that the only real escape from the present lay in the world of verse. The *Eclogues,* despite their contemporary political and social allusions, are essentially an attempt to substitute a world of imagination for that of fact. Thus, in the first Eclogue it is only Tityrus, the poet, who can escape the destruction around him to sing at his leisure in the shade, *lentus sub umbra* (E. 1.4). In the ninth Eclogue, Menalcas, in whose features also we may discern those of Virgil, is spoken of as "strewing the turf with flowering grass, and curtaining the springs with green shade" (*E.* 9.20). Is the phrase simply a literary elegancy, meaning no more than "to sing of the flowering grass and of the springs with their green shade?" Or is it not also a precise description of the landscape of the *Eclogues,* one which the poet's *fiat* creates—he "curtains the springs with shade"—and of which the poet is the only true inhabitant? The last lines of the tenth Eclogue may suggest the autonomous nature of the *Eclogues* as a whole. "Let us rise: the shade is often harmful to singers:" *surgamus: solet esse gravis cantantibus umbra* (*E.* 10.75). The line may be no more than a recommendation that the shepherds return home, now that night is falling. But perhaps Virgil also implies that the time has come to move on to a larger genre: *surgamus.* Shade, characteristic element of the pastoral landscape that the poet creates, has at last proven too private, too isolating.

Certainly the *Georgics,* published some eight years later, are less exclusive. The relationship between man and his environment in the *Eclogues* is typified by Silenus, in the sixth Eclogue: to his songs the wild beasts keep time, and the stiff oaks nod in rhythm. In the *Georgics* it is not poetry that relates man to nature, but labor. Through unremitting effort an ordered fertility can be imposed upon the fields: its tacit condition is peace. The end of the first Georgic resumes the theme of the fourth Eclogue, though with a different emphasis. It is now not the Golden Age, but the Iron Age of civil war that is described at length; hope for a reborn future is confined to the mention of a youth, clearly Octavian: "Gods of my country . . . at least do not prevent this youth from rescuing a world uptorn! We have already paid enough with our blood for the perjury of Laomedon at Troy" (*G.* 1.498-502). Virgil's concern—one shared by his contemporary and friend, Horace—with the idea of an original sin, divine vengeance as expressed by the civil wars, and finally a rebirth under a new saviour, suggests a way of looking at the *Georgics,* particularly the last half of the fourth book. The *Georgics,* in the broadest terms, deal with the rebirth of the land, a land depleted by the constant battles of the last hundred years. The peaceful fertility that Virgil evokes will itself be the sign that the guilty heritage of the Trojan-Roman people has been redeemed under Octavian, who, the baroque proem of the first Georgic assures us, will soon himself become a god. The human qualities of the bees described in the fourth Georgic are apparent, not to say ostentatious. Commentators are fond of attributing these anthropomorphic passages to Virgil's desire to "enliven the narrative." Yet there are more precise implications. The characteristics of the bees are those of the Roman ideal: courage, industry, loyalty, and discipline. They, alone of living creatures, lead their life under set laws; they alone have a homeland, *patriam,* and fixed gods, *certos penatis* (*G.* 4.153ff.); most remarkable of all is the surpassing love they bear their leader. While the king is safe, all are of one mind; once he is lost they turn upon one another, tearing down the hive and the stored honey (*G.* 4.22ff.) . The parallel with the description of civil war at the end of the first Georgic has gone oddly unremarked, yet it seems obvious enough to require little explication. We need only remember the reference there to Caesar's death, and the chaos that followed: "And so, Philippi saw Roman armies clash with one another once again" (*G.* 1.489-90).

Professor Palmer Bovie has suggested that an analogy obtains between the royal state of the bees and the new Imperial province of Egypt. Just as honey is valuable to the farmer, so Egypt was a source of revenue to Octavian; and just as the farmer is adjured to take special care of the management of the hive, so Octavian took special pains to insure the orderly administration of Egypt. The parallel is ingenious, but there may also be a less detailed analogy to be drawn. The tale of the beekeeper Aristaeus at the end of the fourth Georgic prescribes a method of generating from a bullock's carcass a new hive of bees in the unhappy event that the original hive has perished. It is, in other words, the description in miniature of how to recreate a state, an ideal polity. An epic invocation to the Muse opens the story; we first see Aristaeus in despair at the loss of his former hive, and prepared to relinquish the whole venture of beekeeping. (We may recall our first view of Aeneas, despairing that he too had not died beneath the walls of Troy when it fell.) Aristaeus complains to his mother, a sea-goddess, who receives him beneath the waves; and, after some initial difficulties, he learns the reason for his hive's failure. Earlier, Aristaeus, pursuing Eurydice with an eye to rape, had been unwittingly responsible for her death; for this reason divine vengeance, *numinis irae,* pursues him now. *Tantaene animis caelestibus irae?* ("Do heavenly minds feel such wrath?" *A.* 1.11) So ends the invocation of the *Aeneid.* After sacrifices to appease the wrath of the goddesses of the wood, and of Eurydice, the curse is removed from Aristaeus; from the bodies of the sacrificed bulls, bees come swarming forth to hang, like fertile grape clusters, from the boughs above. The fourth Georgic ends with a brief epilogue, recalling us to the events of the outside world. "Thus I sang of the care of fields, of herds, and of trees, while great Caesar thundered in war by the deep Euphrates, and, a victor, gave laws to willing nations, and made his way to heaven" (*G.* 4.559-562). The final phrase reminds us that Aristaeus too was destined for Olympus. It would be easy to point out specific parallels between Aristaeus and Aeneas and Octavian. A minor one is the fact that Aristaeus is the son of Apollo, Octavian's patron god; the title Aristaeus uses in referring to his father is *Thymbraeus,* a word found elsewhere in Virgil only in the third Book of the *Aeneid,* where *Thymbraeus Apollo* prophesies to Aeneas Rome's future greatness under Aeneas' descendants, among whom Octavian numbered himself. Or we might notice that the crime responsible for the hive's destruction was an attempted rape; just so was the fall of Troy precipitated by Paris' rape of Helen; just so was Actium, the culminating battle of Rome's civil wars, connected with Antony's adulterous affair with Cleopatra. Yet such specific parallels are unnecessary. What is more important is the similarity of general pattern, which bears witness to the hold that the theme had on Virgil's imagination. In the myth of a faulted past, destruction, and rebirth under a semidivine leader, Virgil's generation could find a parable for its own experience, and for its hopes as well.

The Aristaeus episode ending the *Georgics* is sometimes termed an epyllion, a tiny epic. Now it remained only for Virgil to give the myth definitive form. What is the *Aeneid,* in crudest outline, but the story of a new beginning? But in outline only—for we remember that the story of Aristaeus includes the story of Orpheus, and it is suggestive that Virgil was the first to conflate the two myths. Orpheus is almost the archetype of the man who, overcome by his emotions, could not help looking back. Losing all that he had gained, he spent the rest of his life in vain laments over his dead wife Eurydice, over a vanished past. Aeneas in a sense combines the figures of Aristaeus and Orpheus. Cast in the role of an Aristaeus, or an Augustus, the creator of a new state, he is also all too human in his instincts. As Thomas Greene, author of a recent book on the epic, remarks in another context, "Aeneas has to learn to stop looking over his shoulder." Nor is it, for Aeneas, an easy thing to learn. In mythical or historical terms Troy may represent an infected inheritance; but in human terms it means home, affection, and a fixed identity. Two of Horace's Odes, each clearly written with an eye on Virgil, have a particular interest when read in these terms. In the third Roman Ode (*C*. 3.3), probably written after the *Aeneid* was well under way, Juno, on the occasion of Romulus' deification, cautions the Romans against any attempt to return to their original home, Troy. To do so would demonstrate an excess of piety—*nimium pii:* the adjective is that which habitually characterizes *pius Aeneas.* Only, she warns them, if they renounce the past entirely will she abate her anger, admit Romulus to divinity, and insure Rome's future glory. Here, if we substitute Aeneas for Romulus, is the plot of the *Aeneid.* Yet for a more suggestive, if more oblique, view of Aeneas' situation it is necessary to look to a later Ode, *C*. 1.24, written to Virgil on the occasion of the death of their common friend Quintilius, in 24 B.C. "Quintilius died wept by many good men, but by no one more than you, Virgil. Pious, alas, in vain (*tu frustra pius heu*), you demand Quintilius back from the gods, he who was granted to life on no such terms. What if you were to play the lyre even more tunefully than Thracian Orpheus, would then the life return to that bloodless shade?" The example of Orpheus—Horace even imitates a line from the Orpheus episode of the fourth Georgic—is calculated to remind Virgil of the uselessness of an overattachment to what once was. Similarly, Horace's coupling of *frustra* and *pius* suggests that Virgil is imitating, to no profitable end, the instinctive piety of Aeneas towards a vanished past.

Certainly the early books of the *Aeneid* show Aeneas in that light; yet he is not, as is often claimed, a static character. It is precisely his shift from an allegiance, a piety, to the Trojan past to an allegiance to the Roman future that the *Aeneid* charts. (So much is implicit in the poem's opening sentence, which moves, as Aeneas himself will, from "the shores of Troy," *Troiae . . . ab oris,* to "the walls of lofty Rome," *altae moenia Romae.*) Consider Aeneas' first words: "O three and four times blest were those fated to fall before their fathers' eyes beneath the high walls of Troy!" (*A.* 1.94-96) Imitating Odysseus' speech in the fifth Odyssey (306ff.), Virgil makes a significant change. Odysseus wishes only that he might have died at Troy, instead of at sea, so that he might receive fitting funeral rites, and have the Achaeans spread his glory. Aeneas is concerned not with glory, but with a death among his companions, in known surroundings—for we must remember everywhere that, as Dryden observed, where Odysseus is going home, Aeneas is leaving it behind. Throughout the second Book, the storming of Troy, Aeneas wishes only to die with his city: "Let us rush into battle and die," he cries (*A.* 2.353), in the very tones of a Homeric warrior. But to be an epic hero, living—and dying—for his own glory, is no longer enough. Aeneas is not fated to achieve undying renown as a dead Trojan, like Hector or Sarpedon; rather he must live on until he kills Troy in himself. Thus it is that at one stage in the battle he dons Greek armor, only to find himself killing Trojans in the confusion; thus too, at one point the Trojans hurl down their own city walls in an attempt to beat back the invading Greeks. The paradox of Troy's destruction and re-creation assumes its most concise form toward the second Book's end in the flames that play about the head of Aeneas' son Ascanius. Fire, the element by which Troy was destroyed, now reappears as a harmless omen, suggestive of the new future awaiting Aeneas' descendants. The closing picture of the Book shows us Aeneas in a characteristic posture, bearing his father, the weight of the past, upon his back, and leading his son, the hope of Rome's future, forward by the hand. The fact that during the battle Aeneas loses his wife Creusa rather carelessly, as it seems, has often been urged against him, but the event's justification lies in the logic of the poem as a whole. As Aeneas' wife, Creusa represents all the stability of home. Her function in the life Aeneas must lead is over once she has borne him a son, thus insuring the perpetuation of his descendants, the Romans. And, fittingly, it is Creusa, at the Book's close, who appears to Aeneas in a vision, urging him on to Rome.

The third Book, the description of Aeneas' wanderings, is one of mysterious prophecies, half truths, and thwarted attempts; the atmosphere in part creates, in part reflects, the bewilderment of Aeneas himself. Equally important, the Book illustrates the impossibility of any return to the Trojan past. Though it opens with a farewell to the land "where once was Troy" (*ubi Troia fuit, A.* 3.11), one suspects that the verb, for Aeneas at least, does not really indicate a finished action; it is, we might say, a Greek perfect. He first attempts to settle in Thrace, formerly allied with Troy, only to find that its ruler has gone over to the Greeks. Polydorus, a son of king Priam in whom Priam attempted to preserve the Trojan line, has been slaughtered there. The episode's significance is clear. Proceeding to Crete, Aeneas builds a city and calls it Pergamea, or Troy. His followers rejoice in the familiar name—and a plague descends upon the city. The Delian Apollo's ambiguous prophecy of a new homeland ("Seek out your ancient mother," he had counselled them, *A.* 3.96) was not to be so easily fulfilled. The Trojans might better have taken a lesson from Apollo's shrine itself, for the island of Delos had wandered over the sea for many years before the god gave it a permanent home in one place. The major incident of the Book is the visit to Andromache, formerly Hector's wife, and her new husband Helenus. Here the impossibility of a merely retrospective life becomes most apparent. Helenus and Andromache have built a miniature Troy, complete with an imitation citadel and a brook named after the Xanthus river—but the brook is dry. Aeneas' farewell to Helenus and Andromache sets the terms of the contrast between their destiny and his own: *Vivite felices* . . . "May you live happy, you whose destiny is completed; we are called on from one fate to the next" (*A.* 3.493-4). Helenus and Andromache seem happy, *felices,* to Aeneas, in that they have found a permanent home; but *felices* in the word's root sense of "fertile" they can never be. They are among the living dead. Childless, Andromache still refers to herself, rather tactlessly perhaps, as the wife of Hector, and she still sacrifices at his empty tomb, *inanem tumulum.*

Infandum, regina, iubes renovare dolorem: "Unspeakable, O Queen, is the grief you bid me renew" (*A.* 2.3). So begins Aeneas' account of the fall of Troy and his subsequent wanderings. It is appropriate that Dido's palace should be the setting for his narrative, for Dido's Carthage will prove to be a new, and the most seductive, alternative to Aeneas' destined future. We see him first in Carthage gazing nostalgically at the temple frescoes picturing the fall of Troy: "He fed his mind upon the empty (*inani*) picture, with many a groan" (*A.* 1.464-65). *Inani*—the word is the same as that used of Hector's cenotaph, still piously tended by Andromache, and it has here the same implied reference to the emptiness of the whole Trojan past. It is as the ruler of a kingdom that Dido first appears to Aeneas. "Fortunate people, whose walls are already rising!" (*A.* 1.437) Such was Aeneas' cry upon seeing Carthage; he is captivated as much with Dido's city as with herself. She offers him, in effect, an already achieved destiny, and it is when Aeneas is happily assisting in founding the towers of Dido's new city that Mercury appears to urge him on toward his own. As he descends from heaven, Mercury passes Atlas, Aeneas' ancestor, who supports the sky upon his shoulders. Atlas may never put down his burden, and Mercury's words to Aeneas are calculated to point the contrast: "If for your own fame's sake you will not shoulder the burden (*moliris laborem*), think of Ascanius" (*A.* 4.273-75). *Moliris*—the leaving of Dido for an intangible future is the heaviest burden (*moles*) that Aeneas must assume, because it is an internal one. "Such a burden it was to found the Roman race" (*tantae molis erat Romanam condere gentem, A.* 1.33): the ramifications of the poem's thematic line become increasingly evident.

Not until the sixth Book does Aeneas fully accept his future. Compared to his descent into the underworld, Odysseus' corresponding experience seems almost a sentimental journey. It is significant that Odysseus does not pass beyond the threshold of Hades; he remains unchanged. Aeneas' journey is more profound. He must descend into himself, into his own past, and then re-emerge: *hoc opus, hic labor est.* He must turn his back, finally and forever, upon the past, as Orpheus could not. With each encounter in the underworld Aeneas moves further into his past, from his helmsman Palinurus, to Dido, to Deiphobus, who died fighting at Troy. Dido's silence at Aeneas' explanations, as impressive as that of Ajax before Odysseus in the *Odyssey*, incarnates the irrevocability of the past. With Deiphobus, Aeneas would have spent his whole time in reliving the past; the Sibyl must warn him: "Night is rushing on, Aeneas, while we draw out the hours with tears" (*A.* 6.539). And Deiphobus' farewell—"Go, go, our glory, and enjoy a better fate" (*A.* 6.546)—is itself the past's benediction upon the future. Only now may Aeneas go on to his father, and the vision of his future descendants. After the pageant of Roman heroes, culminating in Augustus, the restorer of the Golden Age to Italy, Aeneas has, for the first time, a real sense of his mission. He has been reborn, and, appropriately enough, receives a new name, *Romanus,* "Roman." We tend to forget that in Anchises' famous description of Rome's future he is addressing, first of all, his son:

> tu regere imperio populos, Romane, memento
> (hae tibi erunt artes), pacisque imponere morem,
> parcere subiectis et debellare superbos.

> (You, Roman, must remember to rule the nations beneath
> your sway—these will be your arts—and to impose the habit

of peace, to be merciful to the vanquished, and to overcome
the mighty.)

In the second Book Pantheus, the high priest of Troy, pronounced
what seemed to be Troy's definitive epitaph: "We Trojans are no
more, no more is Troy and the great glory of the Trojans" (*A.*
2.325-26). Yet not until the twelfth Book is the process of Troy's
death complete. There, Juno finally abandons her anger against the
Trojans, provided that they give up their name and become Latins.
"Let there be a Roman stock," she cries, "strong in Italian valor;
fallen is Troy, and fallen let her be, together with her name!" *Sit
Romana potens Itala virtute propago:/occidit, occideritque sinas
cum nomine Troia!* (*A.* 12.827-28) The idea of a new beginning was
popular in the twenties in Augustan Rome. Horace, in the third
Roman Ode, proclaimed the future glories of the Romans, provided
that the Trojan past remain dead, and even the politically recal-
citrant Propertius was prevailed upon to make at least a perfunctory
contribution to the legend: "Troy shall fall, and Trojan Rome
arise!" *Troia cades, et Troica Roma resurges* (4.1.87). In the *Aeneid*
it is somehow appropriate that the definitive statement of death and
rebirth should be made by Juno in heaven, for the transition from
a fallen past to a golden future is more persuasive in abstract or
historical terms than in human ones. Seen from a distant perspective, the story of Aeneas is a tale of progress, progress to which
figures like Dido and Turnus are simply obstacles. They represent
disorder, passion, *furor;* both are constantly associated with fire, a
symbol of the irrational. Dido would remind Roman readers of
another Eastern temptress, Cleopatra; to enforce the comparison
Virgil uses almost identical phrases to describe both: "pallid with
approaching death," *pallida morte futura* of Dido (*A.* 4.644) , and
pallentem morte futura of Cleopatra (*A.* 8.709). Or, it is implied,
Dido is another Helen; when she begs Aeneas to remain in Carthage
"by the marriage we have begun" (*per inceptos hymenaeos, A.* 4.316),
we remember the veil presented to her by Aeneas, a veil once worn
by Helen "when she sought a marriage not to be allowed" (*cum
peteret inconcessosque hymenaeos, A.* 1.651). In a somewhat similar
fashion Turnus is formally associated with irrational forces block-
ing the Trojans' ascendancy. He appears first at midnight, inflamed
by the goddess Allecto, and raging with frenzy for war. Emblazoned
upon his helmet is a fire-breathing Chimaera, recalling one of the
monsters seen by Aeneas in the underworld. In the eighth Book the
terms of the contrast become, at least by implication, still more ex-

treme. When Aeneas visits Evander at the future site of Rome, he arrives on the day of a celebration in honor of Hercules—the same day, by a curious coincidence, on which Augustus celebrated his triumph over Antony—and is favored with a protracted description of Hercules' slaying of the monster Cacus. The parallels are clear: Aeneas is a second Hercules, Augustus a third. There was virtually a cult of Augustus-Hercules at Rome, and Aeneas is something of a Hercules throughout, a hero who, by enduring his many labors, finally overcomes the anger of Juno and is deified. Correspondingly, Cacus, the fire-breathing monster (his name seems to be formed from the Greek word for "evil"), is made to seem an avatar of Turnus. The phrase "he fled more swiftly than the East wind," *fugit ocior Euro,* is used of both (*A.* 8.223, 12.733) and occurs nowhere else in the *Aeneid.* Yet the alignment of Dido and Turnus on the side of passion, disorder, and darkness is thematic only; our sympathy rebels against such terms. Few readers, except Dryden, have preferred to champion Aeneas' cause rather than Dido's; and Dante considered Turnus, along with Nisus, Euryalus, and Camilla, one of the great heroes of Italy. Turnus' real fault is that he has outlived his age. A heroic and even tragic figure, fighting for his own country and glory, he is simply one of the casualties of civilization.

Aeneas' conquest of Italy demands from us the same qualified response. Historically, we may grant that the development from the huts of Evander to the marble buildings of the Forum marked a triumph of civilization over primitive simplicity, and the eighth Book dwells upon the contrast between the two. Yet we feel not so much a sense of progress as one of loss; we are constant witnesses to the violation of the land. An extraordinary simile compares Aeneas in the final battle to a tempest bringing ruin to the crops and trees. The description recalls the picture of civil war at the end of the first Georgic, and it is important to remember that the war in Italy is presented as a civil war since Italy, by a complicated genealogy, is the "ancient mother" of the Trojan people. Before the Trojans' arrival the Italians had lived in a state of pastoral peace. Nearly all the Italian warriors are associated with springs or groves, and even Turnus has a sister who is a nymph of the Numicus river. (By Augustus' time she had been domesticated into a small spring in the Forum, just as the mysterious wood of Avernus, entrance to the underworld, had been cut down to furnish material for Agrippa's shipyard.) In the *Iliad* the plain outside Troy is neutral ground, but in Italy we are made to feel everywhere the land's resistance to the invader. During the final battle Aeneas' spear, missing Turnus, impales itself in a sacred olive tree, which the Trojans, in order to have a clearer battlefield, have already shorn of its leaves. Aeneas is unable to withdraw his spear, so fiercely does the tree resist, until the logic of history, in the form of Venus, comes to his aid. Even the opening episode of the war, Ascanius' shooting of a pet stag belonging to the Latins, suggests the same thing. It was censured by Macrobius, an ancient commentator, as being an insufficiently powerful motive for the beginning of the war. Yet the incident is a microcosm of all that is to follow, the destruction of the Italians' pastoral civilization. It takes on added poignancy if we remember Dido, who had wished to live apart from men, "like a wild animal" (*more ferae, A.* 4.551), only to be pierced and destroyed by her love for Aeneas: "Unhappy Dido wanders through the city like a deer smitten by an arrow, that a shepherd, all unwitting, has pierced from afar" (*A.* 4.68-72).

If, then, the *Aeneid is a story* of success, it is also a story of what success costs: the cost to the land, the cost in lives—and it is characteristic of Virgil that we should remember not the victors but the defeated, Camilla, Nisus and Euryalus, Pallas, Lausus, Turnus, even Mezentius, *contemptor deorum*—and, finally, the cost to Aeneas himself. He is reborn, to be sure, as the ideal Roman incarnate, but by this very fact he becomes increasingly isolated from any human contact. He loses his wife, his father, even his nurse Caieta; the only human relationship he is allowed is with his son, and that seems less personal than dynastic. Venus begs from Jove honor, not for her son Aeneas, as Thetis does for her son Achilles, but only for Aeneas' descendants. To the bees of the fourth Georgic the state was a labor of love, but in the *Aeneid* duty and inclination are constantly opposed. Aeneas' one hope of happiness lies with Dido, but when he is most himself Mercury terms him "forgetful of your kingdom and affairs" (*A.* 4.267). He is never allowed to say, all for love, or the world well lost; rather he must cast Dido aside for the sake of his heir. Lavinia, Aeneas' destined bride, is little more than an eponym for the Italian land, Lavinium, and the dimness with which she is characterized is deliberate. We are meant to realize how faint Aeneas' future as an individual will be. In killing Dido—for it is on his sword that she dies—and Turnus, Aeneas in a sense kills part of himself. He cuts off, as it were, the possibilities of his own intransigence, the heroic responsibility to one's own conception of oneself that Dido and Turnus share, and pay for with their lives. We remember Dido's proud independence, Turnus' unreconstructed individualism, and we recall, by contrast, how rarely Aeneas is even graced with an active verb. He becomes the creator of Rome, but only at the price of becoming a creature of destiny. It is tempting to apply to him the description of the consul Brutus (*A.* 6.822), who unhesitatingly killed his sons for treachery to the state: "Unhappy man, however posterity may extol the deed," *infelix, utcumque ferent ea facta minores.*

The *Aeneid* has often been called an epic of fate. The word fate, *fatum,* comes from the verb *fari,* "to speak," and means, strictly, "that which has been spoken." Fate, then, is an utterance, in this case the utterance of Jove. Yet perhaps the most important point about Jove's utterances, the *fata* of which Aeneas must be the instrument, is the fact that Aeneas is rarely privileged to hear them. In the first Book, when Jove unfolds the glorious future of Rome, it is to another Olympian, Venus, that he speaks: *fabor.* "Spare your fear, Cytherean Venus, the fate I ordained for your children remains to you unchanged": *manent immota tuorum fata tibi* (*A.* 1.257-8). There is a constant and unhappy gap between divine plan, the evolution of history, and the human actors' knowledge of that plan. After Jove's speech we descend abruptly to "Dido, ignorant of fate," *fati nescia Dido* (*A.* 1.299), a phrase which is to become virtually her Homeric epithet. Practically the only time mortals are allowed clear knowledge is when facing death; only when she is preparing her funeral pyre is Dido termed *haud ignara futuri,* "not ignorant of the future" (*A.* 4.508). Aeneas, to be sure, has a glimmering of his fate. The Penates prophesy to him in Book 3—but in a dream. He admires the future glories of Roman history emblazoned upon the shield he receives from Vulcan in Book 8—Vulcan, who is described as *haud ignarus*—but when Aeneas shoulders the burden of the shield (the scene is a miniature of the action of the whole poem) he is termed *rerum ignarus* "ignorant of the events themselves" (*A.* 8.730). And, in the sixth Book, after Aeneas enjoys his fullest vision of the future, it is by the gate of false dreams that he leaves Hades. *Manent immota tuorum fata tibi* were Jove's words to Venus, but for Aeneas very few things "remain" (*manent*) in the sense of being known or fixed. Only the past is certain, and *Priami dum regna manebant* ("while the kingdom of Priam remained") is his constant refrain. *Maneo* as used by human beings usually either refers to the past—"Had I not been so foolish," cries Aeneas, "the lofty citadel of Priam would remain," *Priami arx alta maneret* (*A.* 2.56)—or it may refer to a still unrealized future— thus Aeneas' prayer for a "city destined to remain," *mansuram urbem* (*A.* 3.86)—or it may be rendered ironic by its context—thus Aeneas' promise to Dido that praise shall always attend her name, in whatever land he may be, *laudesque manebunt, quae me cumque vocant terrae* (*A.* 609-610). The human condition in the *Aeneid* might find an epitome in the description of the Sibyl's cave. For the priestess, the prophetic leaves remain fixed in their places, giving a coherent account: *manent immota locis neque ab ordine cedunt (A.* 3.447). But as soon as a mortal tries to consult them the wind from the opened door scatters them in confusion.

Cardinal Newman spoke of Virgil as "giving utterance, as the voice of Nature herself, to that pain and weariness, yet hope of better things, which is the experience of her children in every time." And when we consider Aeneas, pursuing, in his words, the shores of a perpetually receding Italy, and then engaged in wars for which he has no heart, we would be justified in terming the *Aeneid* not only an epic of fate, *fatum,* but an epic of the unspeakable, *infandum.* *Infandum, regina, iubes renovare dolorem* introduces the description of Troy's fall; *infandos labores (A.* 1.597) summarizes Aeneas' wanderings in the Odyssean half of the poem; and *infandum bellum (A.* 7.583) introduces the second or Iliadic half. So many questions remain unanswered and unanswerable: "Was it your will, Jupiter, that in so fierce a battle should clash nations destined to dwell in everlasting peace?" (12.503) "Perhaps on the unhappy, happier days shall wait"; so Juno comforts herself: *forsan miseros meliora sequentur (A.* 12.153). A perpetual *forsan,* "perhaps," hovers over the *Aeneid.* (We remember that Virgil added the word to Homer in his famous imitation: *forsan et haec olim meminisse iuvabit,* "perhaps, some day, it will be a pleasure to remember these things.") Is Rome, *pulcherrima rerum,* really worth the agony— *sunt lacrimae rerum*—that went into its making? The *Aeneid* ends, we should remember, not with Juno's ringing speech in heaven proclaiming Rome's birth, but on earth, with the pathetic and ill-deserved death of Turnus: *vitaque cum gemitu fugit indignata sub umbras,* "and with a groan his resentful soul fled to the shades beneath." [1]

[1] Among the many studies of Virgil that have influenced me, I should like to mention in particular an as yet unpublished dissertation by A. A. Berman, "The Transmigrations of Form: Recurrent Patterns of Imagination in the Odyssey and the Aeneid" (Harvard University, 1960), to which I am indebted for many points of interpretation of the *Aeneid.*

Arcadia: The Discovery
of a Spiritual Landscape

by Bruno Snell

Arcadia was discovered in the year 42 or 41 B.C. Not, of course, the Arcadia of which the encyclopedia says: 'The central alpine region of the Peloponnesus, limited off on all sides from the other areas of the peninsula by mountains, some of them very high. In the interior, numerous ridges divide the secetion into a number of small cantons.' This humdrum Arcadia had always been known; in fact it was regarded as the home of Pelasgus, the earliest man. But the Arcadia which the name suggests to the minds of most of us to-day is a different one; it is the land of shepherds and shepherdesses, the land of poetry and love, and its discoverer is Virgil. How he found it, we are able to tell in some detail, thanks to the researches of Ernst Kapp.[1] The historian Polybius who came from the humdrum Arcadia cherished a great affection for his country. Although there was not much of interest to be related of this land behind the hills, he could at least report (4.20) that the Arcadians were, from the days of their infancy onwards, accustomed to practice the art of singing, and that they displayed much eagerness in organizing musical contests. Virgil came across this passage when he was composing his shepherd songs, the *Eclogues,* and at once understood it to refer to the Arcadian shepherds, for Arcadia was shepherds' country and the home of Pan, the god of the herdsmen, inventor of the syrinx. And so Virgil located the lives and the poetic contests of his shepherds in Arcadia.

[1] E. Panofsky, *'Et in Arcadia ego,'* Festschrift E. Cassirer. Cf. *Hermes,* LXXIII (1938), 242.1.

'You Arcadians,' he says (10.32), 'who are alone experienced in song.' He mentions two Arcadians 'who are equal in song, and equal to giving response in turn' (7.5). He remarks on mount Maenalus in Arcadia 'which ever hears the love songs of the shepherds and Pan blowing his pipe' (8.23). He calls upon Arcadia to judge a contest between the singers (4.58). The shepherds whom Virgil introduces in his earliest eclogue are not Arcadian but Sicilian (2.21): this setting comes to him from the idylls of Theocritus, the Hellenistic poet who served as the model for all Roman pastoral poetry. Since the shepherds of Theocritus, too, indulged in responsive singing and competitions, Virgil had no difficulty in linking them with the Arcadians of Polybius.

Theocritus who was born in Syracuse had written about the herdsmen of his own country. Meanwhile, however, Sicily had become a Roman province, and her shepherds had entered the service of the big Roman landlords. In this new capacity they had also made their way into Roman literature; witness Lucilius' satire on his trip to Sicily. But they could no longer be mistaken for the shepherds of song and love. Thus Virgil needed a new home for his herdsmen, a land far distant from the sordid realities of the present. Because, too, pastoral poetry did not mean to him what it had meant to Theocritus, he needed a far-away land overlaid with the golden haze of unreality. Theocritus had given a realistic and slightly ironical description of the herdsmen of his country engaged in their daily chores; Virgil regarded the life of the Theocritean shepherds as a sublime and inspired existence. If we look at the beginning of his earliest bucolic poem: 'The shepherd Corydon loved fair Alexis,' it has a different ring from anything comparable that Theocritus might have said. In Greek these names were hardened by daily usage; in Virgil they are borrowed words, cultured and strange, with a literary, an exotic flavour, like the names of the mythical heroes which Virgil had drawn from Greek poetry. The effect of this upon the persons of the shepherds was decisive. Later, when Virgil himself had become an example to be followed, the shepherds of European literature were called Daphnis and Amyntas, but they too were awkwardly out of place in the Cotswolds, or the Cornish heath. In the end, when Johann Heinrich Voss bypassed Virgil and re-established Theocritus as his model, he gave the protagonists of his idylls the good German peasant names Krischen and Lene.

Virgil, then, did not aspire to furnish a realistic portrayal of everyday life, but searched for a land which could harbour herdsmen named Corydon and Alexis, Meliboeus and Tityrus, a land

which might be a fitting domicile for everything that seems to be
implied in such poetic names. In the tenth Eclogue, the latest in
date of writing, which more than any other pastoral piece by
Virgil stresses the Arcadian milieu, the poet Gallus has been set
down in Arcady and there finds himself in the company of the gods
and shepherds. The Roman god Silvanus and two Greeks, Apollo
god of song and Pan the deity of the Arcadian herdsmen, express
their sympathy with his unhappy love. How would this be possible
in so near and familiar a setting as Sicily? This scene too has its
precedent in Theocritus, but there (1.77ff.) the gods Hermes,
Priapus, and Aphrodite are shown paying a visit to the mythical
shepherd Daphnis, not just to an ordinary human, much less to an
identifiable contemporary of the writer. Theocritus' scene is mythical, and he keeps that mythical atmosphere clear of any intrusions.
In Virgil's Arcadia the currents of myth and empirical reality flow
one into another; gods and modern men stage meetings in a manner which would have been repugnant to Greek poetry. In actual
fact this half-way land is neither mythical nor empirical; to the
Roman Virgil and his Roman public, Apollo and Pan convey even
less of their divinity, as objects of genuine faith, than they had to
Theocritus and his Hellenistic audience. Arcadia is not an area on
the map, either; even the person of Gallus appears misty and un-
real, which has not, of course, prevented the scholars from trying
to penetrate through the mist and identify the historical Gallus.

The air of unreality which hangs over Virgil's poems is thus
explained by the fact that he seeks to approximate the world of
Theocritus and that of myth, and that therefore he manipulates the
traditional mythology with a greater licence than would have been
possible for a Greek. The tragedians of the fifth century, to be sure,
had begun to elaborate the ancient tales and to interpret them
anew, but they had nevertheless maintained the fiction that they
were discussing events of the hoary past. Plato's inventions in the
mythical genre are often no longer connected with the ancient
motifs, but they are always profoundly significant tales, genuinely
mythical in tenor and aim. Callimachus says that when he first put
his writing-tablet on his knees, Apollo gave him some useful hints
for his poetry. But that is obviously a joke; and when he reports
that the lock of Queen Berenice was placed among the stars, he
bases that on the belief of his time that a great man may after his
death be received among the gods. But nobody, prior to Virgil,
seriously shows men of the present in close contact, and on an equal
footing, with divine beings.

When the early age, during which the Greeks had accepted myth as history, came to a close the tragic writers and the historians of the fifth century divorced the two fields from each other. Myth retired beyond the world of man, and though at first it retained its old function of providing a standard of explanation and interpretation for human experiences, tragedy turned it into a poetic counterpart of reality. With the emancipation of myth came two important changes. On the one hand the ancient heroes and events were interpreted realistically—the psychological approach to the myths is part of this trend—in order to render them more useful to men in their daily lives; and secondly new dramatic situations were invented to the end of adapting the old myths to the stage. Hellenistic poetry carried the psychological interpretation of mythical characters even further, and it made the setting more naturalistic than ever before; but as against this, it also discovered new aesthetic possibilities for the myths. From these up-to-date versions of the ancient tradition, poetry learned to turn its aesthetic energies into the glorification and embellishment of the objects of commonplace reality. In the end, Theocritus domesticated the Sicilian shepherds and made them acceptable to his sensitive art. Virgil, in a certain sense, set about reversing this order of events, and in fact he finally wound up restoring the grand form of the epic. The *Eclogues* contain the first indications of his role which was to exalt the realistic writing which served as his point of departure, *viz.* the idylls of Theocritus, by suffusing it with elements of myth. Myth and reality are thus once more joined together, albeit in a manner never before witnessed in Greece.

Virgil arranges the meeting between his friend Gallus and Pan and Apollo because Gallus is a poet. As a poet he is on excellent terms with the Arcadian shepherds; Virgil had transferred his shepherds to Arcadia because the inhabitants of that country, as Polybius had informed him, were especially well versed in song. The shepherds of Theocritus, too, delight in song; but the ancestry of the musical herdsman is older yet. To trace it all the way back, we must turn to the age before Homer, for on the shield of Achilles (*Il.* 18.525) we find shepherds rejoicing in the sound of the syrinx. We have already mentioned the fact that it was the Arcadian deity Pan who was responsible for the invention of this instrument. Bucolic poetry, also, is of an ancient vintage. It appears that, about the year 600 B.C., Stesichorus introduced it into the repertory of Greek literature, with a choral ode in which he told the story of Daphnis. Daphnis was loved by a nymph; but when, in a bout of drunkenness, he became unfaithful to her, he suffered the punishment reserved for him: he was blinded. This account is obviously based on a simple rustic tale, localized in the vicinity of Himera, the city where Stesichorus lived. In his version, as we might expect in a Greek poetic treatment, the folk-tale is changed into a divine myth, for Daphnis is said to be the son—or, according to others, the beloved—of Hermes, and he tends the cattle of Helios. Our information about the poem is, unfortunately, late and imperfect, but we know that an important section of it was a lament for Daphnis. From that time onward the shepherds have been in love, usually without hope of success; either they indulge in their own suffering, or they wring a poetic expression of sympathy from their friends. We cannot say for sure how Stesichorus formulated all this, but it may be supposed that he endowed the pastoral life with some of the subdued lustre which Homer allows to the figure of Eumaeus, the faithful swineherd of Odysseus. The familiar and self-sufficient world of the simple shepherd is rendered in a myth which, though evidently sprung from a folk-tale, is for all that no less real than the myths which tell of heroes and heroic deeds.

More than three hundred years later, Theocritus composes yet another lament for Daphnis. This time it is given out as a song of the Sicilian shepherd Tityrus (7.72), and again as a composition of the herdsman Thyrsis (1.66). Theocritus takes some pains to present a realistic picture of the life led by Sicilian shepherds. But in one respect they are anything rather than country folk: their mood is a literary one. Theocritus engineers a kind of masquerade; he wishes us to recognize poets of his own circle behind the rustic disguise. He adopts the classic motif of the singing and playing shepherd, and develops the scope of the pastoral poem by voicing the literary themes of the day. All this is done in a spirit of good-natured jesting; the dissonance between the bucolic simplicity of the pasture and the literary refinement of the city is never completely resolved, nor was it ever intended to be, for the whole point of Theocritus' humour lies in this dissonance. In the lament for Daphnis we read: 'The trees mourned for him, those which grew along the Himera river, when he melted away like snow on mount Haemus or Athos or Rhodope or on the furthest Caucasus.' This is the speech of the literati, for it is not customary with shepherds to discuss Haemus or Athos, Rhodope or Caucasus; it is the grand style of tragedy.

This high-flown diction must not be compared with the Greek geographical nomenclature with which Horace, who is our best example for this technique, equips his poems. To a Roman ear his place names do not convey the parody of tragedy, but respect for a noble tradition. And that is the spirit in which Virgil purloined his characters from Theocritus. The Roman poets use these strange-sounding names, dignified, as they thought, by the Greek passages in which they had occurred, to add to the stateliness of their speech; for the Latin tongue has no poetic diction of its own. The names help to lift the writing to a higher plane of literary art. As far as the Romans were concerned, if we may venture a paradox, all these mountains lie in Arcadia, in the land of Corydon and Alexis, of Pan and Apollo. It would not be fair to suggest that in the Augustan period such places had already degenerated into a kind of scenic backdrop for a poetic stage which may be exchanged at will. But it is certain that they have nothing whatever to do with any real landscape outside the theatre, where you might find ordinary, nonfictional men.

When Theocritus has his shepherds enumerate these mountains, he creates roughly the same impression as when Menander puts his quotations from tragedy in the mouths of uneducated slaves. With deliberate irony he makes his Sicilian shepherds live above their intellectual means. But when Virgil read these passages and others like them, he accepted them in the spirit of the more solemn context from which they had originally come, as expressions of genuine feeling. The tension between the real and the literary world which Theocritus had exploited for its peculiar charms, is brought to nought, and everything shifts back to the even plane of an undifferentiated majesty.

In Theocritus, Daphnis is the shepherd from the myth of Stesichorus. In other works he is just an ordinary herdsman, like Tityrus or Corydon. But he is always either the one or the other. Virgil mentions him already in his earliest eclogue: there he is unquestionably the mythical shepherd (2.26). In two other passages (7.1 and 9.46) he is a common herdsman. But what is his identity in the fifth Eclogue? As in other bucolic poems, two shepherds, Menalcas and Mopsus, want to stage a singing contest. They sing of the death and apotheosis of Daphnis, i.e. apparently the Daphnis of the myth. But this Daphnis had been the friend of Menalcas and Mopsus (line 52); thus he also belongs to the immediate environment of the competing herdsmen. Now at the end of the poem we discover that Virgil is using one of the two men as a mask for his own person. Once Virgil had placed his shepherds in Arcadia, it seems, it was but a short step to blend the bucolic with the mythical. This transition was, of course, facilitated by the fact that Theocritus himself had used the figure of Daphnis in both capacities.

In Theocritus, as in Virgil, the shepherds are less concerned with their flocks than they are interested in poetry and love. In both writers, therefore, they are gifted with passion and intellect, but in different ways. Theocritus' herdsmen, notwithstanding their pastoral status, often prove to be urban intellectuals in disguise. Virgil's shepherds, on the other hand—and it is charming to follow the steady progress from ecologue to eclogue—become increasingly more delicate and sensitive: they become Arcadian shepherds. Theocritus, too, stands at a distance from his shepherds; being a man from the city, he looks down upon them partly with a feeling of superiority, partly with an open mind for the straight simplicity of their primitive life. The simplicity is more ideal than fact, and so his shepherds, in spite of all realism, remain fairly remote from the true life in the fields. But this remoteness is as it should be, for a genuine summons back to nature would silence the whole of pastoral poetry; as it turned out, that is exactly what happened in a later age. Above all, these shepherds are not really taken seriously. Their quarrels have something comical about them; how different from the harsh wrangling between Eumaeus and Melanthius in the *Odyssey*! The violent head-on conflicts which we find in tragedy, even between kings, do not exist in Theocritus, and Virgil goes even further in smoothing the differences. From Theocritus on the shepherds display a courtly behaviour, and this courtliness, or courtesy, remains true of all bucolic poetry. The rustic life is made palatable to good society by its acquisition of manners and taste; if there are any embarrassing features left, the poet neutralizes them by making them appear droll, by smiling at them. Virgil is even more intent than Theocritus on toning down the crudeness and coarseness of the shepherds; as a result, he has less occasion to feel superior to them. Furthermore, while endowing the herdsmen with good manners and delicate feelings, he also makes them more serious-minded. But their seriousness differs from that of a Eumaeus; they have no strength to stand up for their genuine interests, nor do they ever clash with one another in open conflict. They are no more conversant with the true elemental passions than the heroes of the *Aeneid* were to be. And it is significant that in those ages when Arcadian poetry was in fashion, and when courtly manners were the order of the day, the *Aeneid* has always been more highly favoured than the *Iliad* or the *Odyssey*.

Virgil's Arcadia is ruled by tender feeling. His herdsmen lack the crudeness of the peasant life as well as the oversophistication of the city. In their rural idyll the peaceful calm of the leisurely evening hours stands out more clearly than the labour for their daily bread, the cool shade is more real than the harshness of the elements, and the soft turf by the brook plays a larger role than the wild mountain crags. The herdsmen spend more time playing the pipe and singing their tunes than in the production of milk and cheese. All this is incipient in Theocritus, but the Alexandrian still shows some interest in realistic detail. Virgil has ceased to see anything but what is important to him: tenderness and warmth and delicacy of feeling. Arcadia knows no reckoning in numbers, no precise reasoning of any kind. There is only feeling, which suffuses everything with its glow; not a fierce or passionate feeling: even love is but a delicate desire, gentle and sad.

Virgil, the discoverer of Arcadia, did not set out to explore new lands. He was no adventurer of the spirit who listens to the call of foreign shores. With utmost modesty he admits that he is proud to have been chosen by the Muse to introduce the Theocritean pastoral among the Romans (6.1). It was not any wish to be an innovator or reformer which caused him to swerve off the path of Theocritus. We must assume that when in his reading of Theocritus he found the grotesque tale of Polyphemus who tried to find a cure for his love in singing, the figure of the Cyclops changed under his very eyes, while he was yet perusing the tale, and turned into a lonely shepherd who voices his longing (*Ecl.* 2). Theocritus says (11.12) that the herds of Polyphemus had to make their way home by themselves in the evenings, because the herdsman forgot all else over his singing. Virgil interprets this as a picture of the golden age when the flocks were able to return to the stables of their own accord, without any herdsman to look after them (4.21). Or again: Virgil has read that during the noon heat lizards sleep in the thornbush. He had found this in Theocritus, where someone expresses his amazement that another person is up and about during that hour, 'while even the lizards take their siesta' (7.22). Virgil has a shepherd who is unhappily in love sing as follows: 'While the flocks seek the cool shade and the lizards hide in the bushes, I must continually sing of my love' (2.8). Thus the sensible beasts have become the happy beasts. Theocritus concludes a jocular prayer to Pan (7.111) with these words: 'If you do not comply with my prayer, I hope you will pasture your flocks during the winter in icy Thrace on the Hebrus, and during the summer among the Ethiopians in the furthest south.' In Virgil, Gallus mourns (10.65ff.): 'Nor will my unhappy love subside if I drink from the Hebrus in midwinter or if I plough through the snowfalls of the Thracian winter, nor if I pasture the sheep of the Ethiopians under the sign of Cancer (i.e. in mid-summer).' The drastic punishment threatened to the shepherd's god is transformed into the sorrows of the unhappy lover who roams through the whole wide world and cannot find a hardship extreme enough to free him from his tortures. These subtle changes are numerous; little by little, without drawing our attention to it, Virgil varies the Theocritean motifs. The transformation is so slight that it took a long time before it was noticed how far Virgil had progressed in his *Eclogues* beyond the pleasantries of the Hellenistic poet. He admired and acknowledged the work of Theocritus, he dwelt lovingly on his scenes; but because he read them with the eyes of the new classicistic age, he slowly came back to the classical Greek poetry, with its earnestness, its deep feeling, its drama. Virgil had not intended to be original; he merely re-moulded Theocritus in the image of what he considered to be characteristically Greek. This was the route by which Virgil discovered Arcadia: without searching for it, without proclaiming his arrival; and so we, for our part, have no easy time in discovering that it was he who discovered the land, and what its discovery means to us.

*   *   *

About six hundred years before Virgil, the early Greek lyrists had awoken to the fact that man has a *soul;* they were the first to discover certain features in the feelings of men which distinguished those feelings sharply from the functions of the physical organs, and which placed them at opposite poles from the realm of empirical reality. For the first time it was noticed that these feelings do not represent the intercession of a deity or some other similar reaction, but that they are a very personal matter, something that each individual experiences in his own peculiar fashion, and that originates from no other source but his own person. Further they had found out that different men may be united with one another through their feelings, that a number of separate people may harbour the same emotions, memories, or opinions. And finally they discovered that a feeling may be divided against itself, distraught with an internal tension; and this led to the notion that the soul has intensity, and a dimension of its own, *viz.* depth. Now everything that we have so far remarked about Virgil's Arcadian world may be summed up by saying that Virgil developed these three basic modes which the early lyric had ascribed to the soul, and interpreted them afresh.

Under Virgil's hands, the spontaneity of the soul becomes the swirling tide of the dream, the creative flux of poetic fancy. The feeling which transcends the individual and forges a link between many men becomes Virgil's longing for peace and his love for his country through which even the beasts and the trees and the mountains are welcomed as fellow-creatures. And finally, the dissonance and depth of the emotions unfold into the conscious suffering of the sensitive man, his awareness that his tender and vulnerable soul lies at the mercy of a harsh and cruel world.

Later on Virgil himself appears to have sensed the futility of pursuing further such an indulgence in the feelings; but the three functions of the soul which he had brought into the open: poetic reverie, unifying love, and sensitive suffering, point far into the future. It was not merely because of his prophecy in the fourth Eclogue that Virgil was, in the Middle Ages, regarded as a pioneer of Christianity. His Arcadia is set half-way between myth and reality; it is also a no-man's land between two ages, an earthly beyond, a land of the soul yearning for its distant home in the past. However, in his later years Virgil avoided the regions discovered by him. For in his later poems he acquired a temper of severe manly restraint which led him to draw closer to the classical Greek expressions of feeling and thought; but many a trace of his earlier sensibility remained.

Along with his new understanding of the soul, Arcadia also furnished the poet with a radically new consciousness of his artistic role. Virgil, for his own person, was too modest to boast loudly of his achievement, but in his portrait of Gallus in the tenth Eclogue he gives us a general idea of his views on the special function of the poet. The reasons, he hints, why the poet takes his stand among the gods, and why he receives the sympathy of nature, is because his feelings are more profound than those of other men, and because therefore he suffers more grievously under the cruelties of the world. Virgil does not actually spell out these ideas which were to become so important in modern poetry, but even his hinting at them is new. At the beginning of the sixth Eclogue Virgil for once formulates a programme of poetic art, but, as is his manner, he is careful not to make too much of himself or his poetry. Following the traces of Callimachus, he refuses to have anything to do with the great epic—later, of course, he was to reverse himself—and he confines himself to the delicate pastime of brief compositions. But in this connexion he accidentally drops a remark which is quite unlike anything that Callimachus ever said; he expresses the hope that his lines, insignificant as their theme is, may be read by someone 'captured by love.' This sympathetic affection is the mark of the poet, and the poet seeks to transmit his compassion to his reader.

* * *

. . . Horace does not speak of Arcadia, but he too envisages a
realm to which the poet alone has access and which is closed to ordinary mortals; a place where dignity of intellect, delicacy of soul and
bodily beauty thrive and flourish. The poet who seeks this place
is a stranger among men. This land in which the Roman poet finds
the objects of his striving is the realm of Greek culture and literature. It follows, of course, that the Greek motifs lose their ancient
contact with reality; the Muses cease to be real divinities, the priest
is no longer a practising priest, the mystery cult is no longer a
genuine worship, and the teacher has no actual disciples before him.
Each image acquires a metaphorical meaning, and in this land of
literary hopes everything, as in Arcadia, must be taken with a grain
of salt. Myth and reality intrude upon each other; concrete existence gives way before significance. The heritage of the Greeks is
turned into allegory, and literature is transformed into a kingdom
of symbols.

This uncovers a deep cleavage between the factual and the significant. The concrete world of experience finds itself face to face
with a new world of art. True, even in Greek literature allegory
and symbols had not been unknown, but they had been innocuous
and unproblematic by comparison. A Greek writer who speaks of
Hephaestus may actually mean a fire. The evolution of that formula
might roughly be sketched as follows. In an early period it was
possible to say: 'Hephaestus destroyed a city,' in the firm belief that
the god's fury was in the fire. Then came the enlightenment which
taught that there were no gods, and that Hephaestus 'signified' fire,
for only fire was real. In the same fashion it became possible to
'explain' all other gods. Finally there was the theory of poetry which
stipulated that the writer must use a picturesque and dynamic
style, and that it was more beautiful and more poetic to use the
name Hephaestus rather than speak of fire. Rationalism on the
one hand, poetic theory and the desire for embellishment on the
other, were responsible for the metonymic use of the names of the
gods.

These considerations prevailed also upon Virgil and Horace, but
in one essential the Romans differed from the Greeks. A Greek
poet, so long as he is a believer, recognizes a reality in the name;
for one who has ceased to believe, the name becomes a sylistic
device or merely poetic play. But the Romans employ these names
to create their Arcadia, the land of the spirit and of poetry; without the names, the land could not exist. It is true that the names
had already lost much of their original impact in Attic tragedy;

since the myth is not related, but acted out or played, the gulf between reality and signification was apparent even then. The drama, that which is happening on the stage, leads us beyond its own limits to a spiritual meaning; it expounds a problem which cannot be expressed directly. But despite this, the outlines of the mythical figures do not vanish behind a mist of unreality; on the contrary, they stand in the very centre of a grimly tangible plot.

Another reason why the characters of Attic tragedy could never be mere allegories is that they were always accepted as real creatures of flesh and blood. Although the ancient myths are no longer enacted as if they were history pure and simple, and although the straightforward limitation of mythical events was gradually forsaken in favour of an added emphasis upon the intellectual and spiritual sides of the action, the dramatic figures remain with their feet firmly planted on the ground. They are no longer regarded as *real,* but every effort is directed at making them appear *possible.* And as the belief in the reality of the myth dwindled, poetry tried hard to preserve at least a semblance of reality by resorting to the devices of realism and psychology. Allegory, on the other hand, does not insist on this kind of semblance; within its realm, the function of a figure is only to convey one specific meaning. In Virgil the nymphs and the Muses, Pan and Apollo are very close to the level of allegory, for they embody the idyllic life of Arcadia, the peace which fills its pastures and the romantic poetry to which its shepherds are dedicated.

Thus the ancient gods are, so to speak, reduced to the form of *sigla:* they are deprived of their primeval mysterious power, and all that is left to them is an ideality which no longer springs from religious awe but from literary erudition. They have taken on a Utopian quality, embodying the spiritual truths which are not to be found in this world. A similar change in the thinking concerning the gods is indicated in many examples of the classicistic painting and sculpture which flourished in Attica at the time of Virgil. We do not know enough about the Greek literature of this epoch to be able to tell to what extent Virgil was indebted to it in his allegorization of the gods. But what was least as important was this, that for the Romans the gods and the myths of the Greeks had never been real. They adopted them as part of their cultural heritage from Greek literature and art, and they found in them the world of the spirit which the Greeks had discovered. Among the Romans, therefore, these figures are emphasized chiefly for whatever meaning they may hold for the life of man; they are allegories

in the real sense of the word, for they signify something entirely
different from what they had originally meant. They are like loan-
words taken into another language, which are called upon to translate a strange legacy for the benefit of the heirs and their thoughts
and feelings, if such a thing is possible in matters of the mind. The
gods become allegories at the very moment when Greek literature
gives birth to a literature of the world.

A similar development occurred also in the East. Allegorical
interpretation helped Philo to incorporate Greek myth and Greek
wisdom into Hellenistic Judaism, and Clement of Alexandria performed the same office for Christianity. Much was accepted, but the
religious and philosophical core was rendered harmless by this re-
formulation. The world of the Greek spirit was, perforce, a stranger
in the cultures which absorbed it, and the allegorical interpretation was needed to permit the Greek heritage to be accepted by nations and ages whose beliefs were in many respects diametrically
opposed to Greek thought.

The special importance of Virgil, which distinguishes his accomplishment from the Jewish and the Christian assimilation of Greek
culture, and which places him squarely in the Roman tradition
leading from Ennius to Catullus, is the fact that he uses the arts,
viz. poetry, to channel the Greek heritage into the body of Roman
thought. But further than that, his *Eclogues* represent the first
serious attempt in literature to mould the Greek motifs into self-
contained forms of beauty whose reality lies within themselves.
Thus art became 'symbol.' Comparable tendencies do not exist in
Greek literature. At most we might establish a certain similarity
with the myths of Plato; but even this last comparison serves only
to stress the special quality of Virgil's achievement. Plato's myths,
too, had been concerned with 'significance' rather than with reality.
But they are not self-contained poetry; on the contrary, their objective is to illustrate something else. They refer to a specific argument
which Plato would like to express rationally, but for which his
language does not suffice. That is why Plato deprecates his myths
and calls them mere play. In Greek literature this species of myth-
making had no successors.

Arcadia was a land of symbols, far distant from the quarrels and
the acrimony of the present. In this land the antique pagan world
was permitted to live on without injury to anybody's feelings.
Arcadia was so remote that it was no more in danger of clashing
with the See of Rome or with the Holy Roman Empire than it had
run afoul of the *Imperium Romanum* of Augustus. Only when

Europe began to be dissatisfied with the goods handed down to her, and when she took thought upon her own spiritual substance, did Arcadia run into trouble. But that was also the time when the genuine Greece was restored to her rightful place.

The *Georgics*

by Jacques Perret

Between the publication of the *Eclogues* and that of the *Georgics* some ten years passed, a period in Virgil's life of which we know nothing. The tree had borne its fruit; now friends are gone, the laughter is over; at forty, Virgil seemed alone forever. There was only a far-away Maecenas, the sole relic of his former friends, to keep him in touch with the vast stirrings of the universe: Alfenus Varus, Gallus, Pollio, Horace—all had disappeared, and no one had taken their places. All about him lay the oppressive scenery of the Gulf of Naples, a boundless space on which to fix his gaze.

The Decisive Change

In order to understand the *Georgics,* we must begin with the *Eclogues.* There Virgil defines poetry as the sole task worthy of man, the only one by which he can fulfill himself and take his place in nature without dishonoring it. It is through poetry, too, that man can bring nature to its fullest being. Beside poetry, all other endeavor seems futile and unbefitting: in the Golden Age described in the fourth Eclogue, agriculture has no more place than do commerce or war. In the *Georgics,* however, we learn that there is another way for man to be in harmony with the universe, through work. The poet discovers the possibility of becoming interested in something other than poetry. Poetic composition ceases to have as its sole conceivable end simply the writing of poetry.

It is not to be expected that these new intuitions can emerge, in Virgil's mind, except at the expense of earlier dreams, which have had to fall into ruin and be to some extent abandoned. After ten years of solitary reflection, the beautiful edifice of the *Eclogues,*

"The Georgics." (Original title: *"Le Poème des patiences."*) From *Virgile* by Jacques Perret. Copyright © 1959 by Editions du Seuil. Reprinted by permission of Editions du Seuil. Translated by M. Brooks.

built in a fervor of discoveries and friendship, no longer gives the
same security to the poet. The fragility of the Arcadian universe
seen in the *Eclogues* is due to several things. The most immediately
obvious is that, given the conditions of actual existence, it is a
magical universe; but magic does not last. It is of the utmost importance in opening the doors of our prison a little way, and in
showing us that they can be opened; but it does not actually open
them in any permanent way. Furthermore, the Arcadian universe
exists only on a momentary basis, at the level of the mountain-tops;
it lasts as long as man can keep himself at this height, but these
privileged moments, whatever the value of the revelations they
bring, do not last long. The singer has seen the tops of the ash
trees rock in cadence, he has repeated the wondrous feats of Orpheus; but when he comes back down to earth, it is almost as if he
had never sung. Finally, the experiencing of these privileged moments, of the summits of life, has no actual effect on the real world,
which continues to follow its dreary and indifferent course; and it is
possible only for a few. And so the poetic adventurer finds himself
isolated in nature, a stranger to himself, alone among men. The
assertion that he will not always be alone, the hope of a great change
in the universe that will create for all men forever the harmony
fleetingly glimpsed by a few, is a means to hide his failure from
himself temporarily. It is the shield with which he protects his
faith. But one day, inevitably, he must ask himself whether this
faith is not all merely an empty show.

Virgil gives us a picture of this decomposition of the Arcadian
universe in the tenth Eclogue, which is explicitly presented as the
last, as a farewell to the whole work. Seen from a distance, it appears,
in fact as the work's annulment. The story is familiar: Gallus, an
Arcadian, one day discovers passion—real passion, not the love of
a Phyllis or an Amyntas, which is only a pretext for songs and graceful fancies, but the kind of love that drives a man mad, that cuts
him off from both his friends and the gods. (A similar misfortune
has befallen the poor goatherd of the eighth Eclogue, but he is a
rustic, a naive soul insufficiently purified by poetry.) Both men and
gods, astonished and distressed by this misfortune for which there
is no remedy, gather helplessly around Gallus. With their help,
Gallus tries to regain possession of himself. But love is too strong,
so Gallus must depart; poetry has not been able to save one of its
most faithful followers, and for Gallus Arcadia is henceforth nothing but a dream.

The same pessimistic representation of the ineffectiveness of
poetry—and finally of its failure—appears again in the *Georgics*;

here it is found in Virgil's treatment of the legend of Orpheus. In almost all, if not all, former traditions, Orpheus' rescue of Eurydice from hell symbolizes the victory of poetry over death: what matter death or the stupid accidents that separate lovers, since in poetry the lovers live again and eternally? But Virgil shows the victory of poetry as a false victory, an illusion put to flight by the first beam of daylight. Orpheus returns alone from his perilous journey; he has lost not only Eurydice, but hope as well. He can only retire into icy deserts that recall very closely the sinister landscapes evoked in the tenth Eclogue. Poetry has been defeated. While in the Eclogue it was defeated by love, here it is defeated by death. No one should die in Arcadia; and if one does, then Arcadia is an illusion.

It seems quite obvious that the tenth Eclogue has biographical foundations. Gallus was a friend who shared the Arcadian ideal; Virgil was grieved to see him depart from it with no hope of returning. It would be interesting to know whether, in the same way, personal experience of the death and final loss of someone close to him animates the myth of Orpheus. But, however that may be, it is not irrelevant to point out that when the pastoral was revived in the Renaissance, the same painful opposition appeared. At first glance, Poussin's *Shepherds of Arcadia* seems an evocation of a luminous atmosphere: a noble tree, youthful figures happily arranged, a little monument, stele or altar that centers the painting and gives it religious character. But, alas, upon closer inspection, the little monument is a tomb and the shepherds are trying to decipher an inscription that we understand only too well: *Et in Arcadia ego.* . . . "I too was an Arcadian," says the dead man, "and now where is Arcadia for me?" Other works of the same period deal with the same subject, and in a form still more emphatic.

It is easy to see why this contrast is so shocking: the pastoral world is that of eternity in an instant, the world of perfect moments, when time suspends its flight. Death, the coarse temporal phenomenon that establishes a "before" and an "after" equally undefined and unlimited, has no meaning there, and no place.

The lost Gallus, the hopeless Orpheus—what a gulf separates these pictures from the luminous splendors of the seventh or the fifth Eclogue! But we may guess at other shipwrecks, in less tragic waters, if only from the dispersion of the little group of Arcadians: still another proof that Arcadia was only a dream. Virgil alone, perhaps, retains this dream in himself, even when he is elsewhere. The name of Arcadia disappears forever from his work; but the reality of Arcadia reappears constantly, in flashes, to guide his progress. The brilliance of the privileged moments fades into the strain of long patient waiting, but the goal is the same. Tedious roundabout paths, tiresome shifts and evasions, will at least permit all of humanity (in the double sense of the word—all men and, in each man, all the levels of his being) to recuperate. At the same time, Augustus, too, in his role of restorer, has begun his own course of patient waiting.

As is natural in a poet, the change in Virgil's spiritual outlook makes itself felt immediately in his imagery. When we turn from the *Eclogues* to the *Georgics* the change is arresting: even the light is different. The *Eclogues* are the poems of sentient hours. Essentially, they are poems of midday, the hour when Pan works his wonders; in this hour of leisure the cricket chirps, everything seems to be alive. Can one imagine Eclogues 2, 3, 6, and 7 as set otherwise than under a brilliant sun, among honey-colored swarms of words? It is a world of violent activity, even when the shepherd reposes, even in the repose itself. Night is absent, night that is duration, while the day is made up of moments. Absent, too, are the soothing stars; instead, the sun exalts. There are no seasons, but only a timeless summer, a nature of wonders that mingles all fruits and flowers. The *Georgics,* however, move with a different rhythm: they evoke the nocturnal sky, the sovereign calm of its revolutions, the periodic returns of festivals and chores, all the reality of the country. Yes, there are indeed two ways whereby one may attain to the absolute: like an archer, with a shot straight into the sky; or by gathering up and embracing the totality of the world.

The supernatural has also taken another form. In the *Eclogues* the gods seldom make an appearance; not because the poet is irreligious, but because the gods are everywhere in nature. Characteristically, it is only when the Arcadian dream is undone that one sees them, as in the tenth Eclogue, appear in visible form, poor actors in a dislocated drama, powerless, almost pitiable mechanisms of a dead magic. From the beginning of the *Georgics,* however, the whole Olympic pantheon, exactly as it is constituted in official religion, is distinctly and precisely invoked; the poet insists on the importance of due religious observance. There exists, then, a means other than poetry to put oneself in accord with the universe. The accord reached by this means is totally different from ecstatic response to a nature animated by divine presences; it is rather a confidence and trust that makes daily life possible; it is faith in the morality of the universe: *iustissima tellus.* The order of the world no longer appears in the flash of an interior illumination; now it is represented by an immense, lasting, and regular machinery. It is no longer exalting; it is beneficial. And, on the part of man, the reply that must be made, the only reply that is harmonious and right, is no longer poetry and song, but work.

Labor Improbus

Virgil elaborated his concept of the positive value of work in a famous myth (G. 1.121ff.), in which his new convictions are mingled with a residue of old ideas. After the bliss of the Golden Age, a jealous Jupiter takes the reins of the world. Where formerly the earth yielded its fruits uncultivated, Jupiter now makes thorns grow there; he divests man of the secret of fire and spreads abroad the races of savage beasts. The jealousy of the gods, the decline from the Golden Age to the present—these old and pessimistic themes seem somewhat jarring in a poet whose hopefulness is his unfailing support. But then we discover that, in so acting, Jupiter is attempting to force man to invent technology, and to wrench him from the torpor that would have stifled his intelligence.

Many elements remain obscure here. Recently an argument arose as to whether the famous formula *labor omnia vicit improbus* really does mean that work overcomes all difficulties. Perhaps this *labor* is instead not the efforts of man, but the trials imposed upon him by god; perhaps the "victory" is not man's victory over a hostile world, but that of the god, triumphing over men's laziness by the ordeals he has set for them. The discussion is not without interest, since it shows us how, even in this important passage, Virgil has difficulty in rehabilitating the word *labor*. Even understood in the way suggested, however, the text surely implies a positive divine intention forcing man in the direction of technology and acting for his good. It is undoubtedly significant that this god with rather obscure intentions is called, in the beginning of the passage, by the name *Pater,* Father; and it is also important that a few lines later Ceres, a benign goddess, guides mankind's first steps in the discovery of agricultural technology. The obscurities of this beautiful passage are a moving testament to the difficulty that any new idea has when it must take definite form and fit itself into a previously constituted universe.

From all this, however, one fact clearly emerges: technology and the necessity for labor are not simply a *pis-aller*, not a burden man must bear in consequence of the universe's gradual decline. On the contrary, the very evil against which we must struggle was introduced into the world only in order that there be work and tech-

nology—and this work is conjointly ordained to beautify the world
and to exalt the human race.

Let us recall here the *Eclogues,* where the only honorable occupation for man is apparently poetry, where all technology is to disappear with the coming of the new order. But let us remember, too,
the positions taken by the contemporary schools of philosophy.
Lucretius and the Epicureans insisted strongly on the idea that all
man's inventions, all his technological improvements, produce in
him new needs, artificial and imaginary, that further enslave him.
Even when these improvements are defensible, when they enable
man to avoid starvation and freezing, to survive, in short, in un-
favorable conditions, they merely testify to our physical decline and
to the indifferent hostility of the natural milieu in which we live.
It would be preferable to have exterior conditions be more favorable, as they were when a younger world enjoyed a perpetual spring-
time; it would be better if we were stronger and could live like so
many animals, free from the cares that only increase our misery.
According to Lucretius, it was the invention of fire that made us
chilly; and here we are not far from Rousseau's dictum: for the
poet it is gold and silver, but for the philosopher iron and wheat
that civilized man and wrecked the human race.

Virgil certainly had no share in these romantic puerilities, and
his position is equally opposed to that of the Stoics. According to
Seneca, it was the sages who, nourished on the contemplation of
abstract ideas, originally invented the technology thanks to which
man can feed and warm himself. This theory, in conformity with
all the thought of antiquity, implies that the material is fixed on
a lower plane than the spiritual, and that the meeting of spirit and
matter demands a descent to the lower plane. In Virgil, on the
contrary, it is in struggling to nourish his body that man raises
himself towards the light and responds to the ideal a fatherly god
has set for him; from human effort exercised on the material world
is born the light of the spirit.

If the ancients always thought material work degrading, it was
because they thought of matter as the negative pole of reality, the
opposite of the spirit, or God. When man works with matter, he
inevitably bears the marks of what he fashions: he becomes more
corporeal and less spiritual; he sinks farther from light, deeper into
darkness. In Virgilian perspective, on the contrary, the enhancement
of work entails an enhancement of matter. To a new conception of
work must correspond a new cosmology.

When the ancient philosophers reflected upon the order of the world, the image they bore in mind was that of the night sky with its stars. The beauty of this night, the comprehensible order and regularity that were manifested there, seemed to them a direct invitation to man to live on the level of the spirit, in contemplation. The principal moral lesson that seemed to follow was that of the primacy of necessity: the stars obey their laws, and thus man, too, should accept in his life the burden of the necessities that surround him and drive him on. The Stoics had integrated this notion into their belief in a Providence mindful of the existence of man, and the result of their contemplation of nature was to make them wholeheartedly grateful. But in no thinker of antiquity except Virgil does one find the idea, so often implied in the first book of the *Georgics,* that nature, like human endeavor, is working towards definite ends, and that contemplation of the universe ought therefore to inspire men to work. Astronomy is no longer a stage where abstract laws are displayed; it has become the description of an immense agricultural machine. To conform to the order of the world is not to contemplate it; it is not to accept the idea of necessity; it is only incidentally to be grateful and give thanks. Instead, what is essential is to act in harmony with the warmth of spring in order to help the young plants grow: to work. Order is not only intelligibility; it is also fecundity, dynamism. Here again the set of abstract laws taught in the schoolroom moves into a new register. Order becomes the reforestation of a hill or the irrigation of a dry field. The poet gives maximum importance to the demiurgic role of the countryman, who attempts by work to act his part on earth side by side with the constellations.

Work, then, is no longer a cause of man's degradation, no longer the struggle of the spirit, forced to descend to its lowest level, against the matter that is alien to it. Instead, work plays its full part in the unity of a dynamic world, a world where it is through matter, too, worked by God, that the divine touches man. Of course, the idea of a world imbued with the divine is far from uncommon in antiquity, but elsewhere one experiences this divinity only through contemplation—it is never through physical work that its effects are visible in mankind.

Hence comes the atmosphere of intimacy, of happiness, of confidence, in which Virgil describes the world of the farmer. Although he hides neither its hardships nor its disappointments, nevertheless he conveys a feeling that beside the laborer stands an unseen force that upholds his arm, puts his tool in his hand, and welcomes him to the land he is to order. Overhead, the immense machinery of the stars is also at work: God approaches man through nature. Beneath the subtle counterpoint of different and often unexpected motifs, it is easy to recognize that the argument of the poem is formed and directed by the interplay of these two themes. The theme of man's work, strongly stated in the first book, is progressively blurred by the description of nature's responses and the animation of the natural world. In Book 2, the trees and especially vineyards begin to manifest an inherent dynamism. The description of the animal world in the third Book adds to the density of existence surrounding the man of the field. The beekeeper of Book 4 is certainly not an idler, but in the marvels of the tiny industrious world of the bees, nature at work, the divine presence is revealed to him in almost tangible form. The poem, beginning with an evocation of the most severe hardship, ends with the story of a miracle, the response of God at work in nature.

Esthetically, it seems that Virgil's positive conception of work enables him to avoid the paradox that often hindered the development of a feeling for nature in antiquity. On the one hand, there can be nothing superior to nature: hence the primacy accorded to its most spontaneous forms and most irrational elements, the grotto full of mysteries, the spring, the tangle of plants in the sacred enclosure where the tree has never known the pruner's hand. On the other hand, art is indispensable to nature's fulfillment. The combination of these two ideas is often seen in paintings of the countryside: statues and steles set in such wild and deserted places that they seem to bear witness to the hand of God rather than that of man. The nature that Virgil's poems evokes is the joint work of man and the gods; far from refusing the imprint of man, it summons him to bring it to fulfillment. On a small scale, it is the garden of the old man of Tarentum; on a larger scale, it is the wheat that waves on the hillsides of Italy as far as the eye can see: the whole expanse of the land included in this round of benedictions. Few of the privileged will know the joy of hearing the pines talk at noon, but everyone can welcome God, master and author of order in their fields.

A Human Vocation

Thus the poet, no longer enchanted by the magic of Arcadia, and no longer believing in the miraculous and universal founding of a new order, nevertheless preserves hope—and even the same hope; the means, however, are no longer the same. The concepts of time and continuity enter Virgil's work. The reasons for this change will surely never be known. A man's whole life can change in a single night when, under the open sky, he hears the music of the spheres differently, sees with different eyes the slow turn of a millstone. We do know, however, that at the same time the world around Virgil was likewise undergoing a change. After the battle of Actium, all of Augustus' efforts seem to have gone into first bringing under his control and then re-orienting towards a fruitful and enduring activity the disorganized forces that had almost engulfed the nation. Thus we are not surprised that in the *Georgics* the name of Maecenas, one of Augustus' advisers, keeps appearing as that of inspirer and patron.

Literary historians tend to be upset by this: can a poet, they ask, write upon command? Can a poet's muse be the slave of a political program? In fact, the passages where Maecenas is mentioned contain nothing that is not very natural, and, indeed, very honorable, as much for Virgil as for Maecenas. In the genesis of literary works, indeed of all human works, the part played by the occasion is much more important than the romantic aesthetic would have it. A commission entrusted by a friend can be of inestimable value for a poet, in helping him to believe in himself and giving him encouragement as he begins a new path. If Maecenas gave Virgil the assurance to write the *Georgics*, that is a proof of his intuition, and one for which we should be grateful. As for becoming aware, through friendly association with someone active in political circles, of the importance of certain problems on a national scale, nothing can be more inspiring for the poet, for then he sees that his own internal debates, his efforts to see things clearly, are not meaningful for himself alone, but should resound throughout the state.

It would undoubtedly have been desirable at that time to put a stop to the desertion of the countryside, which had been aggravated by the civil wars and was already a serious obstacle to the rebuilding of Italy. As recent experience had shown, there was danger of starvation the moment grain convoys stopped coming from Sicily or Egypt. But what could a poem do about it? Would not Maecenas have been better advised to promote agriculture in Italy by imposing high duties on imported wheat, or by taking measures to regulate the exportation of Italian wine? But the ancient world was not so expert in the field of economics as we are today. And what an error to attribute efficacy exclusively to economic measures! When a man leaves a trade because of poor pay, it is almost always because he sees the low wages as an indignity: *Nullus aratro dignus honos,* the plough does not have the respect it deserves. We have a greater need for respect than for money. To help someone respect himself in his occupation—*ignaros viae miseratus agrestes,* to take pity on farmers ignorant of the right way—to show him its merits and pay homage to them, is to strengthen his commitment to it and to improve his condition, even his material condition. Of course, to suggest that such action is possible is not to suggest that the *Georgics* were intended to reach a rural proletariat torn apart by the civil wars. Those who read the *Georgics* were the members of the educated classes, large and small land-owners from the villages and towns of Italy, provincial leaders who were more or less permanently settled in Rome, but who still remained very much attached to their rural investments. To inspire their respect for the land and for those who lived by it was to save through them the thousands who would not read the poem.

Perhaps Maecenas and Virgil saw still further. In addition to ensuring Italy's food supply, a new problem was arising in the Roman world: that of the balance between town and country. It was no longer simply a question of mass migration to Rome; in all the provinces men were leaving the land, and the population was becoming concentrated in the cities. How could anyone who wanted to become cultured remain a countryman and live far from schools and amusements? All the values of ancient civilization—leisure, fine arts, politics—were urban values. There was an increasing tendency to identify general prosperity with the prosperity of the cities. It was because of the countryside, under-populated, wretched and demoralized, that the Empire began to decline; it was the existence of all this uninhabited land that made the invasions possible, and let them pass almost unnoticed. In Virgil's time it was still not too late to take steps; this helps to explain why, in order to avert the dangers he foresaw for the future, he so strongly emphasized the vitality of the Italy of former times.

In any case, the *Georgics* go well beyond the problems of farming. This is obvious to anyone who is sensitive to the tone, urgent, pressing, hortatory, taken by the poet. The subject of the *Georgics* is not "what it is best to do when one wants to cultivate the land"; it is instead an "exhortation to cultivate the land." There is an ardor, a faith in the importance of the work begun, that recalls Lucretius. It is because of this intensity that the moving prayer at the end of the first Book—one of the most beautiful religious passages in all of classical literature—or, again, the lyric praise of Italy in Book 2, fit harmoniously with precepts on agricultural methods or the study of meteorology. In fact, through this evocation of rural life an entire philosophy is proposed to us. Virgil's laborer becomes a symbol of all human life, with the result that the poet's exhortations and vehemence produce an immediate emotional response in

us, at the same time that his imagination is stimulating ours. I myself may have no feeling for the work of the farmer; yet the images
of the poet move me nonetheless: a countryside to recreate, a land to
make fruitful, order to establish, a national ideal to animate, a
Golden Age to give birth to. No school of philosophy proposed these
things to the contemporaries of Virgil; rather they all—and Cicero
fought against this—recommended to their adherents the practice
of *otium*, of studious retreat. We may well wonder whether, in the
long run, the Roman world did not collapse for lack of having set
its people a common goal that would at once have satisfied the best
hopes of the best people, while remaining near enough and concrete
enough so that all could work towards it.

It is only quite recently that it has again become possible for us
to interpret the *Georgics* in this way, as a poem of human effort, of
the building of a country and of the world, as a poem of God's
presence in and response to human labor. When one reads poems
on rural themes of the French classical tradition, one is astonished
to see how little esteem the authors, often very philanthropic, have
for the work of the fields. Work was no more than raw material for
genre paintings—material, indeed, to be framed within a nature
that was itself only seen as a setting for pleasure-trips and excursions
—and it was obviously impossible to discern in it the shape of
human destiny. On this point, at least, the development of sensibility during the nineteenth century had some literary value. Anyone who has read the dialogue between the architect and the laborer
at the end of *The Annunciation to Mary*, or who takes pleasure
in Giono's *Vraies Richesses*, runs no risk of mistaking the character
of the *Georgics*. But the very fact that this sort of appreciation has
been so slow to return helps us to gauge the novelty of Virgil's
achievement. It took a Roman, sprung from a race of working-men,
to adopt a view of the world in which God communicates with
man through work.

The Inner Quality of Things

It is difficult for us today to approach without scepticism a descriptive poem more than two thousand lines long. The poetry of the
last hundred years or so, whenever it deals with externals, is almost
exclusively concerned with the recording, in relatively short pieces
or by pointillist notations, of instantaneous perceptions. In most
cases, the poet's intention is to show the uncertainty or reality of the
world to which we are accustomed, and then, with a quick feat of
legerdemain, to replace it with some other creation. Apart from

this, there seems to be only dull, flat didacticism, servile worship of the object.

Classical poetry holds much more closely to everyday perceptions. Of course, we must not suppose that ancient writers regaled themselves with mere lists, like inventories or science textbooks; but, unlike us, they felt no need to get away from appearances. For them, appearances were rooted in reality: everything had an inside, a secret, a being, which was not apparent at first glance but not arbitrary either, and which was such that man could give it whatever name he pleased as the fancy took him. The external world was not devalued. The task of the poet was, starting from what is seen, to say what is.

In the metaphysical disorder of the modern world, endeavors of this sort can no longer be possible. Baudelaire perceived that the world was a forest of symbols. But symbols of what? The affirmation is made, but the poet goes no further. He falls back into his solitude, into his gratuitous creations, into artificial paradises. But the relation of a Virgil to the world, a relation founded on firmer principles, is one of confident and unvarying attentiveness: he has some deeper understanding and some moments when his perceptions are superficial; but all are part of a gradual progress towards the innerness, the meaning of things. The universe no longer resembles a House of Mirrors. Objects carry their message, they are to be known—first some, then others; the long narrative or descriptive poem has its *raison d'etre*. In reading these works, we are a little reminded of the engravings left us by the eighteenth century and the Romantic period: although documentary in theory, they are nevertheless, be they of Piranesi or Gustave Doré, deeply embued with soul. It cannot be doubted that a great deal has been lost with this form of art; today the only choice left us is between impressionist or nonrepresentational painting and a photograph album. And yet how could it be otherwise, if the subject is without consistency? Our metaphysics deprive us of one way of grasping the world, a way by which possibilities for perception and enjoyment that are lost to us were once realized, in the union of human perception and the objectivity of things. More submissive to the object, less strained, less tiring—this art was an enchanted promenade, the stuff that memories are made of.

Certainly the adoption of any one metaphysic does not suffice to remove all the obstacles. The descriptive poem holds its course between two dangers. To remain on the level of appearances is to fall back, to mark time; to apprehend a transcendence in things is to risk having their singularity disappear. Even on the epistemological level there is only one escape from this contradiction inherent to our mode of perception: love. Love alone can see things and beings for what they are, without being put off; it alone can perceive a beyond, an extension of what they are, without making them vanish. The literary success of the *Georgics,* one of the rare successful descriptive poems in the archives of man, is linked much more closely than is at first apparent to a certain quality of the soul.

On Translating the *Aeneid*:
Yif that I Can

by R. W. B. Lewis

> But as I romed up and doun,
> I fond that on a wal ther was
> Thus writen, on a table of bras:
> 'I wol now singe, yif that I can,
> The armes, and al-so the man. . .'
> *The House of Fame*, 1.140-44

The lines descried by Chaucer's visionary dreamer on the walls of the Temple of Venus are not only an English rendering in a fourteen-word couplet of the opening three words of Virgil's *Aeneid*: *Arma virumque cano*. They also manage to say, or imply, a good deal about the difficulty of translating the whole or any part of that extraordinary poem. The words Chaucer has added are wonderfully suggestive. They comprise a sort of built-in awareness by the first of the great English poet-translators of the utter precariousness of the task he now proposes to attempt, and one of the major reasons therefor; all with the equally untranslatable Chaucerian air of serenest and most knowing amusement. The cautionary phrase, "Yif that I can" (or "gif" in another variant, or elsewhere, more modernly, "if") is addressed by Chaucer to himself. The translator, while Englishing the first three words, adds his own comment in his own voice: yif that he can—not sing, but translate; recreate in another language the complex beauty of the Latin song. And the grounds for caution are hinted at in the well placed vocables of the next line: "And al-so." Those words are likewise commentary, or built-in footnote. For this poem challenges any translator by dealing not only with warfare, but also with other vast reaches of human

"On Translating the *Aeneid*: Yif that I Can." From *Yearbook of Comparative and General Literature*, X (1961), 7-15. Copyright © 1961 by the Comparative Literature Committee of Indiana University. Reprinted by permission of the Comparative Literature Committee of Indiana University.

experience, including a heroic human character. So massive a task
has it always been to compose a translation of the *Aeneid*; or even
to paraphrase Chaucer's compressed and witty little critical essay on
the problem.

Chaucer, in point of fact, gave up after the third line of the
poem; and the balance of the first book of *The House of Fame*
offers, instead, the dreamer's account of a series of "curious portrey-
tures" and "queynt maner of figures" he saw adorning the temple
walls, illustrations of the Virgilian epic through to the final triumph
of the hero—with Chaucer plucking only occasionally at the Latin
for his English purposes, as in the lines admired by Ezra Pound
describing the appearance of Venus to her son (1.319):

> Goinge in a queynt array,
> As she had ben an hunteresse,
> With wind blowinge upon hir tresse.

Chaucer was wise; and in the present note, I should like to borrow
his self-admonition, and maybe even a small portion of his wisdom:
and attach that admonition to an effort, not to translate myself
(much less to sing); but to reflect upon the virtual impossibility of
anything like a *complete* translation of the *Aeneid*; which is to
reflect, of necessity, on some aspects of the poem's peculiar greatness
and its beauty. Yif that I can. The caution will, I hope, be remembered: partly because I can refer only to a handful of translations
into English, wilfully including Douglas's sixteenth century Scottish
under that head, and leaving aside other English versions and versions in any other language. Partly, also, because this observer is
not in any way a classical scholar, but in every sense an *amateur* of
Virgil, albeit of reasonably long standing. So it should be clear that
I come not to scold translators of the *Aeneid,* nor to rank them in-
vidiously; but mainly, to sympathize.

Among the many kinds of difficulties that confront the translator
of Virgil, I want to focus on that phase of his mastery of language
that is revealed in an almost Shakespearian exploitation of imagery:
exploitation, that is, to intensify, to illuminate (often by way of
irony) and to carry forward the *action* of the poem. (A superior and
indeed pioneering example [in English] of the study of this aspect of
the *Aeneid*—and a work to the contents and author of which I am
much indebted—is "The Serpent and the Flame" [on the imagery
of *Aeneid* II] by Bernard M. W. Knox in *American Journal of Philology*, LXXI [October 1950), 4. See also the invaluable book-
length study of image and symbol in the *Aeneid, Die Dichtkunst
Virgils* by Viktor Poeschl [Wiesbaden: Rohrer Verlag, 1950].) Virgil's

imagery has been sometimes, though by no means regularly, admired; and his action has been investigated within a variety of allegorical frames; but the relation between imagery and action has rarely been detected in criticism or caught in translation. John Dryden, in the lengthy dedication of his 1697 *Aeneid,* offered some of the most incisive comments ever made on Virgil's "similitudes"; Dryden was the first, and arguably the best, of the new critics; no one has noticed more accurately, for example, how Virgil's figures "are not placed, as our unobserving critics tell us, in the heat of any action; but commonly in its declining, when he has warned us in his description, as much as possible he can; then, lest that warmth should languish, he renews it by some apt similitude"—the one Dryden chooses being that of Neptune calming the storm (in Book 1), as a venerable man calms an urban uprising with his eloquence. But for the most part, Dryden restricts his rhetorical analysis to the sweet harmony of Virgil's verses: "His words are not only chosen, but the places in which he ranks them for the sound; he who removes them from the station wherein their master sets them, spoils the harmony." Again, Dryden's feeling for, and in fact his intellectual comprehension of, verbal harmony was uncommonly keen. He has much to say, and always shrewdly, about the relative balance of vowels and consonants in Latin, Italian, French, and English. Yet he does not indicate in his preface nor suggest in his translation the manner in which Virgil's figurative language participates vitally in the essential action that unfolds and consummates itself in the course of the poem. More recently, Rolfe Humphries, in the introduction to his 1951 version, has stressed the vigorous movement that characterises the *Aeneid*. "This is a composition . . . that *moves* in more senses than one. . . . Hear how the themes vary and recur; how the tone lightens and darkens, the volume swells or dies, the tempo rushes or lingers." But in practice (as, later, I shall briefly illustrate), Mr. Humphries tends to limit all that activity to the narrative alone, reducing the element of metaphor to mere static, or inactive, quality. But the poem's activity has both its source and to a great extent its very meaning within the dimension of imagery; even though it is perhaps my main point that that is the dimension least accessible to satisfactory translation.

Here are two exemplary passages (cf. the English versions by C. Day Lewis at the conclusion of this article), containing two key figures, that may be offered as representative both of the poem and of its special difficulty. Taken individually and together, the passages comprise two interplaying synecdoches, so to say, of the entire epic. The first gives us the initial appearance of Queen Dido (following

the picture of the Amazon Queen Penthesilea that Aeneas sees on
the wall of the Temple of Juno)—1.490-504:

> Ducit Amazonidum lunatis agmina peltis
> Penthesilea furens, mediisque in milibus ardet,
> aurea subnectens exsertae cingula mammae,
> bellatrix, audetque viris concurrere virgo.

> Haec dum Dardanio Aeneae miranda videntur,
> dum stupet, obtutuque haeret defixus in uno,
> regina ad templum, forma pulcherrima Dido,
> incessit magna iuvenum stipante caterva.
> Qualis in Eurotae ripis aut per iuga Cynthi
> exercet Diana choros, quam mille secutae
> hinc atque hinc glomerantur Oreades; illa pharetram
> fert umero, gradiensque deas supereminet omnis;
> Latonae tacitum pertemptant gaudia pectus:
> talis erat Dido, talem se laeta ferebat
> per medios, instans operi regnisque futuris.

The second passage, lines 141 to 150 in Book 4, give us the look of
Prince Aeneas, as he rides forth on the fateful day to join in the
hunt with Dido:

> Ipse ante alios pulcherrimus omnis
> Infert se socium Aeneas atque agmina iungit.
> Qualis ubi hibernam Lyciam Xanthique fluenta
> deserit ac Delum maternam invisit Apollo,
> instauratque choros, mixtique altaria circum
> Cretesque Dryopesque fremunt, picti Agathyrsi;
> ipse iugis Cynthi graditur, mollique fluentem
> fronde premit crinem fingens atque implicat auro;
> tela sonant umeris; haud illo segnior ibat
> Aeneas; tantum egregio decus enitet ore.

An ideal, or shall we say an angelic, translation of those passages
would not only solve particular questions of phrasing, and seek for
some English equivalent of the intricate variety of rhythm and
tempo. It would also reflect the highly animated paralleling, the
insistent echo of language and of metaphoric structure; the similitude *between* these two similitudes. It would adopt the Jamesian
principle of point-of-view (someone eventually will have to write
an essay called: "Henry James: the Virgil Aspect"), and would suggest—possibly by pace and weight—that the first passage is not direct
description so much as the impression made by a regally beautiful

woman upon a very masculine man; and the second, the impression
made by a princely man upon a very womanly woman. And it would
so manage the language of translation as to make evident to the
reader's imagination, ultimately and in retrospect, the synecdochic
nature of each passage: the way each adumbrates a major part of
the action, and the way the two together adumbrate the whole of
the action. Which is, of course, altogether impossible.

Let me, anyhow, try to justify the conditions laid down. The
echoes and parallels, for example, are at once striking and profound;
nor are they mere formulaic repetitions or epic clichés (it was Dryden's mistake, or his unavoidable choice, so to read them). In the
Aeneid, there are almost no formula-lines in the Homeric manner;
his song was primarily a written one, not dependent on a bardic
memory; and as to the conventional phrase, he tended to recharge it
in a way more reminiscent, for the modern, of T. S. Eliot, and fre-
quently to the same ironic or paradoxical ends. Scrutinising the two
quoted similes, then, we observe that *pulcherrima* Dido is, in the
first of them, presented in her likeness to the goddess Diana, leading
the dances (*choros*) on the ridges (*iuga*) of Mount Cynthus, on the
island of Delos; and *pulcherrimus* Aeneas is described in his likeness
to the god Apollo, restoring the dances (*choros*) on the ridges (*iuga*)
of Mount Cynthus, on the island of Delos. Further similarities gather
about the two divinities themselves. Both carry weapons on their
shoulders (*umero, umeris*); both are depicted as they walk (*gradiens,
graditur*). And, more important, for the kind of knowing reader on
whom Virgil was able to depend, there is the shared allusion to the
mother—to Latona, whose still maternal heart rejoices as Diana,
her daughter, leads the ceremonies; and, implicitly, to Latona again,
as Apollo abandons wintry Lycia and goes back to his mother's
home, the *Delum maternam* where he was born.

Diana and Apollo are, of course, sister and brother, the twin children of Delian Latona. The close similarity in structure and language of the two passages serve to join the *human* figures, Dido and
Aeneas, in a relationship comparable in closeness to that of the
divine figures, according to an almost geometric premise of likeness.
The union accomplished in the imagery is then consummated in
the fact when, fifteen lines later in Book 4 beyond the Apollo simile,
Dido and Aeneas—driven by a divinely contrived storm—bind
themselves in the act of love: in the *coniugium* enacted in the
mountainside cave of Carthage; "for with this name, *coniugium*,"
Virgil remarks gravely, "did Dido cover up her fault."

It was perhaps Gawin Douglas, Bishop of Dunkeld, in his *XII
Bukis of Eneados* (1553), who was most alert, among Virgilian

translators, to the existence and the dramatic value of those multiple parallels. Ezra Pound may be right in his belief (in "Notes on Elizabethan Classicists," *Literary Essays of Ezra Pound*, 1954, p. 245) that Douglas "gets more poetry out of Virgil than any other translator"; though Pound has rendered his opinion suspect in advance by contending tersely and somewhat inanely that "Douglas's *Eneados* (is) better than the original, as Douglas had heard the sea." Pound detested Virgil, and resented having in part to go through him to get at Homer. One does, however, see what Pound means when he adds that Gawin Douglas gives "a clue to Dante's respect for the Mantuan," something that had plainly puzzled him. Douglas's version of the two passages is muscular and alive, and it abounds with meaningful echoes.

> The queyn Dido, excellent in bewte,
> To tempill cumis with a fair menye
> Of lusty yinkeris walkyng her about.
> Lyke to the goddes Dian with hir rowt
> Endlang the flude of Eurot on the bra
> Or undir the toppis of hir hill Cynthia
> Ledand ryng dansys. . . .
>   To Latone her moder this
> Gevis rejosyng and secrete hartis blyss.

And in Book 4:

>   hym self thar kyng
> Enee gan entir in falloschip, but dout,
> And unto thame adjonyt hys large rowt.
> Lyke quhen Apollo list depart or ga
> Furth of hys wyntring realm of Lysya,
> To vissy Delos, his moderis land and ile
> Renewand ryngis and dansys, mony a rowt. . . .
> Als fresch, als lusty dyd Eneas ryde,
> With als gret bewte in hys lordly face.

In addition to the more commonplace references in both passages to *bewte, rowt, lusty* and *flude,* Douglas has caught the binding action of the two images of dancing—"ledand ryng dansys" and "renewand ryngis and dansys"; and of the recurring awareness of the mother—"to Latone her moder" (doubly admirable, since the phrase "her moder" is in fact contributed by Douglas, knowledge of the relationship being, as he saw, essential), and "his moderis land and ile." By contrast, one hundred and forty-odd years later, John Dryden gives almost no suggestion of the extent to which the similes are actively and creatively involved with one another. Dryden aimed first of all at registering his sensibility of the sweet flow and harmony of Virgil's verses (something he went far towards achieving in the melody of his English), so that the harmony of Virgil's concrete subject remained largely unnoticed. The verbal echoes are limited to such conventions as "above the rest" and "lofty mien"; the divine and human persons are transfixed by the bloodless and inactive adjective ("beauteous Dido," "great Aeneas," "fair Apollo"); and the island of Delos suffers a yet further reduction to mere "native." Dryden was a very remarkable judge of certain aspects of Virgil; but his *Aeneid* seems well below his translation, say, of the satires of Juvenal. His talent for vigorous, even aggressive phrase-making was thoroughly stimulated by Juvenal; but his Englishing of Virgil is a demonstration of another of Ezra Pound's notions—namely, that "The quality of translations declined in measure as the translators ceased to be absorbed in the subject-matter of the original. They ended in the 'Miltonian cliché.'"

How valid that notion is becomes clearer when we return to the subject-matter of the *Aeneid* as a whole, taking note, this time, of the participation in it of our two exemplary passages. Looking at them in reverse order, we can now observe that in the Aeneas-Apollo simile, the god is not only leading the dances on the slopes of Mount Cynthus. To do so, Apollo must first abandon his wintry Lycia (*hibernam Lyciam*), go *back* to his mother country, to maternal Delos, and there *renew* the dances (*instaurat*: renew, celebrate again; Douglas, as usual, is exact—"*renewand* ryngis and dansys"). It is with this surprising and seemingly maladroit figure that Virgil characterises the man Aeneas, who is actually dallying in Carthage with Dido, all negligent of duty. This is the sort of image for which Virgil has been accused of incompetence across many centuries; in fact, it is an instance of his greatest strength. The Apollonian image is more dynamic, so to speak, than pictorial; it is at once ironic and prophetic; it implies what Aeneas must himself eventually do, and measures his present erotic idling against that destiny. (This article must perforce—since it deals with Virgil—make frequent use of the helplessly unavoidable term "irony"; and in the present case, assuming the Apollo image to exist in Dido's consciousness, we witness again a deeply Jamesian irony—that of one character recording more and other than she knows, and of a nature that would destroy her if she *did* know.) For Aeneas, too, must soon abandon his winter palace in Carthage; must return to the mother country of his Trojan race (that is, to Italy); and there must renew the ceremonies of his people—while around him will murmur (*fremunt*) the mingled

voices, if not (as with Apollo) of Cretans and Dryopes and Aga-
thrysi, at least of Latins and Arcadians and Trojans.

The same Apollo who returns figuratively to his mother country
in 4.144 also explains to the Trojans in the actual narrative and on
the actual Delos that they must undertake an exactly analogous
journey. Landing at Delos, the Trojans worship at the shrine of
Apollo and beseech his guidance; and the god answers: that the land
which first produced them will in good time take them back.
"Antiquam exquirite matrem," he enjoins (3.96); and though Anchises, already rather senile, supposes this to mean Crete, a later
oracle specifies Italy as the place of tribal origin.

The astuteness of Gawin Douglas's translation, his attunement
with the Virgilian epic, is peculiarly evident at this point. The
references to "Latone her moder" and "Delos his moderis land and
ile" have their dramatic justification in the very nature and design
of the Trojan mission—in the actual statement of Apollo, which
Douglas renders as follows:

> The ilke grond, fra quham the first stok cam
> Of your lynnage, with blyth bosum the sam
> Sal you ressave thiddir returnyng agane:
> To seik your ald moder mak you bane.

(*Bane,* as Professor Helge Kökeritz has been kind enough to explain
to me, is a variant of the word *bain*—and a derivative of the Old
Norse word, *beinn*—meaning ready or prepared. "Make you ready
to seek your old mother.") That last line deserves italicizing, since
it amounts to a definition of the poem's central action. I am here
accepting the concept of "action" as propounded in various essays
by Francis Fergusson: as something best defined by an infinitive of
purpose, as "to find the killer of the king," or "to revenge the murder
of the father." It is in this sense of the term that the action of the
Aeneid has been so sharply identified by Douglas; for it is, exactly,
"to seik your ald moder." And the grounds, or better the sanction,
for such an enterprise, the grandeur, the propriety and indeed the
holiness of it: all this is established by Virgil's reminder, in Book 4,
that a comparable endeavor is characteristic—and according to
legend, annually so—of the god Apollo. Nor is Apollo, for Virgil,
any common sort of divinity. The god whose rhythmic and habitual
movement provides the pattern for the heroic human mission is the
god of poetry: a designation Virgil himself insists upon (especially in
certain lines of *Aeneid* 6, and in the *Georgics*). In seeking out his
race's ancient mother, Aeneas is thus acting in consonance with
nature, with art and with religion, and the significance of his ad-

venture is thereby heightened out of all bounds, made truly epic: while at the same time his momentary dereliction in Carthage is made to appear reprehensible to the edge of sacrilege.

It is just this microcosmic action in the Apollo simile that all but vanishes from the version of it offered by Rolfe Humphries. The potent charm of the latter's translation does not compensate for its dramatic thinning out:

> Aeneas
> Comes to her side, more lordly than Apollo
> Bright along Delos's ridges in the springtime
> With laurel in his hair and golden weapons
> Shining across his shoulders. Equal radiance
> Is all around Aeneas, equal splendor.

The dramatic details have there been dropped in favor of an intense, and beguiling, lyric glitter. The original Latin image, however, participates in the poem's action by itself containing an action (as Virgil's similes almost always do): Apollo leaves, visits, renews, steps. With Humphries, the image is simply a quality, seen variously as bright, shining, radiant, and splendid. Humphries equates the appearance of Aeneas with the appearance of Apollo; but Virgil compares their conduct, what they do. And the reason, as I have suggested, is that Virgil throughout the *Aeneid* is not so much picturing something as pressing towards or enacting something: enacting with all the resources known to poetry and on many different "levels" the classic drama of a necessary and sanctified return—the return of the dead to life, the return of the race to its homeland, the restoration of peace and order out of violence and disorder, along with the renewal of the year, of the ceremonies, of the human spirit.

Or rather, to be precise, he is enacting all that in part: in part, the *Aeneid* steadily mirrors an action of an opposite kind, a self-propelled movement towards defeat and death. It is hard, in our tension-ridden age, not to apprehend the *Aeneid* in terms of an unresolved tension or duality: a duality that persists to the very end, where it is fixed forever in that closing glimpse, not only of the victorious Aeneas but simultaneously (and perhaps more memorably) of Turnus's *vita indignata* ("Unconsenting spirit," C. Day Lewis) fleeing to the shades below. It is that dark underhalf of the poem that is secretly present in the other of our two passages, in the image of Dido-Diana, following immediately, as it does, the portraiture of Penthesilea on the temple wall. I do not myself see how translation could effectively manage to suggest this secret presence; but it may be pointed to, at least, in the language of

criticism. The character and both the present high position and the
tragic future destiny of Queen Dido are here indicated by means of
not one but two similes: one of them (to Diana) explicit, and one
(to Penthesilea) implicit and by juxtaposition.

As to Penthesilea, Virgil assumes one's knowledge of the legend
about her in the epic cycle and in vase paintings: the valiant and
beautiful young virgin warrior and queen, who fought on the
Trojan side in the old war and was slain by Greek Achilles, who,
grieving over her corpse, was taunted by Thersites. Such is the
memory, stimulated by the image, that Virgil asks us to carry into
the first glimpse of Dido; for even as Aeneas stands wondering at
the painted Amazon, the living queen steps into view. Over the
description of Dido's beauty, authority and grace, the image of
Penthesilea casts a very dark shadow. For Dido, too, is a valiant
young queen; herself possibly a virgin, and now altogether chaste
in her widowhood; able, like the Amazon, to hold her own with
the heroes, the dangerous neighboring princes. And Dido, too, will
eventually be slain, or anyhow driven to madness and self-slaughter,
by the man who in this poem takes on the victorious aspects of
Achilles and who will likewise grieve over her speechless ghost (as
he will, incidentally, imitate Achilles as well by slaying the literal
counterpart of Penthesilea in the *Aeneid,* the swift-footed Camilla).

Later, in Book 4, Virgil will attach to Dido some of the language
used here, in Book 1, about Penthesilea. *Aurea subnectens exsertae
cingula mammae,* he says here; and the line is echoed by *aurea
purpuream subnectit fibula vestem* in 4.139, just ten words before
the start of the Apollo simile. (The image of Dido at this moment
also includes the very phrase attached, in the Book 1 simile, to the
goddess Diana: *magna stipante caterva.*) Far more significant are
the key words *furens* and *ardet* that characterise the militant conduct of Penthesilea and that then turn up, in Book 4, to characterise
the behavior of Dido. But it is exactly at this point that the full
force of the two similes in Book 1—the implicit and the explicit—
realises itself. The nature of that force is, as poetically it should be,
the opposite of the force of the Aeneas-Apollo simile. The latter is
immediately ironic (considering Aeneas's actual occupation), but it
is ultimately descriptive, or perhaps *pre*scriptive. The two similes
involving Dido, on the contrary, are immediately descriptive, but
ultimately ironic, and very tragically so. When *furens* and *ardet*
are associated with Dido in Book 4, they represent not (as with
Penthesilea) the flaming heroics of a virgin warrior—but the sexual
fires of a woman raging with physical passion. *Totaque vagatur
urbe furens,* Virgil reports in 4.69; and *"Ardet amans Dido, traxit-*

que per ossa furorem," exults Juno, in 4.101. ("She wanders raging
through the city. . . . 'Dido burns and her whole frame rages with
love,' " C. Day Lewis). Dido, likened initially to the virgin warrior
and the rites-observing goddess of chastity, has by line 300 of Book
4 pulled so far away from both, has so far betrayed her political
and religious duties, as to be comparable to "some Bacchante driven
wild and drawn at night to the Bacchic orgies"; and by line 470 to
Pentheus (is there a slight twisty echo of Penthesilea in that familiar
name?), raving on the Theban hills, destined to be torn in pieces by
the Bacchae.

The Aeneas-Apollo simile, I have argued, participates in the
action of the *Aeneid* by providing a divine archetype which it is
the business of Aeneas and his followers to emulate—in their huge
enactment of the personal, moral, racial, and national *return*. In
a considerably more complex and even paradoxical manner, the
Penthesilea-Dido simile combines with the Dido-Diana simile to
participate in an action of an opposite kind: in the multiple movement towards personal and moral and national death which the
poem embraces. Just as, for example, the allusions to the mother
Latona are grounded in the divine injunction to "seik your ald
moder," so the allusions to *furens* and *ardet* and so on reach their
fulfillment when the individual death and funeral pyre of Dido, in
4.669-671, are analogised to the fall and destruction of the entire
city by fire:

> Non aliter, quam si inmissis ruat hostibus omnis
> Karthago aut antiqua Tyros, flammaeque furentes
> Culmina perque hominum volvantur perque deorum.

Of contemporary translators, C. Day Lewis is probably the one who
has best perceived the crucial continuity of the imagery at work
here:

> It was as if Carthage or ancient Tyre should be falling,
> With enemy troops breaking into the town and a conflagration
> Furiously sweeping over the abodes of men and of gods.

Lewis has grounded that version in his earlier renderings of
Penthesilea "storming through the melee like a fire," and in his
English account (quoted, for example, in an earlier paragraph) of
the burning fury of Queen Dido. The *Aeneid* of C. Day Lewis is
not always exhilarating, nor has it been able to capture very much
of the sheer beauty of the original; it has a somewhat dogged quality. But it also has the merit of leaving nothing out, and of staying
with the exact line-count of the Latin. Beyond that, it is a transla-

tion which usually tries and often succeeds in carrying over into
English the steady, almost relentless drama of the Virgilian poem
—in discovering in English an echo of the active Virgilian echoes.
It is, therefore, by way of a tribute to this version that I borrow
from it a full translation of the passages with which we have been
concerned.

(Aeneas) picked out Penthesilea leading the crescent shields of
The Amazons and storming through the melee like a fire,
Her bare breast thrusting out over the golden girdle,
A warrior queen, a girl who braved heroes in combat.
Now while Aeneas viewed with wonder all these scenes,
And stood at gaze, rooted in a deep trance of attention,
There came in royal state to the temple, a crowd of courtiers
Attending her, queen Dido, most beautiful to see.
As by the banks of Eurotas or over the Cynthian slopes
Diana foots the dance, a thousand Oreads following
Weave a constellation around that arrowy one,
Who in grace of movement excels all goddesses,
And happiness runs through the still heart of Latona—
So Dido was, even as she went her radiant way
Through the crowds, eager to forward the work and growth of her realm.

(1.490-504)

                                But by far the handsomest of them all
Was Aeneas, who came to her side now and joined forces with hers.
It was like when Apollo leaves Lycia, his winter palace,
And Xanthus river to visit Delos, his mother's home,
And renew the dances, while round his altar Cretans and Dryopes
And the tattooed Agathyrsi are raising a polyglot din:
The god himself steps out on the Cynthian range, a circlet
Of gold and a wreath of pliant bay on his flowing hair,
The jangling weapons slung from his shoulder. Nimble as he,
Aeneas moved, with the same fine glow on his handsome face.   (4.141-50)

Some Characteristics
of Literary Epic

by C. M. Bowra

In the disputable and usually futile task of classifying the forms
of poetry there is no great quarrel about the epic. An epic poem
is by common consent a narrative of some length and deals with
events which have a certain grandeur and importance and come
from a life of action, especially of violent action such as war. It
gives a special pleasure because its events and persons enhance our
belief in the worth of human achievement and in the dignity and
nobility of man. Inside this field it is easy to make distinctions, and
everyone is familiar with that between "authentic" and "literary"
epic. Such a distinction may invite distrust. For in the fine arts no
rules are binding, and it is dangerous to be too precise in saying
what a thing is or what it ought to be. And this particular distinction may well arouse other misgivings; for we may suspect that the
adjectives are not chosen impartially but betray a liking for one
kind of poetry and a dislike for another. While "authentic" suggests the wild wood-notes of pure poetry, the inspired, direct and
unpremeditated song of the poet whom culture has not corrupted,
"literary" suggests the derivative and the manufactured, the poverty
of *le vers calculé* against the wealth of *le vers donné*, the reliance
on books instead of on life, all that Verlaine meant when, after
sketching his ideal poem, he said

Et tout le reste est littérature.

When the innocent student is first confronted by the antithesis between "authentic" and "literary" epic, he must surely feel that he
should admire the first and be suspicious, if not contemptuous, of

the second, while those experienced in the ways of critics must no less surely feel that the distinction is prejudiced if not false, and is perhaps dictated by irrational beliefs in *Volksgeist* and *Volkspoesie* and by theories which in the interests of racial mysticism ascribe all excellences to the anonymous activities of a community rather than to the deliberate work of individual poets.

Yet though this distinction rightly arouses distrust, it would be wrong to dismiss it as worthless. There is undeniably a great difference between *Beowulf* and the *Song of Roland* on the one hand and the *Aeneid* and *Paradise Lost* on the other. But this difference is not primarily one of poetical quality. If the *Aeneid* can show nothing so stark or so sublime as Roland's refusal to blow his horn, the *Song of Roland* has nothing so intimate or so tragic as the last hours and death of Dido. Each poem succeeds in its own way; each makes its special contribution to the vision and understanding of life. We cannot say that the one kind is necessarily better than the other; we can merely mark the differences between them and enjoy the pleasure that each has to give. But though it is easy to recognise a distinction between two kinds of epic, that is not enough to justify us in calling the one "authentic" and the other "literary." Such a division must be made on more solid grounds than a vague dissimilarity between two kinds of aesthetic enjoyment. And in fact such grounds exist. The two classes of epic are really distinct because their technique is different and because each owes its character to special methods of composition.

The distinction between *Beowulf* and *Paradise Lost,* to take two extreme examples, is mainly that between oral and written epic, between what is meant to be heard and what is meant to be read, between what is recited and what is put down in a book. Oral epic is the mature form of improvised lays such as still survive in Jugoslavia and were once popular in many parts of the world. In such countries the bard, like Homer's Demodocus, composes his poem as he recites it. He improvises impromptu, and his art requires a long and elaborate training. To tell a tale in this way he must have at his complete command a large number of lines and phrases to deal with any situation in his story; he may have stock passages for such recurring themes as the throwing of a weapon, the putting of a boat to sea, the coming of morning or evening, and all the other machinery of story-telling; he must have a rich supply of stories, for he may be called to recite any of them; he may have to be master of a traditional language which bears little relation to the vernacular of his home and has been created by generations of bards simply as the language of poetry. In his case the Greek fancy that Memory

is the Mother of the Muses is true. For unless his technique is at
his finger-tips, unless he can surmount with immediate and unnoticed ease whatever difficulties his theme presents, he will hesitate
and stumble and fail. His task is to use as best as he can for his
immediate purpose the phrases and lines which he has learned in
his apprenticeship. Of such an art Homer shows a transcendent
development. It is impossible to believe that the *Iliad* and the
Odyssey, as we know them, were ever improvised, but their technique is largely that of improvisation and comes directly from it.
The famous constant epithets, the repeated lines and blocks of lines,
the copious store of synonyms and of alternative word-forms, are a
heritage from improvisation. Homer practises on a grand scale an
oral art which has grown out of improvised poetry, and this art is
in many technical respects the art of *Beowulf* and the *Song of
Roland*. The conditions of improvisation and of recitation have
created a kind of poetry which can be recognised by its use of repetitions and formulas. And this poetry is far removed from that of
Virgil or Milton. If they sometimes show traces of it, it is because
they are following Homer in the conscious conviction that they
ought to do so, not because their conditions compel them to use
devices which are indispensable to oral poetry and make it what it
is.

This difference in conditions of composition leads to a difference
in the character of the poetry. Because Homer composed for recitation, his composition is in some ways freerer and looser than Virgil's.
Both his poems have a majestic plan; both pass through crisis to a
conclusion. But they are less closely woven than the *Aeneid*; their
episodes are more easily detached from the whole and may be
enjoyed as separate poems. The Greek epic poet might compose on
a grand scale, but he could not always or even often expect to recite
his poem in its entirety. He must be prepared to select from it, to
recite only a section which must be relatively complete in itself
and not require too much explanation for its understanding. Because Homer, especially in the *Iliad*, has a loose method of composition, his art has been misjudged, and it has even been thought
that his poems are collections of separate lays fastened together, as
philologists of the nineteenth century fashioned the Finnish *Kale-
vala* from lays by different authors. But the *Iliad* is a single poem
with a single plan and a remarkably consistent use of language. Its
looseness of construction and of texture is the product of the circumstances in which it was composed; it might be used for piece-
meal recitations and must be ready for them. Even Homer's apparent carelessness about details, which might seem a fault in a

novelist, is part of his oral art. He must concentrate severely on what is really relevant, and if he were to give too much attention to small points, he would confuse his listeners and lose their attention. Modern critics, for instance, may complain that at an important crisis Achilles puts down his spear only to be found with it in his hand later, but Homer knew that the taking up of a spear is in itself of no interest, provided that Achilles has his spear when he needs it.

Between Homer's oral and Virgil's written art there is an enormous difference. The poet who writes for readers operates less with phrases and formulas than with single words. He fashions his sentences carefully and individually; he takes care to avoid omissions and contradictions, to harmonise the details of his plot, to secure an interwoven unity for his whole design. Even when he follows Homer in using the oral device of repetition, Virgil goes his own way and makes variations on a given form. For him the artifices of oral poetry are valuable for their archaic elegance; their beauty is no longer functional. Virgil is seldom wholehearted in his attempts at repetition. He prefers to vary the words and to show in how many different ways he can describe such familiar matters as the coming of dawn or of evening. Even when his characters speak to each other, they do so not with Homer's regular forms of address but with elaborate variations, no two of which are quite alike. The old formulas were of no real use to Virgil and were even a hindrance; for his aim was to compose a poem which could be read with exact and appreciative care, and for that reason he gains more by variation than by repetition.

Virgil's art is in fact akin to other modern poetry. Its aim is to pack each line with as much significance as possible, to make each word do its utmost work and to secure that careful attention which the reader, unlike the listener, can give. If the oral epic triumphs through its simplicity and strength and straightforwardness, through the unhesitating sweep of its narrative and a brilliant clarity in its main effects, the written epic appeals by its poetical texture, by its exquisite or apt or impressive choice of words, by the rich significance of phrases and lines and paragraphs. Homer sweeps us away by the irresistible movement of lines through a whole passage to a splendid climax. What counts is the singleness of his effect, the unbroken maintenance of a heroic or tragic mood, the concentration on some action vividly imagined and clearly portrayed without irrelevance or second thoughts or even those hints that lure into bypaths of fancy and suggest that there is more in the words than is obvious at first sight. But in Virgil, great though the paragraphs are, compelling though the climax is when it is reached, we are more concerned with the details, with each small effect and each deftly placed word, than with the whole. We linger over the richness of single phrases, over the "pathetic half-lines," over the precision or potency with which a word illuminates a sentence or a happy sequence of sounds imparts an inexplicable charm to something that might otherwise have been trivial. Of course Homer has his magical phrases and Virgil his bold effects, but the distinction stands. It is a matter of composition, of art, and it marks the real difference between the two kinds of epic, which are not so much "authentic" and "literary" as oral and written.

*   *   *

The difference in the methods of epic composition coincides on the whole with another difference which is social and even spiritual. For most oral epics display what is commonly and rightly called a heroic spirit and come from societies which holds heroic standards of conduct, while literary epics, though they have their "heroes," have a different conception of heroism and of human greatness and come from societies which cannot really be called heroic. The heroic world holds nothing so important as the prowess and fame of the individual hero. The single man, Achilles or Beowulf or Roland, surpasses others in strength and courage. His chief, almost his only, aim is to win honour and renown through his achievements and to be remembered for them after his death. He is ruthless to any who frustrate or deride him. In his more than human strength he seems to be cut off from the intercourse of common men and consorts with a few companions only less noble than himself. He lacks allegiance, except in a modified sense, to suzerain or cause. What matters is his prowess. Even morality hardly concerns him; for he lives in a world where what counts is not morality but honour. Historically, this ideal seems to have grown in societies which have burst through the stiff forms of primitive life. It is the reflection of men's desire to be in the last degree themselves, to satisfy their ambitions in lives of abundant adventure, to be greater than other men in their superior gifts, and to be bound by no obligation except to do their uttermost in valour and endurance. If they succeeded, such men were thought to be comparable almost to gods. This ideal, outmoded though it has long been in most parts of the world and intolerable as it is in civilised society, had its uses when peoples were on the move, as the Greeks were in the dawn of their history or the Angles and Saxons were when they came to England from their continental homes. In such times the hero, the superman, is the leader who inspires and commands others in the work of war which precedes the establishment of a new order.

The claim of this heroic ideal is that after all it is an ideal and that its adherents are ready to make any sacrifice for it. Even though Achilles lives mainly to win glory and assumes that it is his right, his life is darkened by suffering and at the end he dies for his belief in his heroic manhood. His aim is not ease but glory, and glory makes exacting demands. A man who is willing to give his life for it wins the respect of his fellows, and when he makes his last sacrifice, they honour him. Even Roland, who ostensibly fights for Charlemagne and for Christendom, comes to his heroic end simply because his honour has been wounded and he feels that he must make amends by facing incalculable odds. In fact, what counts in the high estimate in which such men are held is not so much their power to destroy as their readiness to die. Their heroism is the greater because they sacrifice pre-eminent gifts of strength or beauty or eloquence or counsel. The doom of a short and glorious life which hangs over Achilles is tragic in its menace that he, the noblest and most gifted of men, is soon to go down to the dust and be made equal to the humblest servant. The memory of Roland haunted the Middle Ages because he, the greatest of soldiers, was willing to give his life for something that he valued above everything else,— his honour. It is because they are ready to make this last annihilating sacrifice that heroes are honoured. Compared with this even their courage and prowess are of secondary importance.

The truly heroic ideal and standards of conduct did not exist for the writers of literary epic. Though Virgil was a devoted student of Homer and owed much to him, he had quite a different conception of human worth and lived in a society from which Homer's heroes were remote and alien. When he took the traditional epic form, he had to adapt it to the changed conditions of his own day. Between him and his heroic models lay a vast tract of history. He looked to the past for inspiration, but his work was inevitably shaped by the present. His epic has rightly been called "secondary"; for it was an attempt to use again in new circumstances what had already been a complete and satisfactory form of poetry. Virgil differs from Homer in at least two essential points. First, his method of composition, as we have seen, is meant for readers, and in consequence the whole texture of his poetry is different. Secondly, his conception of heroism is equally different. He has one, but it is not Homer's, or indeed that of any heroic age. The whole temper of the *Aeneid* is far from that of the *Iliad*. Virgil created a poetry which was epic in its scope and nobility and sense of human worth but was unlike any other epic before it. So great was his success that other poets have followed his example, and their performance is such that we can mark a whole class of literary epic, discern its special characteristics and consider it as a whole.

It may seem artificial to class the work of such men as Camões, Tasso and Milton with that of Virgil,—for the good reason that not only did they write after him but they knew his work well and consciously imitated it in many ways. Indeed the whole theory of epic in the Renaissance was built upon Virgil's practice. When the "immortal" Vida wrote his *Ars Poetica,* he laid down rules for epic of an exact and exacting kind, and insisted that any modern epic must closely follow a Virgilian model. To these rules the epic poets of the Renaissance were in their different ways obedient. Epic had become almost a standard form, and the poets competed in the new turns which they gave to a traditional theme or device. It might therefore be claimed that these poets model themselves on Virgil and are his successors and imitators but not his peers in the same kind of poetry. This might well be true, but the facts suggest a different conclusion. The epic poets of the Renaissance were indeed Virgilians both in their desire to rival him and in their dependence on him, but they were also his peers because they did in their own way what he had done in his and because the conditions in which they worked were often like his and led to independent results which are comparable to his. Literary epic is the work of a real class of poets who resemble each other in aim and outlook, and it is widely separated from heroic epic both ancient and modern.

The fundamental difference between literary and oral epic is in the circumstances of origin. The writers of literary epic lived in highly organised societies where unfettered individualism had no place. Neither Virgil under the all-pervading influence of Augustus Caesar, nor Camões under the Catholic monarchy of Portugal, nor Tasso under the Counter-Reformation, nor Milton under Cromwell and the Puritans, was likely to praise the virtues of a noble barbarian. Even their lords and patrons did not claim to be heroes in the old sense. Augustus liked to be thought the first citizen of Rome, bound by all the decencies of conventional morality; the potentates and prelates of the Renaissance, Reformation and Counter-Reformation were Christian rulers who believed that they were at least subordinate to God. Man had changed his place in the universe. His life was no longer a short span of light in the encompassing darkness, his duty no longer towards himself. From the eminence of his own glory he had been reduced to a subordinate position where he was much inferior to the state or the church to which he belonged. Cosmogonies and theologies had arisen which displayed his insignificance before the vast abyss of time, the claims of empire, or the will of God. The very qualities for which the old heroes had been honoured were themselves suspect or barely understood. That Achilles or Roland should harm their sovereign lieges from motives of injured pride was not a notion to appeal to the potentates of imperial Rome or Renaissance Europe. Nor in such times could individual prowess have the significance that it had for Homer. The great prince was not the warrior who defeated his enemies in hand-to-hand encounter but the organiser of victory and the administrator who imposed his will upon other men. It was impossible for the epic poet to treat his subject in the old heroic spirit. If he wished to present a heroic theme, he must create a new type of hero and a new ideal of heroism.

It is certainly paradoxical that civilised societies and their poets should claim for those whom they admire names and titles which belong to ages very unlike their own, and that the conception of heroic man should appeal as it did to the Augustan age and the Renaissance. In such a quest different forces were at work. Both at Rome and in the Renaissance the epic was thought to be the grandest and noblest form of poetry and the right means to celebrate great achievements. No doubt its scale was felt to be appropriate to such subjects. Its mere size appealed to a love of grandeur and magnificence. But more important was the spirit of the epic, its attempt to find significance in the achievements of man and to show him in his essential nobility. The writers of literary epic held new and different conceptions of human greatness, but such was their concern for it that epic alone could suffice to portray it. Moreover they were particularly impressed by the special form which the old heroic outlook took. The great hero, Achilles or Roland, appeals to two deep impulses of the human heart, the desire for glory and the respect for sacrifice. Through the second the first is satisfied; the hero sacrifices his life and wins thereby an immortal glory. When this happens, the human state gains in dignity, and the value of its efforts is triumphantly affirmed. It must have been for this reason more than for any other that Virgil and his successors believed that only through epic could they say all that they wished. It was the right means for them to assert their belief in human greatness and to show the special form of it which they honoured.

Virgil revealed a new field both for glory and for sacrifice. The cause which deserves the one and inspires the other was for him not an ideal of individual prowess but of service to Rome. It is Rome to whom in the last resort the glory of her sons belongs, and it is for her that they make their sacrifices not merely of life but of happiness and personal ambitions and all that the old heroic type took for granted as its right. Virgil abandons the scheme of life by which the hero lives and dies for his own glory, and replaces a personal by a social ideal. The old concept of a man's honour is merged in a scheme of morality where duties are laid down with precision and must be fulfilled if the gods' will is to be done. Virgil revealed an entirely new use for epic to an age for which the old heroic outlook was too anarchic and anti-social. With him the epic became national, and though later it was to extend its scope beyond the boundaries of nations and of continents, his was the first step in a new direction. Moreover, because he had a new outlook on human greatness, he brought into the epic much that earlier poets denied or neglected. Above all he made it contain almost a philosophy of life and death, a view of the universe which answered many desires in the heart of man and provided an impressive background to the new ideal. Virgil's epic is still epic because it treats of what is greatest and noblest in man; it is of a new kind because this greatness and this nobility are themselves new.

Virgil and the Subject
of Secondary Epic

by C. S. Lewis

> This visage tells thee that my doom is past;
> Nor should the change be mourned, even if the joys
> Of sense were able to return as fast
> And surely as they vanish. Earth destroys
> Those raptures duly—Erebus disdains:
> Calm pleasures there abide—majestic pains.
>
> Wordsworth

The epic subject, as later critics came to understand it, is Virgil's invention; he has altered the very meaning of the word epic. Starting from the desire that the Romans should have a great poem to rival the *Iliad,* he had to ask himself what kind of poem would really express and satisfy the Roman spirit. The answer to this question he doubtless found in his own heart; we can find it by considering the earlier Roman attempts in this kind. The two previous Latin epics had been quite remarkably unlike Homer. Naevius had told the story of the first Punic War, but apparently on so large a scale that he could begin with the legend of Aeneas. Ennius, starting with the same legend, had worked steadily through the history of his people down to his own time. It is clear that both poets wrote what we should call metrical chronicles, things very much more like the work of Layamon and Robert of Gloucester than that of Homer. They catered for a taste common to the Romans and ourselves, but curiously lacking among the Greeks. Neither Herodotus nor Thucydides attempted to trace the history of even a single Greek state from its origins. The phenomena of growth, the slow process by which some great thing has taken its present shape, does not seem to have interested the Greeks. Their heart's desire was the timeless, the unchangeable, and they saw time as mere flux. But the Romans were different. Whether directly or (as Dr. Tillyard would say) 'obliquely' their great poem, unless it was to be a mere pastiche of Homer, would have to deal with the same sort of material as Naevius and Ennius. Yet, on the other hand, so true an artist as Virgil could not be content with the clumsiness and monotony of a mere chronicle. His solution of the problem— one of the most important revolutions in the history of poetry— was to take one single national legend and treat it in such a way that we feel the vaster theme to be somehow implicit in it. He has to tell a comparatively short story and give us the illusion of having lived through a great space of time. He has to deal with a limited number of personages and make us feel as if national, or almost cosmic, issues are involved. He must locate his action in a legendary past and yet make us feel the present, and the intervening centuries, already foreshadowed. After Virgil and Milton, this procedure seems obvious enough. But it is obvious only because a great poet, faced with an all but insoluble problem, discovered this answer and with it discovered new possibilities for poetry itself.

Partly as the result of romantic primitivism a silly habit has grown up of making Homer a kind of norm by which Virgil is to be measured. But the radical differences between them begin to appear on the very first page of the *Aeneid*. The third paragraph of the poem (ll. 12 to 33) furnishes us with examples of nearly all the methods whereby he makes his comparatively simple fable carry the weight of so much destiny. Notice the key words. Carthage is an *ancient* city, facing the Tiber's mouth a *long way off*. He is already spreading out his story both in time and space. Juno hoped to give it *empire* of the earth, if the *fates* allow: but she has already heard a rumour that *one day* (*olim*) the Trojan seed will bruise it. The whole Punic War has come in. But Juno is not thinking only of the future; an *older war* is rankling in her mind—she thinks of her Argives at Troy wall, of the Judgement of Paris, 'and Ganymede exalted to immortal place.' We are not, you see, at the beginning. The story on which we are embarked fades backward into an even remoter past. The heroes whose adventures we are to follow are the *remnant* (*reliquias*) of some earlier order, destroyed before the curtain rose; survivors, and, as it were ghosts, hunted (and here wideness in space comes in again) *maria omnia circum*, while Juno bars them from Latium,

> Leading them far, for-wandered, over alien foam;
> So mighty was the labour of the birth of Rome.

The labour, the *moles,* is the point. These men are not fighting
for their own land like Homeric heroes; they are men with a vocation, men on whom a burden is laid.

The more obvious instances of this enlargement of Virgil's subject have, no doubt, often been noticed—the glimpses of the future
in Jove's prophecy in Book 1, or in the vision of Anchises, or in
the shield, or again the connexion of the whole fourth Book with
the Punic Wars. Perhaps the most moving of all these forward links
is the visit of Aeneas to the site of Rome in Book 8. The backward
links are of equal importance in determining the poetical quality
of the *Aeneid.* If I am not mistaken it is almost the first poem which
carries a real sense of the 'abysm of time.' *Priscus, vetus,* and *antiquus*
are key-words in Virgil. In Books 6 to 8—the true heart of the poem
—we are never allowed to forget that Latium—*Lurkwood,* the
hiding place of aged Saturn—has been waiting for the Trojans from
the beginning of the world. The palace of King Latinus is very unlike any house in Homer: 'Awful with woods and piety of elder days,'

> Where carved in ancient cedar their old sires appear
> In order: father Italus and grey Sabine
> Bearing his hook in token how he loved the vine,
> And Saturn old and Janus with his double face . . .   (8.180)

There is a poetry that reiterated readings cannot exhaust in all these
early Italian scenes; in the first sight of the Tiber, the lonely prayer to
that unknown river, and the long river journey on which the ships
startle those hitherto unviolated forests. I do not know a better example of imagination, in the highest sense, than when Charon
wonders at the Golden Bough 'so long unseen'; dark centuries of
that unhistoried lower world are conjured up in half a line (6.409).

But Virgil uses something more subtle than mere *length* of time.
Our life has bends as well as extension: moments at which we
realize that we have just turned some great corner, and that
everything, for better or worse, will always henceforth be different.
In a sense, as we have already seen, the whole *Aeneid* is the story
of just such a transition in the world-order, the shift of civilisation
from the East to the West, the transformation of the little remnant,
the *reliquias,* of the old, into the germ of the new. Hence the sadness of farewells and the alacrity of new beginnings, so conspicuously brought together at the opening of Book 3, dominate the
whole poem. Sometimes the sense of *paes ofereode* is made explicit,
as when the Trojans arrive at Actium and find themselves at last,
beyond hope, disengaged from the Greek world, and this important
moment is underlined by a change of season,

> Meanwhile the sun had rolled through the delaying year
> And icy winter, roughing the dark waves, was here.   (3.285)

Sometimes it is an infinitesimal change of language which may pass the reader's conscious mind unnoticed, but which doubtless plays its part in colouring his total experience, as when the old Aegean hatreds have slipped far enough behind for *crafty Ulysses* to become *unfortunate Ulysses*. Perhaps one of Virgil's most daring successes is the appearance of Creusa's ghost in Book 2. The sad, ineffectual creature, shouldered aside by destiny, must come to prophesy the wife who will replace her and the fortunes of her husband in which she will have no share. If she were a living woman it would be inexcusable cruelty. But she is not a woman, she is a ghost, the wraith of all that which, whether regretted or unregretted, is throughout the poem drifting away, settling down, into the irrevocable past, not, as in elegiac poets, that we may luxuriate in melancholy reflections on mutability, but because the *fates of Jove* so order it, because, thus and not otherwise, some great thing comes about. Aeneas himself is mistaken for a ghost in the next book. In a sense he *is* a ghost of Troy until he becomes the father of Rome. All through the poem we are turning that corner. It is this which gives the reader of the *Aeneid* the sense of having lived through so much. No man who has once read it with full perception remains an adolescent.

This theme of the great transition is, of course, closely connected with the Virgilian sense of Vocation. Nothing separates him so sharply from Homer, and that, sometimes, in places where they are superficially most alike. Aeneas' speech encouraging his men in Book 1 (198) is closely modelled on Odysseus' speech in *Odyssey* 12 (208). Both remind their followers that they have been in tighter places before. But Odysseus speaks simply as any captain to any crew; safety is the goal. Aeneas adds something quite un-Homeric:

> One day it will be pastime to recall this woe,
> Through all these freaks of fortune and hard straits we go
> Right onward to the promised home, the Latian earth,
> Where we shall rest and Ilium have her second birth.   (1.206)

Vicit iter durum pietas ("piety has conquered this hard road"); with this conception Virgil has added a new dimension to poetry. I have read that his Aeneas, so guided by dreams and omens, is hardly the shadow of a man beside Homer's Achilles. But a man, an adult, is precisely what he is: Achilles had been little more than a passionate boy. You may, of course, prefer the poetry of spontaneous

passion to the poetry of passion at war with vocation, and finally
reconciled. Every man to his taste. But we must not blame the
second for not being the first. With Virgil European poetry grows
up. For there are certain moods in which all that had gone before
seems, as it were, boys' poetry, depending both for its charm and for
its limitations on a certain naivety, seen alike in its heady ecstasies
and in its heady despairs, which we certainly cannot, perhaps should
not, recover. *Mens immota manet,* 'the mind remains unshaken
while the vain tears fall.' That is the Virgilian note. But in Homer
there was nothing, in the long run, to be unshaken *about*. You were
unhappy, or you were happy, and that was all. Aeneas lives in a different world; he is compelled to see something more important than
happiness.

It is the nature of a vocation to appear to men in the double
character of a duty and a desire, and Virgil does justice to both.
The element of desire is brought out in all those passages where
the Hesperian land is hinted, prophesied, and 'dimdiscovered.' First
through the lips of Hector's ghost, a land still without a name; then
by Creusa's ghost, with the names *Hesperia* and *Tiber* added; then
comes the all-important third Book, the reluctant yet unfaltering
search for the *abiding city* (*mansuram urbem*), always supposed to
be so near and always in reality so distant, and our slowly increasing
knowledge of it. It is our *ancient mother*—it is a *terra antiqua,*
mighty in arms and rich in soil—it is quite close, but not for us who
must go many miles about and make a different landfall—now it is
in sight, but not the part of it we seek. This is the very portrait of a
vocation: a thing that calls or beckons, that calls inexorably, yet you
must strain your ears to catch the voice, that insists on being sought,
yet refuses to be found.

In the human response to this we find the element of duty. On
the one hand we have Aeneas, who suffers, but obeys. He has one
moment of real disobedience in the fourth Book, which we read all
amiss because an increased respect for woman and for the sexual
relation have made the hero appear inhuman at the very moment
when Virgil intends to exhibit (and for a historically minded reader
does exhibit) his human weakness. But everywhere else he bears the
yoke well, though with a wistful side-glance at those not called to
bear it.

> Live happy! you whose story is accomplish'd. We
> Commanded, move from destiny to destiny.
> Your rest is won. You wander the wide seas no more,
> Nor seek that ever-vanishing Ausonian shore.   (3.496)

On the other hand, we have the women, who have heard the call, and lived long in painful obedience, and yet desert at last. Virgil perceives their tragedy very clearly. To follow the vocation does not mean happiness: but once it has been heard, there is no happiness for those who do not follow. They are, of course, *allowed* to stay behind. Every arrangement is made for their comfort in Sicily. The result is that agonized parting in which the will remains suspended between two equal intolerables.

> 'Twixt miserable longing for the present land
> And the far realms that call them by the fates' command.   (5.656)

It will be seen that in these two lines Virgil, with no intention of allegory, has described once and for all the very quality of most human life as it is experienced by any one who has not yet risen to holiness or sunk to animality. It is not thanks to the fourth Eclogue alone that he has become almost a great Christian poet. In making his one legend symbolical of the destiny of Rome, he has, willy-nilly, symbolized the destiny of Man. His poem is 'great' in a sense in which no poem of the same type as the *Iliad* can ever be great. The real question is whether any epic development beyond Virgil is possible. But one thing is certain. If we are to have another epic it must go on from Virgil. Any return to the *merely* heroic, any lay, however good, that tells merely of brave men fighting to save their lives or to get home or to avenge their kinsmen, will now be an anachronism. You cannot be young twice. The explicity religious subject for any future epic has been dictated by Virgil; it is the only further development left.

Odysseus and Aeneas

by Theodore Haecker

It was twenty long years before Odysseus at last returned to his homeland—returned poor, naked and a beggar, it is true, but a conqueror. He returned and found again there almost everything that home stands for; he found his island, his earth, the place where as a child he had first known the light and beauty of the world; his old father was still there, his wife and his son, his faithful hound—surely the very picture of a happy home-coming! But what of Aeneas—to what did he come? Does he really resemble Odysseus at any point? No—there is no greater difference within the whole compass of ancient literature; and to understand that is to see how absurd are those critics who would dismiss Virgil contemptuously as a mere plagiarist and imitator of Homer. There is no more profound or astonishing originality in all the literature of antiquity than Virgil's; and that precisely because it operates within the limits imposed by the inherited and traditional forms, which it reverently observes. But to return to Aeneas—does he, like Odysseus, come back to the land of his childhood? We are told incidentally, it is true, that Aeneas's ancestors had once dwelt in Italy, but this is mere political rhetoric, and has nothing to do with the story proper, the personal fate of Aeneas, where in fact it is entirely forgotten. Aeneas did not return to the home of his childhood; on the contrary, he left it, and he left it as a fugitive (*fato profugus*)— witness the fact that Turnus, who had always remained at home in Latium, refers to him contemptuously and reproachfully as *desertorem Asiae,* deserter of Asia, a coward forgetful of his duty, flying from the colours. And this of Aeneas, of the ancestor of Caesar, of the mirror of Augustus! Aeneas was no victorious Greek, but a defeated Trojan like Hector. In that night of horror and desolation in the burning city of Troy, his wife, *dulcis coniunx,* had perished,

"Odysseus and Aeneas." From *Virgil, Father of the West* by Theodore Haecker, published by Sheed and Ward, Inc., New York. Reprinted by permission of Sheed and Ward, Inc., New York.

and alone he had carried away his aged father and the *penates;* beside him, hardly able to keep pace with him, ran his little son. His father died on the journey—the father of *pius Aeneas* whose very life, the inmost spring of whose being was love of his father and his father's love of him—and he buried him. So far as he alone was concerned, so far as concerned only his own selfish will, his personal inclination, his own earth-bound, memory-bound desires, it is true he would rather have turned back to build old Troy again. Yet he dared not; for Fate, the will of the all-powerful, had bidden him seek out a new homeland—Italy. So armed only in the might of *virtus,* he went forward against the malignity of *Fortune;* for Aeneas never had fortune with him in the way that Odysseus always had.

> Disce, puer, virtutem ex me verumque laborem;
> fortunam ex aliis.

> (Learn virtue from me, child, and true toil; learn fortune from others.)

And with the help of war (though a thing in itself hateful) he made his way against the opposition of men; he made it despite the jealousy of the lesser gods, despite the promptings of his own desire, despite even pity; against his own will, and strong only in the strength of submission and the supreme might of Fate, he went on to find Italy, his new home. *Italiam non sponte sequor*—Not of my own will I seek Italy.

> Me si fata meis paterentur ducere vitam
> auspiciis, et sponte mea componere curas;
> urbem Troianam primum, dulcesque meorum
> reliquias colerem

> (Did the Fates but suffer me to shape my life after my own pleasure and order my sorrows at my own will, my first care would be the city of Troy and the sweet relics of my kin.)

In all pre-Christian literature there are no more Christian lines than these. Sainte-Beuve hardly penned a truer line—though a bold one and one open to misunderstanding—than when he wrote: *La venue même du Christ n'a rien qui étonne, quand on a lu Virgile.* Against his will then Aeneas journeyed to that Italy which he knew not, and which was full of perils. But even as he listened to the mysterious, unsearchable higher will, gradually there kindled within him, and burned into the very marrow of his soul, a longing that was prepared for any sacrifice, for this second homeland, for Italy, which as yet was his only in the command of Jupiter, a land of promise from which he was still separated by long, and ever longer, trackless ways, *viae inviae*. Thus Virgil breathed into his hero that love for Italy, not merely for Rome, which was his own; for Virgil was not merely a Roman, he was an Italian also.

How full of paradox, how dialectical is the inner life of Aeneas! Does he in this resemble any of Homer's heroes? Though remote in time, of another race, and of another country, yet in spirit, which knows no distinctions of time or race or country, is he not akin rather to Abraham, the father of the faith? Did not Abraham also have to leave the homeland of his heart, and, for the sake of the faith and in obedience to an inscrutable will, a *fatum*, take upon himself the sorrow and bitter smart of memory, which for star-bound man is the meaning of a change of homeland. So it was with Aeneas.

It is of the essence of the greatness and artistic unity of the Homeric poems—a unity irretrievably lost to us—that these men could say, and in fact did say what they lacked and what they had. (For man this is unity: though he have, yet will he also lack.) And even where they do not say it, but speak falsely, theirs is no more than a simple *dolus*, akin to animal cunning in the animal world. The Homeric heroes can state plainly their truths and their false-hoods, and both are in the nature of self-revelations. But Aeneas cannot do this. Like all reticent men, he can speak only the truth that is in him, and that only occasionally and darkly. And again, like all reticent men, be they so from necessity or of their own free will, he makes no such brave figure as Achilles or Odysseus; it is easy to misunderstand him, as it is not the cunning Odysseus, or the transparent Achilles. Perhaps Virgil is here throwing some light upon the difficult character of Augustus—was he too, and of necessity, reticent? (which is, of course, not the same thing as 'sullen'). Aeneas is a grave man, *gravis*, a man burdened with one idea—for having many thoughts makes a man light, but having few and anxious thoughts makes him grave; and the burden of one thought only will make him grave indeed. It was this that made him a leader; this that made him the founder of Rome. At all events Virgil is not here drawing simply upon his imagination; this is no mere poetic invention. He here makes explicit in truth and in beauty what had for so long lain implicit in the character of Rome itself. And with one accord, without a moment of hesitation, Rome accepted and sanctioned this explanation of herself at the hands of her greatest poet. That is an historical fact, and a highly significant one; for what a people endorses and appropriates forever to itself from the writings of its greatest poet is always something that is at once both a self-confession and a self-revelation. Goethe, for example, would never have been able to foist Faust upon the German people if he had not really belonged to them. Any historian who would omit from his history such a fact brought to light by a poet, leaves out a great deal, and not infrequently the whole; he denies himself a master-key, and seals up the one clear and abundant source of understanding.

Rome had no original speculative philosophers, but she did possess great practical, realistic thinkers, and her greatest was a poet, Virgil. All the great and simple things of our reality have been meditated by him. That ideal of the man of mind, the spiritual man, union of contemplative sage and creative artist, was realised only twice in the classical world—first in Greece by Plato who was thinker and poet, after the Greek fashion; and then in Rome by Virgil who was poet and thinker, after the Roman fashion. (Among the Jews of pre-Christian times, that is of the Old Testament, this union was practically never broken; none was there a poet without being also a sage, and none a sage without being also a poet.) Virgil has demonstrated that Rome was fully conscious of her own character, both as to the things she lacked and as to the things she possessed to overflowing. She acknowledged without envy the superior gifts of the Greeks in the fine arts and in philosophy, though hardly in literature; and with unshakable steadfastness and confidence she devoted herself to her mission—itself also an art—to the mission of governing. But her mission—and here is a fact often ignored and easily forgotten—her mission was not primarily based upon force. Where that alone exists as a foundation, Virgil's condemnation is unequivocal. Not only is Catiline—that true political criminal, *contemptor divum,* despiser of the gods—hateful to him, but for him Sulla and Antony—brutal generals without any of the *magnanimitas* of true statesmen—also share the fate of the political criminals of Dante. He blames even the great Caesar, because he did not rule *more patrum,* after the manner of the fathers. Rome's mission was essentially not founded upon force; it was power rather, and based upon certain great and simple virtues, chief of which was *pietas,* love fulfilling duty, whose political expression is justice. Hence the paradox of a Rome founded not by a conqueror but by a defeated man. Let King Pyrrhus or any other petty tyrant preen himself because Achilles, the unconquered, was his ancestor; Rome was for Hector.

And Aeneas, the fugitive, who after one defeat built a new city, was the ancestor of Caesar and Augustus. No State that would stand, still less an empire that would endure, was made of the Greeks, for all their qualities; neither would Achilles serve, for all his impetuous storming to victory and, equally impetuously, to a profitless death; nor yet Odysseus—he knew too much, he was too fickle and he had too large a sense of humour, a thing which may easily prove an insuperable obstacle to successful statecraft. The ancestors of Rome were required to be builders and rebuilders, not destroyers, of cities. The Greeks built cities too, of course; they gave us the very name and science of politics; they taught us to understand wherein the essence of it lies, namely in that justice which accords to each man his own, not merely to each man the same, but to each man differently, for the reason that each is not only like, but also different from, every other man. The Greeks—I mean the philosophers, not the politicians—understood this science and gave it its name; but a *real* State that should *last* they were unable to build. The Greek did build cities, it is true, but he built them only once; when they were destroyed he did not build them again. But Aeneas would have built Troy again had Fate willed it; instead he built Latin towns. Though Rome was to be destroyed many times, it would always be built up again.

It is truths of this order that lie hidden in the *Aeneid*; truths which, though through long periods they may fail to be appreciated, will again suddenly flash out brilliantly in the light of their own truth, touched anew into life by some catastrophe of the time. Virgil is the only pagan who takes rank with the Jewish and Christian prophets; the *Aeneid* is the only book, apart from Holy Scriptures, to contain sayings that are valid beyond the particular hour and circumstance of their day, prophecies that re-echo from the doors of eternity, whence they first draw their breath:

> His ego nec metas rerum, nec tempora pono:
> imperium sine fine dedi.

> (To these I have set bounds neither in space nor in time;
> dominion have I given thee without end.)

—so runs the *fatum Jovis*. For, whether we like it or not, whether we know it or not, we are all still members of that *Imperium Romanum*, which finally and after terrible errors accepted Christianity *sua sponte*, of its own free-will—a Christianity which it could not abandon now without abandoning itself and humanism too. The

Imperium Romanum, which Virgil knew in all its natural grandeur and revealed in the splendour of beauty, is no hazy ideal; nor is it merely a true ideal, but a reality, deep though that reality may at times lie buried. The thing 'Rome' is not idea alone, though a true one, but actuality, *res,* a thing of flesh and blood. Wherever there is the will and urge to empire, the measure of its wisdom or its excess, of its blessing or its curse, is to be determined by the standards of the enduring reality of the *Imperium Romanum.* And it is so still even where anarchy and ignorance, the results of a spiritual backsliding, are so great that they despise or fail to see these real relationships.

A revival of this empire, which has never quite perished, could only be effected in one of two ways. It might be brought about through some renewal of the *Pax Romana,* whereby the Western world might be denationalised and levelled; this would be possible only if one nation were by force to gain overwhelming ascendancy over all the rest, and it would be the greatest crime against both humanity and Christianity. For to-day no nation enjoys such pre-eminence above the rest as did the Romans in their day (and even they with their *Pax Romana* did not accomplish any particularly lovely thing). Moreover the value of the 'nation' has been magnified by Christianity, in that the value of the 'individual,' the 'person' thereby came to be infinite. It is *not* required of us that we should denationalise, and thereby renounce, our individuality, our uniqueness. Levelling in the spiritual realm is anti-Christian. Before 'the embannered throne of God' are ranged the angels of each nation— and who will level angels?

The second way which, through mutual understanding, conciliation and respect, would preserve all that is valuable in each nation, thereby uniting all in one higher commonwealth—which could only be a spiritual one—is infinitely the better. But this spiritual commonwealth must omit nothing essential in what has gone before, neither pagan Rome, which in Virgil became adventist, nor Christian Rome, which is also adventist, but must be in the nature of a fulfilment and transcendence to a new age, and in the spiritual form of faith, hope and love.

It has not been difficult to find a *leitmotiv* for the *Bucolics* and the *Georgics;* in the former it is *Amor vincit omnia;* in the latter, *Labor omnia vicit improbus;* in the one, the elemental power of Eros, the force, the urge that is in creative, procreative, fruitful nature to which man himself belongs; in the other—and here we have already entered a more spiritual world—that sublimely antithetic, yet welded, unity of substance and attribute, *labor improbus,* a blessing from a curse, a blessing not to be had except under the compulsion of the curse. The greatness of Virgil's art, one of which only a powerful intellect and no mere impetuous emotion is capable, achieves its zenith in *labor improbus,* this bold, clear and realistic antithesis of a blessing and a curse. But in the *Aeneid,* whose theme is the leader—primarily the political leader and only secondarily the warrior—the implications are still more numerous, so that no one phrase suffices to comprehend or fully to express its content. Yet there is perhaps one; let us examine it. The theme is Aeneas—Aeneas, the leader toward the glory of Rome. But the true leader—and this, be it remembered, was Virgil's opinion after a century of civil war—the true leader is not he who makes himself leader, but he who is called and dedicated to that end by Fate. Whoever would elevate himself to that position without the will of Fate is abhorrent to Virgil's theological soul.

The content of the *Aeneid* is a hazy, inchoate theology expectant of the inseminating spirit—the best of which paganism was capable before the fullness of time was come. Paganism as it existed before Christ is no more to be revived than is the Jewish world before Christ. The decisive difference between the submissive adventist humanity of a Virgil and the pale, decadent humanism of the so-called humanists of the Renaissance lies in the fact that, whereas the one was a material soil awaiting the springing seed, the other was a sort of horticulture occupied with growing cuttings from lovely pot-plants; the one, a womb of longing which cried aloud for fulfilment; the other a mere precautionary measure which, if the worst come to the worst, should serve to hide from men's eyes for a few centuries approaching disaster. The Classicists pretend to see in Virgil their own image; yet, whereas he has denied nothing of his, not an iota of the tragedy and shame, they have often in the ultimate things denied the past of their ancestors, so that it seems unlikely that their opinions will be respected in the future which lies ahead, but rather that they in their turn will be denied by their offspring. A humanism devoid of theology cannot stand. To-day men are searching desperately for 'Man,' but they seek what does not exist, namely autonomous Man. If they would find a *whole* man, they must not mistake the part for the whole, but, what is more important and more essential, must see that man realises his wholeness only in the fact that he is wholly *creature* and cries out *unceasingly* for his Creator when He is not near, even as a child cries for its mother.

An Interpretation of the *Aeneid*

by Wendell Clausen

The *Aeneid* is a literary epic: it refers to a literary tradition and was intended for a literary audience. An ancient reader would hear Virgil's poetry—ancient poetry was read aloud—and simultaneously overhear other poetry, Greek and Latin. No subterfuge was designed, though one malevolent critic, Perellius Faustus, drew up a list of Virgilian *furta*, "thefts." Obvious and successful imitation was for a Latin poet, as for a late Greek poet, a form of originality. Hence the peculiar difficulty of Virgil for the modern reader, who will hardly be a close and constant student of ancient poetry: he must rely on footnotes, and footnotes are a mean and pallid substitute for experience. Virgil uses Homer as he uses other poets—Apollonius of Rhodes, Ennius, Lucretius—but with this difference: Homer was for Virgil the archetypal poet, the grand original. When Homer sings, ἄνδρα μοι ἔννεπε Μοῦσα ("Tell me, Muse, of the man"), he invokes the Muse, daughter of Memory, to help him remember an old story (though Homer himself was most likely following a convention: he was, whoever he was, no primitive singer, no dawn-figure, but rather a late and decadent poet of genius who concluded a long tradition of oral song); when Virgil writes, *arma uirumque cano* ("Arms and the man I sing"), he makes a literary allusion, and in so doing at once defines the character of his poem for the reader. In a sense, the *Aeneid* is a prolonged literary allusion to Homer; and any response to the *Aeneid* will depend in good part on an intimate knowledge of the *Iliad* and the *Odyssey*.

> Arma uirumque cano, Troiae qui primus ab oris
> Italiam fato profugus Lauiniaque uenit
> litora, multum ille et terris iactatus et alto
> ui superum, saeuae memorem Iunonis ob iram,
> multa quoque et bello passus, dum conderet urbem

This paper is essentially a revision of one published in *Harvard Studies in Classical Philology*, LXVIII (1964), 139-47.

inferretque deos Latio, genus unde Latinum
Albanique patres atque altae moenia Romae.

(Arms and the man I sing, who first from Troy's shores, the
exile of destiny, won his way to Italy and her Latin coast;
a man much buffeted on land and on the deep by violence
from above, to sate the unforgetting wrath of Juno; much
scourged, too, in war, as he struggled to build him a city, and
find his gods a home in Latium—himself the father of the
Latian people, and the chiefs of Alba's houses, and the walls
of high-towering Rome.)   (1.1-7)

So begins the *Aeneid,* with an allusion to the *Odyssey:*

Ἄνδρα μοι ἔννεπε, Μοῦσα, πολύτροπον, ὃς μάλα πολλὰ
πλάγχθη, ἐπεὶ Τροίης ἱερὸν πτολίεθρον ἔπερσε·
πολλῶν δ' ἀνθρώπων ἴδεν ἄστεα καὶ νόον ἔγνω,
πολλὰ δ' ὅ γ' ἐν πόντῳ πάθεν ἄλγεα ὃν κατὰ θυμόν,
ἀρνύμενος ἥν τε ψυχὴν καὶ νόστον ἑταίρων.

(Tell me, Muse, of the man, much-travelled, who wandered
widely, after he destroyed the sacred city of Troy, and saw
the cities of many men and learnt their minds; many pains,
too, did he suffer at heart on the deep, striving to secure life
for himself and a return home for his comrades.)   (1.1-5)

There is even a verbal echo of the Greek in the repetition *multum
. . . multa.* Would an ancient reader be aware of this? Certainly;
for he would have the same sort of rhetorical education as the poet.
But he would also be aware of a difference, and this is the meaning
of the allusion: Odysseus is anxious to get home and bring his
companions with him—fools, νήπιοι, who in the outrage of their own
hearts ate the oxen of the Sun, and died. His ambition is personal.
Aeneas is a dispossessed wanderer, fated to march his gods into
Latium and found a city and an empire.

The *Aeneid* is named for Aeneas, as the *Odyssey* is named for
Odysseus. It is an epic about the experience of a hero. What sort
of hero is he? Or what sort of character has Virgil chosen to create?
(I mean by "character" the impression we get from the poem and
call "Aeneas," trying the while to remember that we have been
reading a poem.) Homer's Aeneas is almost characterless, a non-
descript hero, who, however, enjoys special protection on the battlefield because his mother is a goddess. And Virgil's Aeneas? Of him
it is easier to give a negative than a positive description; and per-

haps this in itself is significant. He is not hungry-hearted for experience, like Odysseus; he is not simple-minded, like Ajax; he is not happy; he suffers from melancholia. We see him, middle-aged and a widower, bound to pursue his reluctant way from Troy to Italy, from a past he has lost to a future he will never possess.

Aeneas enters the poem wishing he were dead, the only epic hero to do so; and this is not to be explained away with a mention of the ancient horror of a watery grave. Aeneas is caught in a storm stirred up by the divine malice of Juno in the seas off Sicily. He groans, and stretches out his hands to the stars, and speaks:

> o terque quaterque beati,
> quis ante ora patrum Troiae sub moenibus altis
> contigit oppetere! o Danaum fortissime gentis
> Tydide! mene Iliacis occumbere campis
> non potuisse tuaque animam hanc effundere dextra,
> saeuus ubi Aeacidae telo iacet Hector, ubi ingens
> Sarpedon, ubi tot Simois correpta sub undis
> scuta uirum galeasque et fortia corpora uoluit.

(O happy, thrice and again, whose lot it was, in their fathers' sight, under Troy's high walls to meet death! O thou, bravest of the Danaan race, Tydeus' son, why was it not mine to lay me low on Ilion's plains, and yield this fated life to thy right hand? Aye, there it is that Hector, stern as in life, lies stretched by the spear of Achilles; There lies Sarpedon's giant bulk; there it is that Simois seizes and sweeps beneath its waves those many shields and helms, and bodies of the brave!)   (1.94-101)

A strange speech for a hero to make, especially a hero sailing towards a new world: Aeneas thinks only of the past, of those who fell under Troy's high wall, and wishes he too had died there. Aeneas is more burdened by memory than any other ancient hero; he is unlike Achilles or the typical hero of Greek tragedy, largely careless of the past and only gradually coming to an understanding of the true present. Virgil's Aeneas most resembles Hector and Sarpedon, and it can be no accident that their names figure in this speech; for they, almost alone of Homeric heroes, strike that note of melancholy awareness so characteristic of Virgil's Aeneas:

> εὖ γὰρ ἐγὼ τόδε οἶδα κατὰ φρένα καὶ κατὰ θυμόν·
> ἔσσεται ἦμαρ ὅτ' ἄν ποτ' ὀλώλῃ Ἴλιος ἱρὴ
> καὶ Πρίαμος καὶ λαὸς ἐϋμμελίω Πριάμοιο.

(For I know this well in my mind and in my heart: there
will come a day when even holy Ilion will perish and
Priam and the people of Priam of the good ash spear.)

(6.447-49)

ὦ πέπον, εἰ μὲν γὰρ πόλεμον περὶ τόνδε φυγόντε
αἰεὶ δὴ μέλλοιμεν ἀγήρω τ᾿ ἀθανάτω τε
ἔσσεσθ᾿, οὔτε κεν αὐτὸς ἐνὶ πρώτοισι μαχοίμην
οὔτε κε σὲ στέλλοιμι μάχην ἐς κυδιάνειραν·
νῦν δ᾿ ἔμπης γὰρ κῆρες ἐφεστᾶσιν θανάτοιο
μυρίαι, ἃς οὐκ ἔστι φυγεῖν βροτὸν οὐδ᾿ ὑπαλύξαι,
ἴομεν, ἠέ τῳ εὖχος ὀρέξομεν, ἠέ τις ἡμῖν.

(Friend, if fleeing this battle we two might live forever,
ageless and deathless, I would not fight in the front ranks
myself, nor would I send you into the battle that brings
men renown. But now the demons of death press upon
us in thousands, which a man cannot flee from or escape:
let us go, whether we shall give glory to someone else, or
someone else to us.)   (12.322-28)

It was long ago recognized that Aeneas' first speech is closely
imitated from a speech of Odysseus. Odysseus is immobilized on
Calypso's isle; the gods confer, and send Hermes to order his re-
lease. Calypso offers him a painless immortality if only he will stay
with her, and contrasts her own beauty favorably with that of
Penelope—goddesses (she complacently observes) are necessarily
more beautiful than mortal women. Odysseus agrees, but even so
he chooses the painful reality of returning to Ithaca and his wife.
He makes a raft and sets sail; Poseidon, angered by the blinding of
the Cyclops, stirs up a storm:

τρισμάκαρες Δαναοὶ καὶ τετράκις οἳ τότ᾿ ὄλοντο
Τροίῃ ἐν εὐρείῃ, χάριν Ἀτρείδῃσι φέροντες.
ὡς δὴ ἐγώ γ᾿ ὄφελον θανέειν καὶ πότμον ἐπισπεῖν
ἤματι τῷ ὅτε μοι πλεῖστοι χαλκήρεα δοῦρα
Τρῶες ἐπέρριψαν περὶ Πηλείωνι θανόντι.
τῷ κ᾿ ἔλαχον κτερέων, καί μευ κλέος ἦγον Ἀχαιοί·

(Happy, thrice and again, the Danaans who were killed
before, in broad Troy, doing their service to the Atreidae!
O, that I had died thus and met my fate on that day
when throngs of Trojans hurled their bronze-tipped spears
at me, fighting around the dead son of Peleus; for then I

would have got my funeral rites, and the Achaeans would
have glorified me.)   (5.306-11)

But this is not Odysseus' first utterance in the poem; the reader has
heard him already, speaking to Calypso in an easy and calculating
manner, and knows a great deal about him from Telemachus,
Nestor, and Helen. Odysseus has been in trouble before, and will
get out of this. Odysseus thinks of his own life merely; Aeneas thinks
of all those who died, and wishes he too had died—but not for the
glory. Odysseus is only momentarily retrospective; he does not yearn
for the past, or desire to live it over again.

After the storm, Aeneas and the other survivors land on the coast
of Africa; Aeneas shoots twelve deer, and then soothes the grieving
hearts of his men—*maerentia pectora mulcet*—with a brief speech
very like the first in tone, as if Virgil were concerned at the outset
to enforce a certain impression of Aeneas on the reader. Again there
is a reminiscence of the *Odyssey*. Odysseus cheers his men as they approach Scylla, and reminds them of the Cyclops' cave:

> ῏Ω φίλοι, οὐ γάρ πώ τι κακῶν ἀδαήμονές εἰμεν·
> οὐ μὲν δὴ τόδε μεῖζον ἔπι κακὸν ἢ ὅτε Κύκλωψ
> εἴλει ἐνὶ σπῆϊ γλαφυρῷ κρατερῆφι βίηφιν·

(O my friends, we are certainly not unacquainted with evils;
this is no worse than when the Cyclops with overweening
force shut us up in his hollow cave.)   (12.208-10)

His tone is hopeful; for he confidently plans to evade the danger
that lies ahead. And the speech ends:

> ῝Ως ἐφάμην, οἱ δ᾽ ὦκα ἐμοῖς ἐπέεσσι πίθοντο.

(Thus I spoke, and they swiftly obeyed my words.)
                                            (12.222)

Odysseus' confidence is matched by the lively obedience of his men.
Now consider Aeneas' speech to his men:

> O socii, neque enim ignari sumus ante malorum,
> o passi grauiora, dabit deus his quoque finem.
> uos et Scyllaeam rabiem penitusque sonantis
> accestis scopulos, uos et Cyclopia saxa
> experti: reuocate animos maestumque timorem
> mittite; forsan et haec olim meminisse iuuabit.

per uarios casus, per tot discrimina rerum,
tendimus in Latium, sedes ubi fata quietas
ostendunt; illic fas regna resurgere Troiae.
durate et uosmet rebus seruate secundis.

(Comrades!—for comrades we are, no strangers to hardships
already. Hearts that have felt deeper wounds—for these, too,
heaven will find a balm. Why, men, you have even looked
on Scylla in her madness, and heard those yells that thrill
the rocks; you have even made trial of the crags of the
Cyclopes. Come, call your spirits back, and banish these
doleful fears; who knows but someday this, too, will be remembered with pleasure! Through manifold chances,
through these many perils of fortune, we are making our
way to Latium, where the Fates hold out to us a quiet
settlement; there Troy's empire has leave to rise again from
its ashes. Bear up, and reserve yourselves for brighter days.)
                                                        (1.198-207)

What is the reader's impression of this speech? An impression of
sorrow and suffering in the past, intimately shared—*o socii*, Comrades: the exclamation is more emotional in Latin than it is in
Greek; of the fearfulness of experience; of the burden of fate; and
of longing for the peaceable kingdom. Then follow two verses,
Virgil's comment:

talia uoce refert, curisque ingentibus aeger
spem uultu simulat, premit altum corde dolorem.

(Such were the words his tongue uttered; heartsick with
overwhelming care, he wears the semblance of hope in his
face, but has grief deep-buried in his heart.)   (1.208-9)

And then follow, as if to emphasize the un-Homeric quality of these
two verses, seven verses describing how the men prepared their
meal, approximate renderings of Homeric formula verses: *postquam
exempta fames epulis mensaeque remotae* (Their hunger sated by
the meal, and the boards removed): αὐτὰρ ἐπεὶ πότιος καὶ ἐδητύος ἐξ
ἔρον ἕντο (But when they had satisfied their desires for drink and
food.) I can think of no other place in the *Aeneid* quite like this.
The effect is not to make us feel we are in Homer's world; on the
contrary, we have the sense of a man rather like ourselves—moody,
hesitant, reflective—thrust into a situation that seems to call for

heroic action; and the ritual of feeding and drinking does not brace and comfort him, as it does Homer's heroes. Consider the scene at the end of the *Iliad*: Priam has come to beg the body of Hector from Achilles, and kissed his murderous hands:

> τὼ δὲ μνησαμένω, ὁ μὲν Ἕκτορος ἀνδροφόνοιο
> κλαῖ᾽ ἀδινὰ προπάροιθε ποδῶν Ἀχιλῆος ἐλυσθείς,
> αὐτὰρ Ἀχιλλεὺς κλαῖεν ἐὸν πατέρ᾽, ἄλλοτε δ᾽ αὖτε
> Πάτροκλον· τῶν δὲ στοναχὴ κατὰ δώματ᾽ ὀρώρει.

(They both remembered: the one remembered man-killing Hector and wept plentifully, crouching at the feet of Achilles; but Achilles wept for his own father, and again for Patroclus. And the sound of their groans rose throughout the dwelling.)   (24.509-12)

Presently, Achilles tells Priam he may have his son's body; and then says:

> νῦν δὲ μνησώμεθα δόρπου.
> καὶ γάρ τ᾽ ἠΰκομος Νιόβη ἐμνήσατο σίτου,
> τῇ περ δώδεκα παῖδες ἐνὶ μεγάροισιν ὄλοντο.

(But now let us think about a meal. For fair-haired Niobe took thought for food, even though her twelve children had been slain in her halls.)   (24.602-4)

Private sorrow finds solace and relief in the routine of life: the continuity of life is asserted over the abruptness of death. Priam and Achilles grieve, but put aside their grief to share a meal. Aeneas and his men share a meal, but their communal enjoyment gives way to private reminiscence and sorrow. They are not sustained by any heroic ethic, by any sense that death, if only it result in glory, is tolerable. Aeneas weeps for the dead, or for those he thinks dead, for Orontes, for Amycus, for Gyas, for Cloanthus. *Fortemque Gyan fortemque Cloanthum* (brave Gyas and brave Cloanthum): the cadence is strangely affecting; the repetition somehow and the regretfulness of the tone suggest the futility of what has happened and of what will, in all probability, happen again.

If then, Aeneas is in some sort the hero I have described—profoundly melancholy, half-paralyzed by fate—how is it that a poem which recounts his fortunes should move us so deeply? Chiefly the answer must be that we respond to Virgil's evocative poetry, to verses which, once heard, cannot quite be forgotten.

forsan et haec olim meminisse iuuabit.

(Who knows but someday this, too, will be remembered with pleasure!)

en Priamus. sunt hic etiam sua praemia laudi;
sunt lacrimae rerum et mentem mortalia tangunt.

(See there Priam. Here, too, worth finds its due reward; here, too, there are tears for human fortune, and hearts that are touched by mortality.)

ibant obscuri sola sub nocte per umbram.

(On they went, darkling in solitary night, far into the gloom.)

                          sate sanguine diuum,
Tros Anchisiade, facilis descensus Auerno.

(Heir of the blood of gods, son of Anchises of Troy, easy is the going down to Avernus.)

        salue aeternum mihi, maxime Palla,
aeternumque uale.

(Hail forever, mightiest Pallas, and forever farewell.)

But there is another reason why the *Aeneid* moves us: its larger structure—and now I offer a simple interpretation of the *Aeneid,* ignoring whole books—enlists our sympathy on the side of loneliness, suffering, and defeat. For it is the paradox of the *Aeneid,* the surprise of its greatness, that a poem which celebrates the achievement of an exemplary hero and the founding of Rome itself should be a long history of defeat and loss. Aeneas finally wins—for that is his fate—but he wins at a terrible cost: he sees every human attachment broken except that which binds him to his son, Ascanius, destined to succeed him and inherit the fateful fields of Italy—a cold comfort. We are told of Aeneas' feeling for his son, but only once does he speak to him, the long companion of his wanderings; and while his manner is affectionate, his words are curiously impersonal:

        disce, puer, uirtutem ex me uerumque laborem,
        fortunam ex aliis . . .

> (Learn valor from me, my son, and genuine hardihood,
> success from others . . .)   (12.435-36)

Aeneas is forced to abandon his native city, Troy, and loses his wife
there; his father dies in Sicily; and in Africa he must desert the
woman who loves him. In the Underworld he meets the shade of his
imperious mistress, and she cuts him dead—a scene T. S. Eliot has
denominated the most civilized in Western literature. Aeneas tries
desperately to explain, as Dido turns haughtily away:

> siste gradum teque aspectu ne subtrahe nostro.

> (Stay, and withdraw not from my gaze.)   (6.465)

Dido goes to rejoin her husband Sychaeus in the shadowy grove,
eluding Aeneas as a little later the shade of his father Anchises will
elude him, when almost the same words are repeated (such repetitions are significant in Virgil, as they are not in Homer, at least not
in the same way).

> stant sale Tyrrheno classes. da iungere dextram,
> da, genitor, teque amplexu ne subtrahe nostro.
> sic memorans largo fletu simul ora rigabat.
> ter conatus ibi collo dare bracchia circum;
> ter frustra comprensa manus effugit imago,
> par leuibus uentis uolucrique simillima somno.

> ("In the Tyrrhenian sea my ships are riding at anchor.
> Let us grasp hand in hand—let us, my Father! Oh, with-
> draw not from my embrace!" As he spoke, the streaming
> tears rolled down his face. Thrice he essayed to fling his
> arms round his neck; thrice the phantom escaped the hands
> that caught at it in vain, impalpable as the wind, fleeting
> as the wings of sleep.)   (6.697-702)

Ter conatus ibi . . . (thrice he essayed . . .). Where have we heard
these words before? At the end of the second Book (792-94), when
Aeneas attempted to embrace the elusive image of his wife on the
fatal night of Troy, when he reached out vainly for a human relationship that no longer existed.

Troy, Creusa, Dido, Anchises—these were the sorrows of Aeneas
before he reached Italy, but his experience there is no happier. He
is forced into a war for which he has no stomach and witnesses the
pitiful slaughter of his own people. To survive he solicits help from

the aged Arcadian prince Evander, whose only son Pallas follows Aeneas to the war and in Aeneas' absence is killed by Turnus. As Aeneas gazes on the dead body of Pallas, he expresses a sense of failure and impotence, as if he had somehow betrayed his promise to Evander:

> non haec Euandro de te promissa parenti
> discedens dederam, cum me complexus euntem
> mitteret in magnum imperium.
>
> (Not such was the parting pledge I gave on your behalf to your sire, Evander, when, clasping me to his heart, he sent me on my way to mighty empire.)   (11.45-47)

And a little later:

> hi nostri reditus expectatique triumphi?
> haec mea magna fides?
>
> (And is this the proud return, the triumph we looked for? Has my solemn pledge shrunk to this?)
>
> (11.54-55)

Aeneas weeps; and as the elaborate and stately funeral cortège forms, he raises two coverlets stiff with purple and gold to place over the body of the dead boy.

> tum geminas uestis auroque ostroque rigentis
> extulit Aeneas, quas illi laeta laborum
> ipsa suis quondam manibus Sidonia Dido
> fecerat et tenui telas discreuerat auro.
>
> (Then brought forth Aeneas two coverlets stiff with gold and purple, which Dido had wrought for him in other days with her own hands, delighting in the toil, and had streaked their webs with threads of gold.)   (11.72-75)

At this poignant moment in the poem Virgil reminds the reader of Dido, in the old days, happy in her love for Aeneas.

All this labor and anguish might have been made to seem more endurable were it consummated or justified somehow in a final triumph. But in the closing scenes of the poem, when Aeneas faces Turnus in a mortal duel, there is little suggestion of triumph, and certainly none of personal triumph. It is fated that Turnus shall fall. Turnus knows this and replies to Aeneas' ferocious taunts with something like resignation.

> non me tua feruida terrent
> dicta, ferox; di me terrent et Iuppiter hostis.

> (I quail not at your fiery words, insulting foe; it is
> Heaven that makes me quail, and Jove my enemy.)
>
> (12.894-95)

Finally Turnus lies wounded at Aeneas' feet, and in a brief, noble speech asks for mercy. Aeneas hesitates and is about to relent when he sees, gleaming on Turnus' shoulder, the sword-belt Turnus had stripped from the body of Pallas to wear as a trophy. Maddened by the sight, Aeneas raises his sword:

> Pallas te hoc uulnere, Pallas
> immolet et poenam scelerato ex sanguine sumit.
> hoc dicens ferrum aduerso sub pectore condit
> feruidus. ast illi soluuntur frigore membra
> uitaque cum gemitu fugit indignata sub umbras.

> ("It is Pallas, Pallas, who with this blow makes you his vic-
> tim, and gluts his vengeance with your accursed blood."
> With these words, fierce as flame, he plunged the steel into
> the breast that lay before him. The other's frame grows chill
> and motionless, and the soul, resenting its lot, flies groan-
> ingly to the shades.)   (12.948-52)

The poem ends with an outburst of savage sorrow and a death. The reader is left with no sense of triumph, but rather with a poignant reminder of Pallas and an awareness that the final obstacle has now been overcome: the fateful fields of Italy have been possessed, the long history of monumental achievement and personal grief is complete.

What is the significance of this final scene? I shall try to answer this question obliquely, by discussing Book 6. It is in this Book, the Janus-Book looking to past and future, that Virgil's sense of the Roman fate is most powerfully expressed. (The *Aeneid* is an intensely Roman poem. A Roman poet was most himself, most Roman, precisely when he was imitating a Greek poet, as if he were then most aware of his own individuality.) Aeneas descends into the Underworld, with the Golden Bough as a talisman, to confront his past and his future. He encounters three shadowy figures: Palinurus, his helmsman, who fell overboard just before his arrival in Italy; Dido, his mistress, who killed herself for chagrin and grief; Deiphobus, his comrade in arms, who was brutally murdered on the night of Troy's destruction. These three figures owe something to three in Book 11 of the *Odyssey*, Odysseus' descent into the Underworld: Elpenor, his helmsman, not much of a fighter, not very smart, who got drunk in Circe's palace and fell down a ladder and broke his neck; Achilles, who would not be consoled for his own death; and Ajax, who would not speak because he was angry still that Odysseus had been awarded the armor of Achilles. But Palinurus, Dido, and Deiphobus are more suggestive figures: the reader has a sense of leave-taking—of a farewell to wandering, to love, to Troy—and of a preparation for something to come, the hard and bloody days in Italy. Aeneas crosses over a dividing ridge and meets the shade of his father, and then notices a throng of souls settled by the river Lethe, like bees in a meadow on a serene summer's day: these are the souls of those who shall be born again, he learns, among them the future heroes of Rome. *Tua fata docebo,* "I shall teach you your fate," Anchises tells him; and from the vantage of a low mound Aeneas watches his own posterity file before his eyes: Silvius, Procas, Capys, Numitor, Silvius Aeneas, Romulus, Augustus, Numa, Tullus, Ancus, Brutus, the Decii, the Drusi, Torquatus, Camillus, Caesar, Pompey, Mummius, Aemilius Paulus, Cato, Cossus, the Gracchi, the Scipios, the Fabii, Fabius Maximus, the elder Marcellus. It is a long and splendid pageant of human greatness, but strangely melancholy:

> infelix, utcumque ferent ea facta minores.

> (Unhappy man! let after ages speak of that deed as they will.)   (6.822)

With these words Anchises characterizes Brutus, founder and first consul of the Roman Republic, who put his seditious sons to death "for the sake of beautiful liberty," *pulchra pro libertate:* in the single adjective there is an infinity of regret.

Virgil's vision of Roman history is not propaganda—though some critics have thought it was: for he does not simply proclaim what Rome achieved; nor is it sentimental: for he does not simply dwell on what the achievement cost. Virgil values the Roman achievement —there are those proud lines (6.847-53) in which he renounces every claim for Rome save that of imperial grandeur—and yet he remains aware of the inevitable suffering and loss: it is this perception of Roman history as a long Pyrrhic victory of the human spirit that makes Virgil his country's truest historian. It is a measure of Virgil's greatness that he withstood the temptation to sentimentality; for it is a temptation which those who write or talk about the *Aeneid* rarely withstand. "All had fought well and, according to their best lights, justly. (This is how one critic[1] writes about the end of the *Aeneid*.) All bitterness and all passion was now laid at rest, and all could now join hands as comrades and together walk to meet the shining future." This is sentimental: at the end of the *Aeneid* there is no clasping of hands, no walking together towards the shining future. The light is hard and clear: Aeneas has killed Turnus, and on Turnus' shoulder gleams the sword-belt of Pallas.

Virgil faced a similar temptation, we may suppose, at the end of Book 6: the Book might have ended—were Virgil not Virgil— with the praise of Augustus, which stands earlier, and an optimistic view of the shining future. But the book ends rather with a somber and pathetic laudation of the younger Marcellus, Augustus' nephew and destined successor, who had excited high hopes, but who was dead when these lines were written. In the Underworld Aeneas catches sight of Marcellus, with the shadow of his early death already upon him, and asks who he is. Anchises answers, in the magnificent speech beginning:

> o gnate, ingentem luctum ne quaere tuorum.
> ostendent terris hunc tantum fata neque ultra
> esse sinent.

> (O my son, ask not of the heavy grief that your people must bear. Of him the Fates shall give but a glimpse to earth, nor suffer him to stay.)   (6.686-70)

So closes the vision of Roman greatness, with the sorrowful memorial of Marcellus; and Aeneas leaves the Underworld by a route that has always seemed very strange.

> sunt geminae somni portae, quarum altera fertur
> cornea, qua ueris facilis datur exitus umbris,
> altera candenti perfecta nitens elephanto,
> sed falsa ad caelum mittunt insomnia manes.

> (There are two gates of Sleep: the one, as story tells, of horn, supplying a ready exit for true spirits; the other gleaming with dazzling ivory, but through it the powers below send false dreams to the world above.)   (6.893-96)

---

[1] M. Hadas, *A History of Latin Literature* (New York: Columbia Univ. Press, 1952), p. 159.

Aeneas is sped on his way by the gate of ivory, the gate of false dreams. Why should this be? The gate of horn was closed to Aeneas, one critic has suggested, because he was not a true shade. It was an ancient superstition, another has pointed out, that dreams before midnight were false; after midnight true; so that when Virgil sends Aeneas out by the gate of false dreams, he implies that the other gate was shut, that it was not yet midnight. This explanation may be true in part—the most distinguished modern commentator[2] on Virgil has accepted it—but I have a sense, which I cannot quite put into words, that Virgil was not merely telling the time of night.

[2] E. Norden, *Aeneis* VI (Stuttgart, 1927), *ad loc.*

The Odyssean *Aeneid*
and the Iliadic *Aeneid*

by Brooks Otis

The Odyssean Aeneid

The *Aeneid* seems at first sight something radically different from either the *Eclogues* or the *Georgics*. We can understand why the 'young Virgil,' the Virgil of 42 B.C., should have turned from his projected *res romanae* to the 'soft and pleasing' verse of the eclogues. He was both too immature and too aware of Homer's unapproachable excellence to undertake such a task at the time. But the *Georgics,* the work of the next ten years, seems a most extraordinary approach to epic. Virgil did not, as we might have thought, prepare for the *Aeneid* by extensive experiments in narrative verse: he came to it, instead, by the quite non-narrative route of didactic. How are we to explain such a seemingly paradoxical development?

But this apparent paradox is really the clue to the whole problem of the *Aeneid*. . . . The Dido episode of Books 1 and 4 was a fusion of three elements: the psychologically continuous narrative; the essential symbol-complex of *fatum–furor–pietas;* and the Homeric motifs. The Damon song of the eighth Eclogue and, much more significantly, the Orpheus episode of the fourth Georgic, illustrate Virgil's concern with psychological continuity in narrative. But the scale of these narratives is small;[1] he had certainly not yet tried to use this kind of narrative as the major vehicle of his ideas. Nor had he shown any interest at all (save for the description of

"The Odyssean *Aeneid* and the Iliadic *Aeneid*." From *Virgil: A Study in Civilized Poetry* by Brooks Otis. Copyright © 1964 by the Oxford University Press. Reprinted by permission of The Clarendon Press. The pages reprinted here are only parts of the chapters entitled "The Odyssean *Aeneid*" and "The Iliadic *Aeneid*."

[1] With the scale goes also, of course, a considerable difference of style. The *Aeneid* is *epic* as *Bucolics* and *Georgics* are not.

Proteus in the Aristaeus episode) in Homeric motifs. What did directly concern him, however, was the elaboration of his Augustan symbols. This is in fact the bridge that connects the *Georgics* with the *Aeneid* and, indeed, the *Eclogues* with both. It is only when we take this first and try to see its significance for Virgil and for his whole conception of Roman Epic, that we begin to understand the genesis and actual structure of the *Aeneid*.

In both the *Eclogue Book* and the *Georgics* an evil or corrupt past dominated by destructive passion is opposed to a new hope embodied in a saviour (Caesar-Octavian) who represents the principle of resurrection and rebirth. In each work the resurrection motif comes at the central or decisive point: at 5, the middle piece of the ten Eclogues, or at the *Aristaeus* or second part of Georgics 4 where the antitheses set up between Books 1-3 and 2-4 (first half) are finally resolved. We can represent the ideological scheme of both works somewhat as follows:

MAN	SOCIETY
The passionate man characterized by *indignus amor, furor* and death: Eclogues 6, 8, 10; Georgics 3	The anarchic society (*furor* on a social scale) Georgics 1 (esp. conclusion); Eclogues 6, 9

Caesar-Octavian

Eclogue 5, Georgics 4.281-558
Resurrection
Salvation

The pious or rational man (passion controlled) Eclogues 2, 4; Georgics 2 (the happy swain)	The peaceful, well-ordered society (Saturnia regna) Eclogues 1, 4; Georgics 2, 4 (first part)

This is of course a schematic reduction of a very complex poetic reality and is certainly not to be applied with procrustean literalism. But it is hard to avoid the conviction that it reproduces in some part the actual design of the two works.

What is important in the scheme is Virgil's central emphasis of the death-resurrection motif. Both the *Eclogues* and the *Georgics* fall into antithetic halves that are united or reconciled by the use of this motif. It is profitable here to inspect the arrangements of these poems once more.

Now the scheme of the *Aeneid* certainly corresponds very closely to the scheme of both works, combining as it were the arrangements of each. It falls, as everyone is aware, into two sets of six

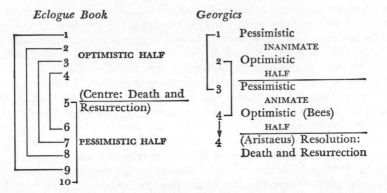

books (1-6, 7-12) corresponding loosely to the *Odyssey* (where Books 1-12 describe Odysseus' actual *nostos* or return to Ithaca and 13-24 describe his actions in Ithaca). This is clearly indicated for example, in the very structure of Book 7 with its new appeal to the Muse and its partial recapitulation of the movement of Book 1 (re-entry of Juno as the major disturbing element). But this 6-6 arrangement of books is paralleled by another which is quite analogous to that of the *Eclogues*:

1		Juno: storm: peace
2		Defeat of the Trojans (Aeneas)
3		Interim of wandering (uncertainty of Aeneas)
4	Odyssean,	Tragedy of Dido
5	PREPARATORY	Interlude of Games: Nisus, etc.
6	HALF	The Future: Show of Heroes
7	Iliadic	Peace: Juno: war
8	FULFILMENT	The Future: shield
9	HALF	Interlude of *Aristeiai*: Nisus, etc.
10		Tragedy of Pallas
11		Interim of movement (uncertainty of Turnus)
12		Victory of the Trojans (Aeneas)

It is not necessary to exaggerate the correspondences between the books in order to see that this scheme must have been, to some degree at least, actually present to Virgil's mind. The deliberate parallelism between 1 and 7, 4 and 10, 5 and 9, 6 and 8 is quite unmistakable: thus 7 reproduces, inversely, the order of 1; 4 and 10 contain the two major tragedies of the poem (Dido, Pallas); 5 and 9 reveal a whole series of correspondences (interventions of Juno via Iris, an attempted ship-burning prevented by a miracle,

an episode involving Nisus and Euryalus, an Ascanius episode, etc.);
6 and 8 each culminate in a major revelation of the Roman future.
The important thing, however, is not so much the arrangement in
itself as the fact that it reveals the centrality of Book 7 and its direct relation to the corresponding 6 and 8. Book 7, of course, brings
Aeneas to Italy and, with Allecto, inaugurates the Latin War. It
is the war for which Aeneas has been prepared in 6 and which he
actively accepts as his predestined duty in 8. In 6 he merely *sees*
the future of Rome; in 8 he takes the future (depicted on the
shield) upon his own shoulders into the Latin War. Thus though
7 is in this sense the centre of the poem (that to which everything
leads, from which everything follows), 6 is the culmination of
Aeneas' preparation *for* the War, inaugurated in 7, and met by
Aeneas' arms in 8. It is surely no coincidence, therefore, that it,
like the correspondingly pivotal portions of the *Eclogues* and *Georgics* (i.e. Eclogue 5 and the *Aristaeus*), is a kind of death and resurrection, a journey to and from the Underworld.

Seen in this way, the ideological similarity of the three works
becomes relatively clear. The sixth Book of the *Aeneid* is the turning point, the death and resurrection piece, that converts the defeat, passion, and uncertainty of Books 1-5 into the victorious and
unshaken valour of Books 8-12. In 4 Aeneas barely escapes from
indignus amor (his own and Dido's); in 10 he wins a great victory
mainly through the effect upon his spirit of his *worthy* affection
for the dead and defeated Pallas. In 2 he is prostrated by the fall
of Troy and loss of Creusa; in 12 he finally wins a new kingdom
and wife. In 1-5 he falters and has to be prodded by Jupiter and
Anchises; in 8-12 he never loses his courage or his resolution. In
short, the *Aeneid* is, like the *Eclogues* and *Georgics,* the story of
death and rebirth by which unworthy love and destructive *furor*
are overcome by the moral activity of a divinized and resurrected
hero.

The difference between the *Aeneid* and the other two works is
that the former is a narrative of human actions whereas the
Eclogues and *Georgics* are not narratives in this sense at all. The
death and rebirth motif in Eclogue 5 or in the *Aristaeus* is isolated; the influence of the saving hero or god is vague and mysterious. The pastoral and agricultural symbolism of the earlier
poems could not, in the nature of the case, be given a fully human
meaning. The bees in one sense stand for the unified, disciplined
state and the *Aristaeus* for its rebirth from death and destructive
passion. But Virgil could not invest Aristaeus with great human
significance—he is an utterly remote and legendary figure—and the

image of defeated resurrection in the *Orpheus* only negatively sug-gests[2] the qualities required for a successful resurrection. Yet once Virgil had seen that his projected epic would require a hero who would at some point in the work reveal the characteristics of Au-gustus or, more accurately, those of the Roman-Augustan ideal, he was forced to relate this hero to all the negative and positive ele-ments of his ideology. Virgil's essential insight, out of which seem-ingly the whole *Aeneid* grew, was the perception that this hero would have to struggle not only against external *furor* and passion but against the same elements within himself and that he could become the Roman-Augustan ideal only by rising above his origi-nal nature to a wholly new and quasi-divine kind of heroism. The death-resurrection motif could then be given a very concrete and very human form and become the central or crucial element in a psychologically continuous narrative of heroic motivation.

The conception of a 'reborn' hero, of the man who by great endurance and action raises himself to divine status, was of course a commonplace of Virgil's era: Caesar and Octavian himself had become divine or semi-divine in virtue of their immense achieve-ments and thus could claim kinship with other *theoi-andres* or divine-men of Roman history, like Hercules, Aeneas and Romulus. No one, however, before Virgil had looked at this kind of man psychologically and seen him as essentially the product of inner struggle and spiritual rebirth. Here Virgil not only combined ele-ments of Stoic psychology with contemporary religion (especially the idea of the divine man) but also brought to them the subjec-tive style of narration whose inchoate and cliptical origins we have descried in the Damon Song and the *Orpheus*.

Thus Virgil certainly humanized or gave psychological reality to the rather formal and austere image of the *theios aner*.[3] But he did

---

[2] But it *does* suggest. Orpheus' *catabasis* is the precursor of that of Aeneas.

[3] The conception of the θεῖος ἀνήρ, the attainment of divinity by noble deeds of philanthropy or humanity, was almost a commonplace of the Augustan age. *Herculis ritu* Augustus sought the laurel of victory (Horace *Carm.* 3.14). *Hac arte* (i.e. the service of the state by resistance to tyranny and sedition) Pollux and Hercules attained the stars among which Augustus reclines and drinks the divine nectar (*Carm.* 3.3. 9). But this divine man is also, to some degree at least, a Stoic stage: *iustum et tenacem propositi virum. . .* It is also no accident that Aeneas, like the Heracles of Euripides, is met by the most infernal of all Juno-Hera's agents (Lyssa, Allecto) just after the accomplishment of the *descensus-ascensus Averni.* The θεῖος ἀνήρ is finally tested by counter-fate itself at the height of his career, but note the *difference* between Euripides and Virgil. . . . Aeneas' *catabasis* is not a mere exploit (like that of Heracles) but is itself the ordeal that finally makes him a true θεῖος ἀνήρ. He is therefore personally invulnerable to Allecto.

not thereby deprive it of cosmic significance. In one sense Aeneas is quite different from Daphnis or Aristaeus. The Daphnis of Eclogue 5 is, like Caesar, deified only *after* death: there is no notion of deification during his lifetime, no conception of a *living* hero's return from the underworld. The transition from a real man to a real god is conceived as a religious or cosmic transformation, rather than the direct result of human *pietas*. The death and resurrection of Aristaeus' bees is also a cosmic symbol, a symbol of nature reflecting and cooperating with human vice and virtue. But though Aeneas is a human figure as these others are not, he is also subject to a cosmic force, to *fatum*, to Rome's ecumenical destiny. The *Aeneid* in fact is the story of the interplay between the cosmic power of fate and human response to it. Rome, we can have no doubt, was in Virgil's eyes really fated to rule the world. But this fate was not designed to operate without regard to human attitudes. There could have been no Rome, as Virgil conceived it, without men like Aeneas, men of supreme *pietas*. In other words *fatum* and *pietas* as well as *fatum* and *violentia* or *furor* (the human opposites of *pietas*) are interdependent. The cosmos (fate) mirrors man as much as man mirrors the cosmos. But this idea, as we have seen, is also a *leitmotif* of the *Georgics*: the degeneration of the soil and of nature in Book 1, with the consequent *labor improbus* it imposes on the farmer, is finally associated with man's own anarchy and wickedness; the farmer can have *secura quies*, can be truly happy but only *sua si bona norint;* only then will nature cooperate with him freely and fully. Resurrection is thus possible but has definite moral prerequisites. This we see not only in the *Orpheus* but also in the designed antithesis of Georgics 1 and 2 and of 3 and 4. All the heavens declare the assassination of Caesar but the heavens also declare his resurrection and cooperate with his divine son's salutary rule. *Pietas* and *furor* work hand in hand with *fatum*.

We see then that the combination of a symbolic system (essentially the *fatum–furor–pietas* complex) with a human, psychologically continuous, narrative was, as it were, potential in the *Georgics* and even to some extent in the *Eclogues*. Yet the narrative element in these two works is only embryonic at best for their symbolism is largely devoid of human content. What was lacking was quite simply Homer—the narrative content, scope, and elevation of epic. We do not, indeed, need to dwell on the crucial importance of this lacuna: the gap between pastoral or didactic and epic is too great and too obvious to be minimized. Yet an approach to the *Aeneid* from the *Eclogues* and *Georgics,* rather than from Homer or other epic 'models', calls attention to a fact that has not yet been adequately recognized. Scholars like Heinze have performed a most fruitful task by comparing the *Iliad* or *Odyssey* with the *Aeneid* and noting the differences. But this kind of study has had the disadvantage of concentrating attention on what Virgil did to Homer rather than on the much more important matter of what Homer did to Virgil. To state the point rather less paradoxically: Virgil did not 'start' with Homer but with his own Augustan 'symbol-complex' and his own subjective style. He did not so much 'copy' Homer as fit Homeric motifs into a radically un-Homeric scheme that he had elaborated without reference to either Homer or the epic genre or indeed any sort of narrative plot or story. Homer really came last in the genesis of the *Aeneid*: he was as it were the necessary model, the high classical model advocated by Horace, but he was a model only in the sense that he was made to fit a pre-existent structure. What he did to Virgil—how Virgil's central design, in other words, was affected by Homeric motifs—is the important question. Homer contributed nothing to the design itself.

It is here, finally, that we reach the true explanation of Virgil's 'success' in epic. He could write a great 'Homeric' epic; he could, as the Antimachi and Choerili could not, assimilate an outmoded form and content to a contemporary subject; he could thus Augustanize Homer and revive heroic myth in truly successful poetry, because he consistently adapted Homer to a thoroughly un-Homeric ideology, always converting the objective narrative of *Iliad* and *Odyssey* to one that was both subjective and symbolic. We have already given an illustration of Virgil's procedure in our analysis above of the Dido episode. But Virgil's real artistry is only revealed in the *Aeneid* as a whole, in its essential architecture and plan.

Essentially the real 'plot' of the *Aeneid* is that of the formation and victory of the *Augustan* hero. Virgil selected Aeneas as his hero because he happened to be the one *theios-aner* (the man who achieved divine status) of Roman tradition who actually belonged to the Homeric saga itself. Hercules was only incidentally connected with Rome; Romulus was already 'historical' and thus alien to the epic-heroic milieu. But Aeneas, of course, is meant to be the prototype as well as the mythical ancestor of Augustus. In the narrative he belongs to his own epic age; Virgil avoided, at all costs, the direct intrusion of contemporary events or persons, of history, into the realm of myth or legend. This would have been fatal to both his symbolic style and his 'prophetic' approach to his own times. Yet the distinction between Aeneas and any genuinely Homeric hero is quite fundamental. His ethos is utterly different from that of Achilles, Hector or Odysseus. Aeneas' goal and object in life is not merely in the near but in the remote future, in Augustan Rome itself. Thus all the intelligible goals of Homeric epic or Greek tragedy, indeed of all Greek literature, are not available to him. His fate is to sacrifice every present enjoyment or satisfaction to an end he cannot hope to witness himself. He bears on his shoulders the *famam . . . et fata nepotum*, not unwittingly as an ordinary ancestor, but quite consciously as the avowed servant of a future which has been finally revealed to him. He is thus the great exhibit of *pietas* or of the willing service of destiny. This is emphatically not a Homeric but a Stoic and, above all, a Roman-Augustan attitude. Augustus, himself, was the avowed founder of the future. The profound difference between such consciousness of and devotion to an historical role and the simple wrath of Achilles, patriotism of Hector or nostalgia of Odysseus hardly needs to be emphasized further.

The *pius Aeneas* is thus the ideal man or hero of Virgil's Augustan ideology. But Virgil could not have shown him to be such had he presented him to us ready formed and complete. His *pietas* had to be an achievement or it would not have been truly *pietas:* hence Virgil's epic had to deal with his hero's formation, his attainment of *pietas,* as well as with his mature performance. The battle between *pietas* and *furor,* between pious acceptance, impious rebellion against fate, had to be fought out inside the hero as well as between the hero and his impious opponents. Thus the pivotal 'rebirth' had to come in the middle of the epic and mark the difference between the hero's preparation for victory and the actual winning of it. This, as we have already seen, dictated in effect the plan of the whole poem: six books depicting the inner struggle for *pietas;* six books depicting the triumph of *pietas* over the *impii.* This is, of course, a rather rough and ready summation of complex material but it brings out the essential division of the whole poem, a subjective, internal or psychological section (Books 1-6) followed by a relatively objective, external and military section (Books 7-12). There are, in other words, three levels of conflict in the epic:

(1) That between Fate (Jupiter) and Counter-Fate (Juno)
(2) That between Aeneas and his own passions
and (3) That between Aeneas and the *impii*

and, though all these levels extend through the entire *Aeneid,* the *second* is emphasized in Books 1-6 and the *third* in Books 7-12.

The design of each of the two sets of six books had thus to be quite different. The first (Books 1-6, the Odyssean *Aeneid*) needed to be subjective in the sense that the essential narrative was psychological and thus dominated the outer events or even reduced them to the status of symbols of the inner events. The second (Books 7-12, the Iliadic *Aeneid*), on the contrary, quite lacked any such subjective-symbolic basis since the action was no longer psychological or mostly so, but overt and visible, and, in large part, could be described directly without further ado. Virgil's problem was to adapt his Homeric motifs to these two distinct sections. His choice of the *Odyssey* for the first part, the *Iliad* for the second, seems almost obvious, once the problem is stated in these terms. The *Odyssey* or at least its first 12 books is essentially an epic of one man's voyage through very strange and exotic territory as he strives, against both divine and human opposition, to reach his home. This clearly fitted both the external (voyage from Troy to Italy) and the internal (progress from incomplete to complete *pietas*) movement of the first six books. On the other hand, the martial *Iliad*, with its multiple cast of characters, its constant warfare and its far less 'romantic' plot, was understandingly better adapted to the last six books.

Thus, what we shall now call the Odyssean *Aeneid* (Books 1-6) is concerned mainly with the first two levels indicated above, the level of fate and counter-fate and the level of internal or psychological action. There is, in other words, the *subjective* or *empathetic narrative* (basically centred in the psyche of Aeneas though the 'empathetic centre' shifts to Dido at the close of Book 1 and stays with her through most of Book 4) *and* an accompanying set of symbols which represent the action of fate and counter-fate and also relate this to the central empathetic narrative. Here Virgil drew on two more or less distinct strands of the objectively continuous Odyssean narrative: the main story of Odysseus (his *nostos*, detention by Calypso, reception by Alcinous, recital of his past adventures) and, on the other hand, the divine machinery and supernatural side of the *Odyssey* (the preliminary council of the gods, the opposition of Poseidon and assistance of Athene, monsters like the Cyclopes, the land of the dead). Virgil adapted the first strand to the main psychological narrative of the *Aeneid*; the second to the cosmic symbolism of the poem, to the action of fate and counter-fate in all its bearings. But, . . . the two levels—the psychologically continuous narrative, the cosmic symbolism—are correlated with each other. It is, in fact, the interplay of the two that constitutes the very heart of the epic.

In order to use the *Odyssey* for his subjective narrative, for the

story of his hero's conversion to complete *pietas*, for what, as we
have seen, was in part at least, a narrative version of the *Georgics*
and *Eclogues*, Virgil had to alter the whole arrangement and to-
nality of his Homeric model. The *nostos* of the *Odyssey*, which is
really the immemorial story of a man's homecoming, was thus con-
verted into what was almost its opposite, a man's progress from his
home, from the emotional centre of his whole affective life, toward
a new, unknown and even dreaded goal. The voyage to Latium
was, as it were, the test and symbol of the hero's willingness to give
up the past for the future, to submit and piously submit to fate.
This is why the story of his departure from home, from Troy, of
the initial and primary cause of his 'inverted nostos', absolutely had
to be introduced even though it (i.e. Book 2) had no Odyssean or
Iliadic precedent.[4] Again the sequence of events in the *Odyssey*
(Calypso–the storm–Alcinous–the recital of the past) had to be
reversed and transposed and given new emphasis: the encounter
with the detaining woman had to become (as it was not in Homer)
the centre of the narrative; the storm had thus to precede this and
the hero's adventures to be told to the woman, not to a comparative
stranger like Alcinous. In this way, as we shall see, the hero's past,
present, and future were linked to the most important spiritual
hazard he had to run and the quite physical action of the *Odyssey*
was given a new psychological meaning. Finally, the *nekuia*—the
hero's encounter with the dead—was not only given a quite different position in the plot (at the very end of the *errores* or wanderings, whereas, in the *Odyssey*, it is followed by a whole book of
subsequent wanderings and is actually part of Odysseus' long recital to Alcinous, not a decisive event of the main narrative) but
was changed to a real *catabasis* or descent of the hero into the
Underworld rather than remaining, as in Homer, a mere coming
of the ghosts to a hero who statically abides their approach. The
changes, in fact, are so drastic that the question arises why Virgil
cared to preserve the Homeric motifs at all: it would seemingly
have been less trouble to abandon them altogether. In fact, however, they play a most important role, as we shall see: Virgil gained
from Homer much more than the cachet of a revered name. But,
the important thing to notice here is the extent to which Homer
yielded to the exacting demands of Virgil's Augustan plot and subjective style of narrative.

The transformation of Homer's gods and monsters—of the su-

---

[4] This point, curiously enough, has seldom been clearly seen or made by critics.
Cf. the discussion of Book 2 in R. Heinze, *Virgils epische Technik* (Leipzig-
Berlin, 1928), chap. i *passim*.

pernatural and miraculous elements of the *Odyssey*—is fully as
radical. It has been generally realized that Virgil's Jupiter is primarily the image of a fate, *fatum,* that is conceived in a funda-
mentally Stoic way.[5] But the relation of Jupiter to the lesser gods
and goddesses (especially Juno and Venus) and the intricate means
by which the two levels of deity are made known to the hero and
to the other human characters of the story, have as yet been left
in a good deal of obscurity. It was, we may say, essential to Virgil's
purpose that Jupiter's or Fate's will should be revealed to Aeneas
according to a scale of increasing clarity, a scale going all the way
from the obscurity of Book 3 (the *errores*) to the final enlightenment of Book 6. It was also essential to his purpose that Aeneas
should be opposed by Juno (or 'counter-fate') and aided by Venus
in such a way as not to make otiose the more direct actions of
Jupiter or the free response to them of Aeneas himself. These two
factors are the very conditions of Aeneas' freedom or of his *pietas*
defined as a human achievement for which he himself is made responsible. For unlike the much simpler divine machinery of Homer,
which is actually a quite integral part of the narrative, Virgil's is
in one sense curiously detached from the human action or parallels
it with the very minimum of overt intervention. We can really
limit Jupiter's overt interferences in the Odyssean *Aeneid* to three:
the oracles at the end of Book 2, the mission of Mercury in Book
4, and the mission of Anchises in Book 5. And even these do not
simply supersede the human will of Aeneas: his conscience was
already active in each of these three cases as we shall see. Certainly
neither Juno's opposition nor Venus' aid are decisive. Most often
they simply cancel each other out.

But it would be just as great an error in the opposite direction
to regard the gods as mere 'reflections' or projections of Aeneas'
psyche. Virgil really believed in a cosmic fate and a cosmic counter-
fate (*ratio* and *furor* on a heavenly scale) and in Rome as much
more than a human achievement. But man was, in his eyes, a
creature whose free response to fate or counter-fate was the indispensable means through which both had to work. The ensuing
correlation of divine and human affairs is thus intricate as well as
necessary; freedom is not an alternative to predestination but an

---

[5] But we must not exaggerate the Stoicism. The full identification of Jupiter-
fatum with Rome is not *per se* a Stoic invention. . . . I would add . . . however, that Virgil's failure wholly to assimilate Jupiter to εἱμαρμένη plus πρόνοια
is not simply the necessity of his Homeric plot: it is also his sense of the complexity of fate, its emergence as the final result of all that both the sub-fates
and human beings can do. In the last analysis, the *Aeneid* is anything but simply
Stoic.

essential component of it. Or put in the terms of the *Aeneid* itself:
both men and gods can accept fate with piety; both men and gods
can reject fate with *furor;* and fate itself is the predestined product
of their interpenetrating acceptances and rejections. It is just this
tangled parallelism, but parallelism without identity, of human and
divine action that permits Virgil to build an intricate structure of
motifs between them. The Storms in Books 1 and 4, Fama and
Allecto, Polydorus, the Harpies, etc. are all intermediary motifs
in this sense: they connect gods and men—the cosmic and human
—in a real blending of inner psychology and outer demonism.
Dreams, oracles, portents, prophecies are used in a similar way.
So too are physical or natural phenomena. Light and darkness,
night and day, colours, sounds, motions, all images of nature in
short, are put on a scale of being that insensibly passes from the
human or psychological to the superhuman or cosmic. The line
between the innermost feelings of men and the outermost activities
of nature or the gods is never fixed, but always open to penetration
from both sides. In short, though we may say that, on the whole,
the divine action of the *Aeneid* is much more symbolic than overt,
we must also say that the symbols possess a truly cosmic dimension
and far exceed a purely human frame of reference.

*   *   *

The *Iliadic* Aeneid

The second half of the *Aeneid* is strikingly different from the
first. The change of model—the substitution of *Iliad* for *Odyssey*
—is but a symptom of another and deeper change. The psychological and subjective emphasis of the first six books is gone: Aeneas
is no more engaged in inner struggle, in the hard task of his remotivation, but in a great war with very tangible human opponents.
His *pietas* has been established: we now see it demonstrated in
action. In this sense the Iliadic *Aeneid* is the obvious climax of
the epic; Aeneas' struggle with the Latins is a *maius opus* and with
it a *maior rerum ordo* begins. But in another sense, the Iliadic
Aeneid contains or seems at first sight to contain an element of
anticlimax: we have been so prepared for the great test in Latium,
so assured of Aeneas' success, so instructed in the designs of fate,
that the actual result seems all but discounted in advance. The
interest of the hero's bitter, personal struggle for self-mastery is, for
at least many moderns, far greater than that of the tangible narrative of a battle whose outcome is certain. Nor does Virgil seem to

make it easy for us: he now presents Aeneas as a quite static figure, unchanging and foursquare in his *pietas,* while it is his opponents, Turnus above all, but also Lausus, Camilla and even Mezentius, who struggle with pathetic heroism in a most unequal combat with fate. Nor does Virgil share with Homer any particular zest for battles or the incidents of battle: he does not in fact hide his aversion to war or his strong preference for peace; all his own tastes and values seem to contradict and discount his martial subject. What then are we to think of the Iliadic *Aeneid?* It is really a *maius opus,* the true climax of the epic, or is it not?

But the answer to this question and the main key to Virgil's purpose has been already given us in the sixth Book. Obvious as in one sense it is, it has often been overlooked, as the curious variety of attempts to 'explain' the Iliadic *Aeneid* to modern sensibilities have repeatedly exemplified. The moral that interprets and sums up the heroic *exempla* of the Roman past is stated in the famous lines:

> Excudent alii spirantia mollius aera
> (credo equidem), vivos ducent de marmore voltus,
> orabunt causas melius, caelique meatus
> describent radio et surgentia sidera dicent:
> tu regere imperio populos, Romane, memento
> (hae tibi erunt artes), pacisque imponere morem,
> parcere subiectis et debellare superbos.

> (Others, I know, will beat out more gently breathing bronzes, and create living faces from marble, others will plead cases better, will mark out the paths of the sky and tell the stars' risings: you, Roman, remember to rule peoples under your sway (these will be your arts), and to impose the habit of peace, to spare the conquered and crush the overbearing.)
> (A. 6.847-53)

The Roman, though he may lack the *arts* of Greek culture, has one great art that is his very own: that of ruling the peoples in one empire and of imposing on them the *habit of peace* by conquering the haughty and sparing the humble.[6] This ideal is thoroughly un-

---

[6] . . . I do not, however, think these famous lines are just a comparison of the Greek βίος θεωρητικός with the Roman βίος πρακτικός. Virgil, I think, uses *artes* (the Greek τέχναι) in a somewhat Pickwickian sense, as if to say: the arts, Roman, are not your forte; your business is to rule—call that your *art* if you will. The real implication is that ruling is *not* an art in the Greek sense but a moral achievement. The Romans are above *art* because they have character like

Homeric and, on the whole, un-Greek. It is certainly true for Homer that the chief virtue (the ἀρετή) of the hero is shown in his *aristeiai*, his great feats on the battlefield. The question of the justification of war—of the opportunity for the *aristeiai*—is not raised except in the most particular and superficial sense. The notion that war is only permissible as an instrument of pacification, of universal good government, was of course quite beyond Homer's ken as, indeed, it was beyond that of anyone who could not envisage humanity as a single society or order for which actual rulers could be held responsible. In any event, it certainly presented a problem for a poet who was concerned to exemplify it not only in an heroic epic but in an avowed imitation of the *Iliad*.

The bearing of the passage just cited on the Iliadic *Aeneid* has often been missed because its concrete applications have not been seen. After all, the only way to conquer the haughty is by battle and all battles are much alike: this has perhaps been the usual view of the matter. But the battles of the Iliadic *Aeneid* are in fact most unusual and the point of view from which they are described and the conduct of the fighters is described, is more unusual still. For the Latin War is seen by Virgil as a simply horrible instance of *furor* or *violentia* on a social scale. It is not only war but civil war, war between destined fellow-citizens and in fact actual fellow-citizens whose *foedus* or plan of union has been impiously disrupted. It is Juno's final and most horrible attempt to thwart fate and it leads to a terrible perversion of human character, both Latin and Trojan.

Aeneas' *pietas* comes out not only in his opposing such violence by fighting it with all necessary courage, but in the *way* he opposes it, in the way he fights and treats his enemies. His is the *humanitas* that sees war as a terrible necessity and a means to its negation, peace. The desire for battle-glory (*aretē* in this sense) or for plunder, the satisfaction of revenge and hatred, the sheer lust of conquest, is, with one apparent exception, conspicuously absent from his conduct. And it is this which in the last analysis gives him the moral superiority that justifies his military superiority over Turnus and the Latins. He is surrounded and seemingly eclipsed by the exploits

---

that of the heroes who have just been described. Cf. G. Radke, *Gymnasium*, LXIV (1957), 176-77, who stresses the connection with Q. Fabius Maximus, the *cunctator* (Fabius refused to participate in the plundering at Tarentum, thus illustrating the principle of *parcere subiectis*). I would also mention the story of Camillus in the fifth Book of Livy (especially his behaviour toward the people of Falerii: cf. 5. 27. 6 *Sunt et belli, sicut pacis iura, iusteque ea non minus quam fortiter didicimus gerere.*

of both Trojans and Latins: he is absent from Book 9, very incon-
spicuous in Book 11, while in Books 10 and 12 he shares the stage
with Turnus, Mezentius, Pallas, Lausus, and others. What gives him
pre-eminence, despite all the competing figures, is his immunity
from the moral failure that fatally stains the conduct of the rest.
Unlike Turnus, Nisus, Euryalus or Camilla he does not succumb to
the lust of plunder. Unlike them also, he does not manifest any
eagerness for fighting, except when dominated by a special emotion
such as his affection for Pallas. Unlike them, he regrets and sorrows
over the war. He alone thinks throughout of the peace to be gained.
He alone realizes the true *pathos* of the *Marcelli,* the noble young
doomed to premature death, and thus pays the price of peace with
some sense of its magnitude. He alone avoids the sin of *hybris* and
feels the sadness of success.

Seen in such a light, the Iliadic *Aeneid* is very far from an anticlimax or a mere tale of events already predicted and of a victory
already guaranteed. In the Odyssean *Aeneid,* the *pietas* that Aeneas
achieves with such difficulty is basically an acceptance of his own
role as the servant of the Roman future. But not until the Show of
Heroes does he really gain any concrete notion of what that future
will be or what it really means to be a Roman. Now his problem
ceases to be merely one of his own remotivation; of internal struggle
with his own individual passion and nostalgia—and becomes, instead, one of leadership, of action, of exemplifying in a great war
the *social* meaning of *pietas* or, still more, of *humanitas.* We are
now to see how the Roman could do what no one else, certainly no
Greek, had done, that is, actually achieve true peace—proleptically
at least the ecumenical peace of Augustus—by setting a new standard of humanity. Whatever the culture of the Greeks (and Virgil
sweepingly grants its superiority in his *excudent alii*) they had not
solved the problem of peace because they lacked the moral prerequisite of a solution.

What gave Aeneas this prerequisite was the ordeal—the ordeal of
the Odyssean *Aeneid*—by which his *humanitas* was changed from an
element of weakness to an element of strength. In the first six books,
Aeneas is certainly humane: he is touched by the 'tears of things'
when he views the sculptures of the Juno temple in Book 1; he
weeps over Dido; he is moved by the work of Daedalus, etc. But
such humanity is compounded with a self-pity that even verges on
despair. He pities the Trojan dead because they are at rest and he
is not; he sees in the rising walls of Carthage the disturbing evidence of his own remoteness from his goal; he bids a reluctant farewell to Helenus' New Troy because *he* has no such home. In the

mythological Hades of the sixth *Aeneid,* he lingers or tries to linger over the pathetic remnants of his past in a 'humanity' of feeling that temporarily displaces any sense of his destiny and of its rigid schedule. But all this is now changed: in the Iliadic *Aeneid* his humanity is never exercised at the expense of his duty. He fights well because he feels it his duty to fight well, but he fights without the violence and cupidity that make war an end in itself or an expression of irrational *furor* indifferent to any peaceful or rational purpose. The obverse of *debellare superbos* is always for him *parcere subiectis* because the final aim is *pacis imponere morem.* To this line of conduct there are exceptions, as we shall see, especially when Aeneas is humanly angered or grieved, but even the exceptions are related to his *humanitas,* his love and pity for Pallas, the great Marcellus figure. At no point, however, does he falter in fighting because of his *humanitas* or exult in the fighting because of sheer *furor* and blood-lust; it is, instead, the combination of *virtus* with *humanitas* that gives him strength and makes him the only hero of the Iliadic *Aeneid* who looks ahead from war to peace, who is able to see in his present foe a future fellow-citizen and Roman. The Augustan meaning of all this is, of course, obvious: we now realize that the 'reborn' hero is a truly Roman hero who stands in the great line that includes Hercules, Romulus and Augustus but who is particularly the Augustan prototype because he, like Augustus, brings peace not only to a world at war but to a *civitas* divided against itself in fratricidal conflict. Here, in short, Aeneas finally emerges as the divine man or 'saviour' of the *Eclogues* and *Georgics.*

The plan of the Iliadic *Aeneid* is itself evidence of the general purpose just described. There are two books of introduction (7, 8) in which the infernal, impiously violent character of the war and Aeneas' role as the divine man, *theios-aner,* designed by fate and his own *pietas* to counteract such violence, are firmly set forth. The last four books then show the violence and the man at work. Their essential aim is to illustrate Aeneas' combined *humanitas* and *virtus* by contrast with the *furor* of both friends and foes. The main Iliadic theme (the parallelism of Achilles-Hector-Patroclus with Aeneas-Turnus-Pallas) is carried by the two major or even books (10, 12) and contrasts the two main heroes, Aeneas and Turnus. The minor or odd books (9, 11) contain, as their central pieces, two great episodes of heroism (a Trojan and a Latin) that establish another sort of contrast with Aeneas: the contrast between his mature *humanitas-virtus* and the immature combination of *virtus* with the battle fury and lust of plunder, with the *caedis cupido* that finally dooms even such heroes as Nisus, Euryalus and Camilla.

But the factor that gives continuity and climax to the whole story is the development of Turnus' character after he has been removed from battle by Juno in Book 10. In one sense Book 12 is a repetition of all that went before, made necessary only because Turnus was not permitted to face Aeneas in the crucial conflict of the tenth book. But, as we shall see, the avoidance of their encounter in 10 is necessary to motivate Turnus' *voluntary* seeking of the encounter in 12. When he *decides* to sacrifice himself 'for the many', the peace and union of Trojans and Latins are assured. Thus, as we shall see, Virgil solved the problem of 'retardation' (the deferring of the climactic duel of the main heroes), as Homer did not.

The purpose and consequent structure of these books thus account for the fact that their use of empathy and of symbolism is so different from that of the Odyssean *Aeneid*. The empathetic 'spotlight' is no longer on Aeneas mainly but on several Trojan and Latin figures and most positively on Turnus. One of Virgil's primary objects is to show *furor* in the mass and in several different individuals and, above all, to show the inner conflict it arouses within such individuals. The opponents of Aeneas are anything but villains or mere *exempla* of violence: they are not only Latins or Italians, whose virtues for obvious reasons must be insisted upon, but human beings whose tragedy is accentuated by their virtues. Even Mezentius, the worst of all, is really glorified in his sacrificial death. But they are nevertheless unable to control their inner *furor* and when they do repent, repent too late. The conflict in their psyches is itself a sign of their malaise. It is indeed the very absence of such inner conflict that makes it unnecessary for us to read Aeneas' mind as we did before. He shows a steadfastness that contrasts favourably with the changing and turbid emotions of Turnus. Yet we see enough of his mind, especially at certain pivotal moments, to understand the difference between him and the others, especially Turnus. Thus the main action is by no means physical, even though there are so many battles, but really a conflict of motivations and it accordingly brings out the essential quality of the divine man who embodies the heroic virtues of Hercules and Romulus and most of all the pacificatory virtues of Augustus.

No one can escape noticing how differently the gods behave in the Iliadic *Aeneid*. The initial action of Juno is of course the climax of her activity in the whole epic: it is the great test of the hero besides which the storms off Africa and at the cave or the shipburning were merely preparatory. Against this is set the action of Venus in Book 8 but, much more, the investment of the hero with the whole future of Rome, not as a show to be passively witnessed but as a burden to be actively borne into battle. Just as Book 7 gives *furor* a social meaning and magnifies the threat to Aeneas into a general attack on the whole Trojan-Latin destiny, so 8 identifies Aeneas with the *Roman* past and future and with Rome's social significance as the opponent of all violence that threatens peace. Venus for once acts like the goddess who had heard the prophecy of Jupiter (Book 1) and now sees in Aeneas the incarnation of Rome's destiny.

The rest of the poem (Books 9-12) might almost be called, at least from the divine viewpoint, the tragedy of Juno, though in the end she is reconciled to Roman victory. Juno now tries, not so much to damn Aeneas as to save Turnus from his fate, but in fact her interventions (especially her crucial intervention in Book 10, which is repeated *via* Juturna in Book 12) only compel him to the insight that his fate is unavoidable. Aeneas, on the other hand, needs no further warning or instigation from Jupiter: the latter actually declares in the gods' council of Book 10 that he will not interfere but let the fates find their own way. In both cases—for both Turnus and Aeneas—the essential decisions come from within; Juno can but defer the outcome; Venus at best helps to cancel the work of Juno. In the end the sub-fates withdrew and the Dirae indicate clearly enough the will of Jupiter. Turnus has no chance, once he has come up against Aeneas (i.e. his fate), but he need never have brought himself to this pass. Acceptance or rejection of fate is free but it is precisely through this freedom that fate works. The divine machinery of the Iliadic *Aeneid* is a most impressive attempt to depict in symbolic terms the inextricable union of free will and predestination. We see the individual and social and demonic aspects of violence brought face to face with *pietas* and humanity, and we see that Fate is finally on the moral side because the moral forces have in fact already put themselves on the side of Fate.

*   *   *

The Two Voices of Virgil's *Aeneid*

by Adam Parry

I want to begin with the particular. Sometimes we come upon a short passage in a poetic work we know well, a passage we have never particularly noticed before, and all at once, as a kind of epiphany, the essential mood of the author seems to be contained in it. Here is a candidate for such a passage in the *Aeneid*.

There is at the end of Book 7 a kind of *Catalogue of Ships,* a muster or roll-call of the Latin leaders and their forces as they are arrayed against Aeneas in the long war which occupies the last books of the poem. One of these leaders is a quite obscure figure named Umbro. The Catalogue is an Homeric form, and Virgil here exploits it in the Homeric fashion, drawing out a ringing sense of power from place-names, epithets of landscape and valor, names of heroes. He endeavors further, again in the Homeric fashion, to give individuality within the sense of multitude by singling out some characteristic of each Latin warrior, a device the *Aeneid* has yet more need of than the *Iliad,* since Virgil has behind him no tradition of Latin song which could give the audience a previous familiarity with the heroes he names.

So Umbro comes from the Marruvian people, and he is most valiant: *fortissimus Umbro.* And he is a priest, who possesses the art of shedding sleep over fierce serpents. But—and here we catch the Homeric pathos—his herbs and his incantation could not save *him,* wounded by the Dardanian spear. Virgil then closes the brief scene with a beautiful lamentation:

> For you the grove of Angitia mourned, and Fucinus' glassy
> > waters,
> And the clear lakes.

> Te nemus Angitiae, vitrea te Fucinus unda,
> Te liquidi flevere lacus.

If we could understand wholly the reasons for this lamentation, so elaborate within its brevity, and what makes it so poignant, and why it is so Virgilian, we should, I think, have grasped much of Virgil's art. First, something I can talk about a little but not translate, there is the absolute mastery of rhetoric. We have a *tricolon*, three successive noun-phrases, here in *asyndeton*, that is, with no grammatical connectives, joined to one verb, *flevere, mourned*; and this device combined with *apostrophe*: the dead warrior is suddenly addressed in the second person. The pronoun *te, you*, is repeated thrice, each time in the beginning of one of the three elements of the tricolon, a repetition we call *anaphora*. So much is developed but standard rhetoric. Virgil's mastery consists not in that, but in the subtle variations of it we see here. The three nouns are all a little different. The first is a grove with the name of the goddess to whom it is sacred in the possessive singular: *nemus Angitiae*, the grove of Angitia. The second is the name of a nearby lake, Fucinus, qualified by a noun and adjective: *Fucinus with glassy wave, vitrea Fucinus unda*. The third, beginning another hexameter line, is a common noun *lacus, lakes*, in the plural, with an adjective only: *liquidi lacus, transparent lakes*. The first two nouns are opposed to the third by being names of places. The second and third are opposed to the first by having adjectives and by having adjective and noun separated, whereas *the grove of Angitia, nemus Angitiae*, comes together. But the first and third are also opposed to the second by the variation of the *anaphora: te, you*, embodying the directness of lamentation, begins the first phrase: *Te nemus Angitiae . . . Te* is repeated in the second phrase, but its directness is modulated, softened, by its coming second in the phrase, after the adjective *vitrea, glassy: vitrea te Fucinus unda*. Then in the third phrase, the tonic note is struck again: *Te liquidi flevere lacus*. And finally, the verse accent falls on the first *te* and the third, but not on the second:

> Te nemus Angitiae, vitrea te Fucinus unda,
> Te liquidi flevere lacus.

If this analysis seems too microcosmic, let me say that Virgil may not be, surely is not, the greatest poet who ever lived; but that in this mastery of the disposition of words within a formal pattern, he has no rivals. The effect of the variation within the symmetry is first to establish a rhythm, whose value might finally have to be analyzed in musical terms; and second, to add emotion to the lines. The tricolon with anaphora is a strong formal device, appropriate to the sounds of public lamentation. The variations, like a gentle yielding within the firm tripartite structure, add the note of genuine grief, invest the far-off place names with something of what used to be called the lyric cry.

For it is the place-names in this passage that show us how Virgil has departed from his Homeric model. The Homeric lines the commentators cite here occur in the Catalogue of the Trojans at the end of Book 2 of the *Iliad*: "The forces from Mysia were led by Chromius and by Ennomus, a diviner of birds. But his birds did not keep *him* from black death. He was to be slain by the hands of swift Achilles at the river, where many another Trojan fell." The moment of death, and the great slaughter of the Trojans when Achilles returned to battle, is the picture we are left with.

Or again this, from the fifth Book of the *Iliad*: "Menelaus son of Atreus caught with his sharp spear Strophius' son Scamandrius, a great hunter. Artemis herself had taught him how to down all the wildlife that the woods nourish. But the huntress goddess Artemis did him no good then, nor did his mastery with the bow for which he was so famous. The son of Atreus, killer Menelaus, struck him with the spear as he fled before him, right between the shoulders, and drove the point out through his chest. And he fell forward, and his armor rang as he fell." Again, and more emphatically in a typical passage such as this, the bitter irony of Homer leaves us with the image of the instant death of the man: the glory of Scamandrius when he lived and was famed as a hunter, then the uselessness of what he was as death comes upon him.

Virgil in the lines about Umbro imitates these scenes. But the image he leaves us with is not a fallen warrior, but a mourning landscape. The dramatic preoccupation of Homer with the single man and the single instant of time gives way to an echoing appeal to the Italian countryside, and an appeal strengthened in wholly unhomeric fashion by historical associations.

The place-names invoked by Virgil, Marruvium, Lake Fucinus, the grove of the goddess Angitia, are from the Marsian country, hill country to the east of Rome, where a few generations earlier than Virgil a tough and warlike Italian people, the Marsi, had lived in independence, as Roman allies. In the Italian or Marsic war of 91-88 B.C., they had been defeated by Rome, and though they had gained citizenship, they had effectively lost their independence. To Virgil, this people represented the original Italian stock. His feeling for them had something in common with what Americans have felt for the American Indian. They were somehow more Italian than the Romans themselves. Proud, independent, with local traditions hallowed by the names they had given to the countryside, they succumbed inevitably to the expansion of Roman power. The explicit message of the *Aeneid* claims that Rome was a happy reconciliation of the natural virtues of the local Italian peoples and the civilized might of the Trojans who came to found the new city. But the tragic movement of the last books of the poem carries a different suggestion: that the formation of Rome's empire involved the loss of the pristine purity of Italy. Thus the plot of the closing books of the poem centers on Turnus, Aeneas' antagonist, who is made the embodiment of a simple valor and love of honor which cannot survive the complex forces of civilization.

In this light we can understand the form which the lamentation for Umbro takes. Umbro himself is not important. He is no more than a made-up name. The real pathos is for the places that mourn him. They are the true victims of Aeneas' war, and in saying that they weep, Virgil calls on us to weep for what to his mind made an earlier Italy fresh and true.

The lamentation of the ancient hallowed places of the Marsi strikes a characteristic Virgilian note of melancholy and nostalgia, a note produced by the personal accents of sorrow over human and heroic values lost. But equally characteristic is the aesthetic resolution of the lines. The lament is presented to us as an object of artistic contemplation. By this I mean not simply that the lines are beautiful, for that is no distinguishing feature of Virgil. Nor do I refer to the vulgar concepts of "word-painting" or "scenic values," concepts often invoked in Virgilian criticism. The unexpected epithets *vitrea, glassy,* and *liquidi, clear,* do not, I think, "paint a picture" for us. But they do create a sense of sublimation, a conscious feeling that the raw emotions of grief have been subsumed in an artistic finality of vision. Not only the death of Umbro but also the loss of Italy itself is at last replaced by an image of bright and clear waters. The word *vitrea* in the middle of the lamentation is particularly noteworthy, for its connotations are those of an artifact. It is as if Virgil were telling us that the way to resolve our personal sorrow over the losses of history is to regard these losses in the same mood as we would a beautifully wrought vessel of clear glass. The perfection of the lines itself imposes a kind of artistic detachment, and we are put in the position of Aeneas himself, as he sees, in Carthage, the destruction of Troy represented as paintings in a gallery of art.

These paintings remind Aeneas of all that has been, of the *tears of human things;* and at the same time, Virgil tells us, they fill him with hope. In a larger way, the whole poem is such a painting. It is about history, but its purpose is not to tell us that history is good, or for that matter that it is bad. Its purpose is rather to impose on us an attitude that can take into account all in history that is both good and bad, and can regard it with the purer emotions of artistic detachment, so that we are given a higher consolation, and sorrow itself becomes a thing to be desired.

Let us now consider the poem from a wider point of view. Here we take care not to let orthodox interpretations of the *Aeneid* obscure our sense of what it really is. The nostalgia for the heroic and Latin past, the pervasive sadness, the regretful sense of the limitations of human action in a world where you've got to end up on the right side or perish, the frequent elegiac note so apparently uncalled for in a panegyric of Roman greatness—like the passage at the end of Book 5 which describes the drowning of the good pilot Palinurus in dark and forgetful waters just before the Trojans reach Italy—the continual opposition of a personal voice which comes to us as if it were Virgil's own to the public voice of Roman success: all this I think is felt by every attentive reader of the poem. But most readers, in making a final judgment on the *Aeneid,* feel nonetheless constrained to put forth a hypothetical "Roman reader" whose eyes were quite unused to the melting mood. *He* would have taken the poem ultimately as a great work of Augustan propaganda, clapped his hands when Aeneas abandons the overemotional Dido, and approved with little qualification the steady march of the Roman state to world dominion and the Principate of Augustus as we see these institutions mirrored in Anchises' speech in Book 6 and in Juno's renunciation in Book 12. This, we are told, is how we should read the poem. After all, what was Augustus giving Virgil all those gold-pieces for?

So Mr. Kevin Guinach, the Rinehart translator, after putting forth these views, adds: "From this it must not be inferred that Virgil was a hireling. . . . It is fairer to suppose that he was an ardent admirer of the First Citizen and his policies, and sought to promote the reconstruction that August had in mind." Apropos of Dido he says: "The ancient Romans did not read this episode as tearfully as we do. . . . From the Roman point of view, Dido was the aggressor in her marriage with Aeneas, an intolerable assumption of a male prerogative." Moreover, he tells us, the Roman would have condemned her for breaking her vow to her first husband, dead these many years. Consider the case of Vestal Virgins. . . .

But what, on the simple glorification of Rome interpretation, do we make of some of the finest passages of the *Aeneid*? What we find, again and again, is not a sense of triumph, but a sense of loss. Con-

sider the three lines at the end of Book 2 which describe Aeneas'
attempts to embrace the ghost of his wife:

> Three times I tried to put my arms around her
> And three times her image fled my arms' embrace,
> As light as the winds; as fleeting as a dream.

Like the lines about the fallen warrior, these lines derive from an
earlier literary tradition. And again a comparison with this tradition will tell us something about the *Aeneid*. Virgil has two Homeric
passages in mind, one in the twenty-third Book of the *Iliad* where
Achilles tries to embrace the hollow wraith of Patroclus:

> So spoke Achilles, and reached for him, but could not
> seize him, and the spirit went underground, like vapor,
> with a thin cry. And Achilles started awake, in amazement,
> and drove his hands together, and spoke, and his words were
>   sorrowful:
> Ah me! even in the house of Hades there is left something
>   of us,
> a soul and an image, but there is no real heart of life in it!

And a passage from the eleventh book of the *Odyssey*, where Odysseus in the Underworld attempts to embrace the shade of his
mother:

> I bit my lip
> rising perplexed, with longing to embrace her,
> and tried three times,
> but she went sifting through my arms, impalpable
> as shadows are, and wavering like a dream.
> And this embittered all the pain I bore . . .

So the Virgilian passage first of all serves to reinforce the identification, operative throughout the poem, of Aeneas with the heroes
of Homer. But the identification only sets in relief the differences.
Virgil's lines are characteristic of the whole mood of his poem, the
sadness, the loss, the frustration, the sense of the insubstantiality of
what could be palpable and satisfying. Virgil emphasizes the *image*
—the word *imago* ends the second line; and we can think of count-
less like passages, such as the appearance of Aeneas' mother in Book
1, not recognized until after she has fled. The Homeric heroes are
made angry by these signs of what lies beyond our physical existence. Achilles *drives* his hands together, Odysseus is *embittered* that
this kind of frustration should be added to his troubles. The
Homeric hero, however beleaguered by fate, loves and enjoys the

warmth of life, and his course of action includes a protest against the evanescence of mortality. But the sense of emptiness is the very heart of the Virgilian mood. After the three lines I have quoted, Aeneas goes on simply:

> The night was over; I went back to my comrades.

And the third of the three lines

> As light as the winds, as fleeting as a dream

receives a delicate emphasis, partly due to the two different words for *as*

> *Par* levibus ventis, volucrique *simillima* somno

that blurs the contours of our waking senses and gives the line a force of poignant resignation absent from both Homeric passages.

One other passage here, which I will speak of again later on. Aeneas comforts his men after the storm in Book 1 with a famous phrase:

> Forsan et haec olim meminisse iuvabit.
> Some day perhaps remembering this too will be a pleasure.

Lifted again from the *Odyssey*. But the Homeric line is quite un-memorable. Odysseus says to his men that some day their troubles now will be a memory. He means only, they will be in the past, don't be overcome by them now. Virgil has made one clear change: the word *iuvabit: it will be a pleasure,* which makes a common-place idea into a profoundly touching one. Not I would insist, because Virgil is a greater poet, but because the kind of sentiment that stands out in the *Aeneid* is different from the kind that stands out in the *Odyssey*.

How much in general is Aeneas like the Greek heroes? We know from the first line that he is cast in the rôle of Achilles and Odysseus:

> Arms and the man I sing . . .

The *arms* are of course the *Iliad,* the *man* is the *Odyssey*. And the first six books of the *Aeneid* retrace the wanderings of Odysseus, the wars of the last six books follow the example of the *Iliad*. But the examples are not followed closely. The *Odyssey* goes on after its first line to tell us about the single man Odysseus; the *Iliad* goes on to describe the quarrel that was the first step in the tragedy of Achilles. The *Aeneid* moves from Aeneas straightway to something larger than himself: Rome:

that man who was tossed about on land and sea
and suffered much in war until
he built his city, brought the gods to Latium
from whence the Alban Fathers, the towering walls of Rome

Aeneas from the start is absorbed in his own destiny, a destiny which does not ultimately relate to him, but to something later, larger, and less personal: the high walls of Rome, stony and grand, the Augustan Empire. And throughout he has no choice. Aeneas never asserts himself like Odysseus. He is always the victim of forces greater than himself, and the one lesson he must learn is, not to resist them. The second book of the poem drills him thoroughly in this lesson. The word Aeneas keeps using, as he tells of the night Troy fell, is *obstipui:* I was *dumbfounded,* shocked into silence. Again and again he tries to assert himself, to act as a hero, and again and again he fails. He leads a band of desperate Trojans against the Greeks, but it all turns sour. The Trojans dress up as Greeks, an unheroic stratagem which works for a while, but then their own countrymen mistake them, and Trojans slaughter each other, while Aeneas himself ends up on the roof of Priam's palace, passive spectator of the terrible violations within. A key passage is the one in which Aeneas is about to kill Helen. At least the personal, if not entirely heroic, emotion of revenge can be satisfied. But his mother stops him, not with a personal plea, as Athena checks Achilles in the *Iliad,* but by revealing for an instant the gods at work destroying the city. Against such overwhelming forces as these, individual feeling has no place. Aeneas must do the *right* thing, the thing destiny demands, and sneak away from Troy.

One of the effects, then, of the epic identifications of Aeneas is ironic contrast: he is cast in a rôle which it is his tragedy not to be able to fulfill. Let us now consider another kind of identification: the historical ones. As well as being cast as Odysseus and Achilles, Aeneas has to be the emperor Augustus. Of many passages, this one in the third book particularly contributes to setting up the connection. Aeneas and his men coast along the western shore of Greece and stop at Actium, where there is a temple of Apollo. There they hold games and Aeneas fastens to the door of the temple spoils taken from the Greeks with the inscription THESE ARMS FROM THE GREEK VICTORS. The reason for this action in this place is that Augustus had won his great victory over Antony and Cleopatra a few years earlier at Actium. He had instituted games in honor of his victory, and he liked to identify himself with Apollo. Moreover THE GREEK VICTORS, who are now vanquished, represent the armies of Antony, who recruited his forces from the eastern Mediterranean, whereas Augustus made himself the champion of Italy. So that the victory Aeneas somewhat illogically claims here by dedicating Greek spoils prefigures the victory that was to establish the power of Augustus.

Some striking verbal parallels confirm the connection; and give us as well insight into Virgil's technique. At the beginning of Book 3, Aeneas sets sail from Troy.

> I am borne forth an exile onto the high seas
> With my comrades, my son, the Penates and the Great Gods
>
> Cum sociis natoque Penatibus et Magnis Dis.

The exact meaning of the phrase *the Penates and the Great Gods* is obscure. But it is clear that they are some sort of cult statues of Troy, destined to become cult statues of the New Troy, or Rome. The oddity of the phrase in fact helps us to remember it—the Romans liked their religious language to be obscure—and so does its remarkable thudding rhythm: *Penatibus et Magnis Dis.* This is Aeneas in his sacral character as bearer of the divine charter of Troy.

At the end of Book 8, Vulcan makes a shield for Aeneas, and on it are engraved scenes from subsequent Roman history. One of these scenes depicts the Battle of Actium:

On one side stands Augustus Caesar leading Italians into battle,
With the Fathers (i.e., the Senate), the People, the Penates and the Great
 Gods

Cum patribus populoque, Penatibus et Magnis Dis.

Aeneas' shield shows the future version of himself.

But Aeneas is not just Augustus. There is also the possibility of his being Augustus' bitter enemy, Mark Antony. Such is the identification we are led to make when, in the fourth book, he has become the consort of Dido, queen of Carthage. Thus the contemptuous description of him by Iarbas, his rival for Dido's love, "that Paris with his effeminate retinue," closely matches the image of Antony and Cleopatra with their corrupt eastern armies which Augustus created for Roman morale.

And Dido is Cleopatra. When she is about to die, she is said to be *pale with imminent death, pallida morte futura.* Cleopatra, in her own person, is described on Aeneas' shield in Book 8 as *paling before imminent death, pallentem morte futura.*

To understand the meaning in the poem of these historical identifications, we must first consider more fully the figure of Aeneas.
We learn from the second line of the poem that he is a man *exiled
by fate, fato profugus,* and we soon learn that fate has for Aeneas
implications that go beyond his personal journey through life. He
is a man blessed—or is it cursed?—with a mission. The mission is
no less than to be the founder of the most powerful state known to
history; and so his every act and his every passion, all that he does,
all that he feels and all that happens to him is in the light or under
the shadow of this immense prophetic future of which he, by no
choice of his own, is the representative elected by the gods. Every
experience he passes through, therefore, has a significance greater
than the events of an ordinary man's life could possibly have. Every
place he visits acquires an eternal fame of one kind or another.
Every action he performs, every word he speaks, is fraught with
consequences of which he himself can only dimly perceive the
enormity.

This sense of pregnant greatness in every detail of experience is
impressed on us too by the rhetorical exaggeration which pervades
the *Aeneid,* and by the unrealism of many of its incidents. Juno's
wrath in Book 1 is magnified far beyond Poseidon's resentment in
the *Odyssey;* Athena's punishment of the lesser Ajax, which Juno
would like to inflict upon Aeneas, is enlarged into a cosmic destruction. When there are storms, the waves rise up and lash the heavens.
Dido is supposed to have arrived in Africa not long before with a
small band of refugees; but already the construction of a tremendous city—the later Carthage, of course—can be seen, complete
with temples and art-galleries. Aeneas is moving through a world
where everything is a symbol of something larger than itself. The
layers of literary and historical allusion reinforce this sense of expansion in space and time which every monumental hexameter
verse imposes on the reader.

The potentialities of ages and empires are alive in the smallest
details of the *Aeneid,* and Aeneas has been made into the keystone
of it all. The inconceivable destiny of Rome rests upon his shoulders. The *Aeneid* can give a literal meaning to that cliché. So line
32 of the first Book:

> Tantae molis erat Romanam condere gentem
> It was a thing of so much *weight* to found the Roman race.

Aeneas can only leave Troy by carrying his aged father upon his
shoulders. And Anchises is more than Aeneas' father. He is the
burden of destiny itself. Thus in Book 6 it is he who unfolds the

panorama of Roman history to his son who has descended to the
Nether World to hear him. And at the end of Book 8, Virgil insists
on Aeneas' rôle as bearer of destiny. The shield which Vulcan makes
for him corresponds to the one he made for Achilles in the *Iliad*.
Only Achilles' shield was adorned with generic pictures of life: a
city at peace, a city at war, a scene of harvest, a scene of dancing,
and so on. Aeneas' shield is adorned with scenes from Roman history, history which is future to him—it is here that we read of
Augustus at the Battle of Actium—and as he puts it on, Virgil says:

> He marvels at the scenes, events unknown to him,
> And lays upon his shoulder the fame and fate of his descendants

> Attollens umero famamque et fata nepotum.

The burden may well be a heavy one to bear, particularly if the
bearer of it himself is permitted only an occasional prophetic
glimpse into its meaning. And when such a glimpse is permitted
him, it is likely to be anything but reassuring.

> Bella, horrida bella . . .

Wars, hideous wars! the Sibyl shrieks at him when he questions
her in Book 6. "You will get to Latium, all right," she tells him,
"but you will wish you had never come!" *Sed non et venisse volent.*
"Go, seek your Italy!" Dido tells him, and then prophesies: "Let
him beg for help in his own land, and when he has accepted the
terms of a shameful peace, let him not enjoy his realm, or that light
he has prayed for, but

> fall before his time, and lie unburied on the sands

> Sed cadat ante diem mediaque inhumatus harena,

whereby Aeneas is included in an almost obsessively recurrent
series of images of disgraceful and nameless death.

Labor, ignorance and suffering are Aeneas' most faithful companions on his journey to Rome. And at once to intensify his own
suffering and lack of fulfillment and to magnify the destiny he is
serving, Aeneas must witness the happiness and success of others.
In the third book he visits his kinsman Helenus in Epirus, and
there he sees a copy of Troy, laid out in miniature. Aeneas is at first
hopeful as he asks the prophetic Helenus for advice: "Now tell me,
for I have divine sanction for all I do, and the gods have promised
me a happy course, tell me the labors I must undergo, and the
dangers I must avoid." But a little later, when Anchises enters, and

he must set sail again, Aeneas falls into despair: "May you live happy, for your destiny is accomplished; but we are called from one fate to another . . . You have peace, you have no need to plow up the sea and follow forever the forever receding shores of Italy."

> Arva neque Ausoniae semper cedentia retro
> Quaerenda.

What this and other like passages impress upon us is something subtly at variance with the stated theme of the poem. Instead of an arduous but certain journey to a fixed and glorious goal, there arises, and gathers strength, a suggestion that the true end of the Trojan and Roman labors will never arrive. It is not that Aeneas will literally never arrive in Latium, found a city, and win his wars. That is as certain as it is that Odysseus will return to Ithaca. But everything in the *Odyssey* prepares us for a fuller end to Odysseus' labors: we are made always to expect his reinstatement in kingship, home, honor and happiness. In the *Aeneid* every prophecy and every episode prepares us for the contrary: Aeneas' end, it is suggested will see him as far from his fulfillment as his beginning. This other Italy will never cease receding into the distance.

There is another dimension to Aeneas' suffering as the bearer of too vast a destiny. Aeneas cannot live his own life. An agent of powers at once high and impersonal, he is successively denied all the attributes of a hero, and even of a man. His every utterance perforce contains a note of history, rather than of individuality. He cannot be himself, because he is wired for sound for all the centuries to come, a fact that is reflected in the speeches of the *Aeneid*. The sonorous lines tend to come out as perfect epigrams, ready to be lifted out of their context and applied to an indefinite number of parallel situations. Aeneas arrives in Carthage and sees the busy construction of the city.

> O fortunate you, whose walls already rise!

he cries out.

> O fortunati, quorum iam moenia surgunt!

The line is memorable, too memorable perhaps for spontaneity. What Virgil has done is to turn to peculiar account what is at once the weakness and the glory of much of Latin verse: its monumentality, and its concomitant lack of dramatic illusion.

But Aeneas' failure as a hero goes deeper than the formality of his speech. As he makes his way through the first six books, we see him successively divested of every personal quality which makes

a man into a hero. We have seen how the weight of his mission is
made to overwhelm him at the very beginning of the poem. In the
second book, he is in a situation which above all calls for self-
sacrifice in the heat of battle. But this is precisely what he is kept
from doing. Hector appears to him in a dream and tells him not to
die for his country, but to flee. "For if Troy could have been saved,"
the ghost says almost with condescension, "my right arm would have
saved it." We understand that Aeneas' words in the first Book, when
he was overwhelmed by the storm, have a deeper meaning than the
parallel lines of the *Odyssey*: "O thrice and four times happy, you
who fell at Troy!" Odysseus spoke out of a momentary despair.
Aeneas' words are true for all his life. His personal ties too are not
kept intact: in his haste to get his father and the state gods out of
Troy, he leaves his wife behind; and when he returns to fetch her,
she is an empty phantom, who can comfort him only with another
prophecy.

But the most dramatic episode and the one in which Aeneas
most loses his claims to heroism is the fourth Book. The tragedy
of Dido is lucid and deeply moving. But the judgment it leads us
to make on Aeneas needs some comment. Generations of Latin
teachers have felt it necessary to defend Aeneas from the charge
of having been a cad. Modern readers are romantic, but a Roman
reader would have known that Aeneas did the right thing. So the
student is asked to forsake his own experience of the poem for that
of a hypothetical Roman. Another theory is that Virgil somehow
fell in love with, and was carried away by, his own heroine. But
we cannot explain Virgil by assuming that he did not intend to
write as he did. It is clear that on the contrary Virgil deliberately
presented Dido as a heroine, and Aeneas as an inglorious deserter.
Dido's speeches are passionate, and, in their operatic way, ring
utterly true. Aeneas can apologize only by urging that his will is
not his own. "If I had had my way," he tells her, "I would never
have left Troy to come here at all." "I would never have fallen in
love with you in the first place," he seems to mean. "I follow Italy
not of my own choice." *Italiam non sponte sequor.* Of course he
is right. Aeneas' will is not his own, and the episode in Carthage
is his last attempt to assert himself as an individual and not as the
agent of an institution. And in his failure, he loses his claim even
to the humbler of the heroic virtues. For piety, in the Roman
sense, meant devotion to persons as well as the state. "Unhappy
Dido!" the queen about to die cries out, "is it now his impious
deeds become clear to you? They should have before, when you
made him your partner in rule. See now his pledge of faith, this

man who carries about his gods, and his ancient father on his back."
For pious Aeneas, as he is called, and calls himself, throughout,
cannot maintain even his piety in a personal way.

Two later passages serve to emphasize this. At the beginning of
the fifth Book, the Trojans sail to Italy, troubled by the death-
fires they see back in Carthage. "For they knew what a woman is
capable of, when insane with the grief of her love dishonored."
The Latin is perhaps more blunt. Dido's love was literally *defiled*,
polluto amore, and Aeneas is its defiler. Later, in the Underworld
in Book 6, Aeneas meets Dido. He wants reconciliation now, and
begs forgiveness. "I did not know the strength of your love for me,"
he says. Again the implication is clear. Aeneas did not know, because he could not feel the same love for her; because he is not
master of himself, but the servant of an abstract destiny. Dido,
speechless in anger, turns away. Aeneas is modelled on Odysseus
here, and Dido's shade is the shade of Ajax in Book 11 of the
Odyssey. Virgil strengthens the emotions this scene creates in us by
recalling the one scene in the *Odyssey* where Odysseus meets a hero
greater than himself, and is put to shame by his silence.

But Dido, we remember, is also Cleopatra, and we must consider
the meaning of that identification. Dido-Cleopatra is the sworn
enemy of Rome:

> Rise thou forth from my bones, some avenger!
> Exoriare aliquis nostris ex ossibus ultor!

invoking the fell shades of Hannibal; but she is a tragic heroine.
Aeneas, on the other hand, could have been, and for a while
seemed to be, Antony, losing a world for love. Only he must in
the end be Augustus, losing love and honor for a dubious world.
The *Aeneid*, the supposed panegyric of Augustus and great propa-
ganda-piece of the new régime, has turned into something quite
different. The processes of history are presented as inevitable, as
indeed they are, but the value of what they achieve is cast into
doubt. Virgil continually insists on the public glory of the Roman
achievement, the establishment of peace and order and civilization,
that *dominion without end* which Jupiter tells Venus he has given
the Romans:

> Imperium sine fine dedi.

But he insists equally on the terrible price one must pay for this
glory. More than blood, sweat and tears, something more precious
is continually being lost by the necessary process; human freedom,
love, personal loyalty, all the qualities which the heroes of Homer

represent, are lost in the service of what is grand, monumental and impersonal: the Roman State.

The sixth Book sets the seal on Aeneas' renunciation of himself. What gives it a depth so much greater than the corresponding book of the *Odyssey* is the unmistakable impression we have that Aeneas has not only gone into the Underworld: he has in some way himself died. He descends carrying the Golden Bough, a symbol of splendor and lifelessness.[1] The bough glitters and it *crackles in the wind:*

> . . . sic leni crepitabat brattea vento.

It sheds, Virgil says, a strange discolored aura of gold; and it is compared to the mistletoe, a *parasitic plant, quod non sua seminat arbos,* a plant with no vital connection to the tree to which it clings. A powerful contrast to the culminating image of the *Odyssey,* that great hidden rooted tree from which the bed-chamber, the house and the kingship of Odysseus draw continuous and organic life.

Aeneas moves through the world of the dead. He listens, again the passive spectator, to the famous Roman policy speech of Anchises, a speech full of eagles and trumpets and a speech renouncing the very things Virgil as a man prized most:

> Let others fashion the lifelike image from bronze and marble;
> Let others have the palm of eloquence;
> Let others describe the wheeling constellations of heaven;
> Thy duty, O Roman, is to rule . . .
>
> Tu regere imperio populos, Romane, memento . . .

When he emerges, so strangely, from the ivory gate of false dreams, he is no longer a living man, but one who has at last understood his mission, and become identified with it. Peace and order are to be had, but Aeneas will not enjoy them, for their price is life itself.

And yet there is something left which is deeper than all this. It is the capacity of the human being to suffer. We hear two distinct voices in the *Aeneid,* a public voice of triumph, and a private voice of regret. The private voice, the personal emotions of a man, is never allowed to motivate action. But it is nonetheless everywhere present. For Aeneas, after all, is something more than an Odysseus manqué, or a prototype of Augustus and myriads of Roman leaders. He is man himself; not man as the brilliant free agent of Homer's

---

[1] See R. A. Brooks, "Discolor Aura," *American Journal of Philology,* **LXXIV** (1953), 260-80, the best article on the *Aeneid* to date.

world, but man of a later stage in civilization, man in a metro-
politan and imperial world, man in a world where the State is
supreme. He cannot resist the forces of history, or even deny them;
but he can be capable of human suffering, and this is where the
personal voice asserts itself.

Someday these things too will be pleasant to think back on

> Forsan et haec olim meminisse iuvabit

he tells his comrades in Book 1. The implication is that when the
great abstract goal is finally somehow reached, these present sufferings, seen in retrospect, will be more precious than it.

And so this pleasure, the only true pleasure left to Aeneas in a
life of betrayals of the self, is envisaged as art. The sufferings of
the Trojans, as Aeneas sees them in Carthage, have become fixed
in art, literally: they are paintings. And it is here first, Virgil tells
us, that Aeneas began to hope for a kind of salvation. Here he can
look back on his own losses, and see them as made beautiful and
given universal meaning because human art has transfigured them.
"Look here!" he cries. "There is Priam; there are tears for suffering,
and the limitations of life can touch the heart."

> Sunt lacrimae rerum et mentem mortalia tangunt.

The pleasure felt here by Aeneas in the midst of his reawakened
grief is the essential paradox and the great human insight of the
Aeneid, a poem as much about the *imperium* of art as about the
imperium of Rome. The images in Carthage make Aeneas feel
Priam's death not less deeply, but more. At the same time they
are a redemption of past suffering, partly because they remove
one element of the nightmare: final obscurity and namelessness,
partly because they mean that we have found a form in which
we can see suffering itself clearly. The brightness of the image and
the power of pleasurable vision it confers, consoles for the pain of
what it represents.

The pleasure of art in fact gives value to the pain itself, because
tragic experience is the content of this art. Virgil continues the
scene in the art-gallery: "He spoke, and with deep sorrow, and
many lamentations, fed his soul on the empty pictures."

> Atque animum pictura pascit inani.

*Empty—inani—*is the key-word here. Consider again how many
times Virgil creates his most touching scenes by dwelling on how
something substantial becomes empty and insubstantial: the phantom of Creusa, old fallen Troy, the apparition of Venus in Book

1, the shade of Dido in the Underworld, the lost pledge to Evander, the outraged life of Turnus. *Inanis* is the very word that describes the tears Aeneas sheds upon leaving Carthage and Dido: "His mind was unmoved; the tears he wept were empty." That is, *of no avail.*

Mens immota manet; lacrimae volvuntur inanes.

Aeneas' tragedy is that he cannot be a hero, being in the service of an impersonal power. What saves him as a man is that all the glory of the solid achievement which he is serving, all the satisfaction of "having arrived" in Italy means less to him than his own sense of personal loss. The *Aeneid* enforces the fine paradox that all the wonders of the most powerful institution the world has ever known are not necessarily of greater importance than the emptiness of human suffering.

The Serpent and the Flame:
The Imagery of the Second Book
of the *Aeneid*

by Bernard M. W. Knox

The second Book of the *Aeneid* displays the full magnificence of Virgil's imagery. In this account of Troy's last night images of raging fire and flood, ravening wolves, storms at sea, the fall of an ancient tree, lend to the events with which they are combined the proportions of a universal cataclysm. Among these tremendous images of destruction there is one which by its emphatic recurrence comes to dominate all the rest. This is the image of the serpent.

Infandum regina iubes renovare dolorem, "Unspeakable, O queen, the grief you bid me recall." Aeneas tells Dido the story of the violence of Troy's fall, engineered by concealment and completed by flames. The ferocity of the attackers, their deceit, and the flames which crown their work are time after time compared, sometimes explicitly but more often by combinations of subdued metaphor, verbal echo, and parallel situation, to the action of the serpent.

For these connotations of the serpent, violence, concealment and flames, Virgil had good precedent in the Latin tradition. It is a commonplace of Latin writing (as it is of English) to compare the serpent and the flame; in English both hiss, creep, and have flickering tongues; in Latin the words *serpere, lambere, labi, volvere,* and *micare* are used of both, often in contexts where one clearly suggests the other.[1] The serpent traditionally strikes from concealment, as

---

"The Serpent and the Flame." From the *American Journal of Philology*, LXXI (1950), 379-400. Reprinted by permission of the *American Journal of Philology*. A number of the footnotes in the original version have been omitted.

[1] Cf. especially Virgil, *Aen.*, 7-346ff. where the serpent thrown by Allecto at Amata produces a (metaphorical) flame in her breast; the words used to describe the motion of the serpent suggest the flame before it is mentioned—*lapsus . . . volvitur . . . errat.*

the Greeks did from the horse; *latere, latebrae,* are clichés used generally of the serpent. Finally, violence as a characteristic of the serpent, common enough elsewhere in the Latin poets, is forced on the reader's attention in the second Book of the *Aeneid* by the description of the fate of Laocoon and his sons.

The serpent is thus an apt comparison for the essential nature of the Greek attackers, ferocity, their typical method, concealment, and their principal weapon, fire. But it is an ambivalent image. Besides suggesting the forces of destruction, it may also stand for rebirth, the renewal which the Latin poetic tradition associated with the casting-off of the serpent's old skin in the spring. And this connotation of the serpent is of the utmost importance for the second Book of the *Aeneid,* which tells of the promise of renewal given in the throes of destruction; the death agonies of Troy are the birth-pangs of Rome.

Only three passages in the book deal explicitly with serpents. In addition to the elaborate description of the death of Laocoon and his sons, there are two serpent similes; Androgeos is compared to a man who comes unaware upon a snake, and Pyrrhus is compared to the snake which has cast away its old skin in the spring. These three passages are the base which supports a complex structure of references to the dominant image; elsewhere in the book the figure of the serpent is evoked by phrase after phrase which reminds us of its presence where it lies half-concealed in the language—*latet anguis in herba,* "a snake lies hidden in the grass." This dominant metaphor creeps into many contexts where its presence is surprising, and the result is in some cases a mixture of imagery which borders on the grotesque—a mixture which is typical of Shakespeare too, and which has recently been explained, in the case of *Macbeth,* as a result of the same process which can be seen in the second Book of the *Aeneid,* the working of a dominant, obsessive metaphor.[2]

The manifestations of the serpent are widely distributed; the suggestions which they make form a pattern full of meaning for the book as a whole. The pattern of the metaphor runs parallel to the pattern of events, the plot; but it does more than enforce the impression made by the events, it interprets them. At the emotional climax of the book, the death of Priam, it is in the image of the serpent that the complete meaning of the event is to be seen. And as the pattern of the metaphor unfolds, an independent process of development is revealed; the imagery has, as it were, a plot of its

[2] Cf. Cleanth Brooks, *The Well-wrought Urn* (New York: Harcourt, Brace & World, Inc., 1947), pp. 27-36.

own. In the course of its many appearances in the book the metaphor undergoes a transformation like that of the serpent which it
evokes, it casts its old skin. At first suggestive of Greek violence
and Trojan doom, it finally announces triumphantly the certainty
of Troy's rebirth.

The first overt appearance of the serpent is the description of
the fate of Laocoon and his sons (199-227). This is one of the events
of the narrative, an incident in the fall of the city; there is, on the
surface, nothing metaphorical about these serpents; they exist, and
destroy. Their action is an essential part of the plot; the death of
Laocoon removes an influential figure who might have barred the
wooden horse's way. But they are something more, as both Servius
and Donatus realized. The incident is a symbolic prophecy of the
fall of Troy as a whole.

The serpents come from Tenedos, where the Greeks, characteristically, are in hiding. (*Huc se provecti deserto in litore condunt,*
"betaking themselves hither, they hide on the deserted shore.") *A
TENEDO,* says Servius, *ideo quod significarent naves inde ven-
turas,* "because they symbolize the ships that will come from there."
ECCE AUTEM GEMINI A TENEDO potuimus hoc signo, says
Donatus, *praevidere manifestam imminere perniciem; significabant
enim hostis venturos a Tenedo et maximos duces et geminos,* "from
this we can foresee manifest destruction threatening; the two snakes
symbolize the enemy that will come from Tenedos, and the two
commanders-in-chief." Henry elaborates this *signum,* the prophetic
significance of the serpents, in the following terms.[3] "The twin serpents prefigure the Grecian armament, which, like them, comes
from Tenedos . . . like them crosses the tranquil deep . . . lands
. . . slaughters the surprised and unsuspecting Trojans (prefigured
by Laocoon's sons) and overturns the religion and drives out the
gods (prefigured by Laocoon)." Henry supports his parallel by reference to "minute particulars," some of them verbal echoes, and
points out finally that "when their work is done they take possession of the citadel under the protection of Pallas," a fact which
he connects with Venus' announcement of the consummation of
the city's fall—*Iam summas arces Tritonia respice Pallas insedit,*
"look, Tritonian Pallas has already taken her seat upon the top of
the citadel" (615).

This "drawing out of the parallel in detail" is censured by Conington as something for which there is "no occasion"; and it is true
that some of Henry's remarks, particularly the distinction between

[3] J. Henry, *Aeneidea* II (Dublin, 1878), 115-16.

Laocoon's sons as the unsuspecting Trojans and Laocoon as religion and the gods, deserve the censure. None the less Henry had the right understanding of this passage—it is much more than an incident in the plot. He concentrated his attention on the parallels between the approach and arrival of the serpents and the approach and arrival of the Greek fleet (250-267), and the limits he thus placed on the significance of the Laocoon passage were perhaps responsible for the forced nature of his interpretation. In fact, however, the echoes of the Laocoon passage in the lines describing the fleet's arrival are only the beginning of a long series of echoes which culminates in the unmistakable parallel between the sea-serpents and Pyrrhus, son of Achilles.

This description of the death of Laocoon and his sons is the principal basis of the subsequent serpent imagery. It is one of Virgil's most impressive descriptive passages, and any echo of it which occurs later in the book brings these terrible serpents back to mind at once. There are many such echoes, and they awaken metaphors which without the connection provided by the echo might have lain dormant or dead.

The description begins (201) with Laocoon sacrificing at the altars, *ad aras. Ecce autem gemini a Tenedo*—they are twin serpents, and this word is repeated later in line 225, *at gemini*. The Atridae are twice described with this word later in the book, *gemini Atridae* (415) and *geminos Atridas* (500). This echo explains Donatus' comment on line 203—*hostis venturos . . . et maximos duces et geminos*. The twin Atridae are compared to the twin serpents; both couples are forces of merciless destruction.

The serpents proceed side by side to the shore, *pariterque ad litora tendunt.* Their bloody crests tower over the waves, *iubaeque sanguineae superant undas;* their length behind wreathes their huge backs in voluminous folds, *pars cetera . . . sinuatque immensa volumine terga.* Their eyes blaze, *ardentisque oculos,* and they lick their hissing mouths with flickering tongues, *sibila lambebant linguis vibrantibus ora.* They make for Laocoon, but first attack his sons. Embracing the childrens' bodies, they twist around them, *corpora natorum serpens amplexus uterque implicat,* and biting deep feed on their wretched limbs, *miseros morsu depascitur artus.* Next Laocoon himself, as he tries to intervene, *auxilio subeuntem ac tela ferentem,* is seized and enfolded; the serpents tower head and neck above him, *superant capite et cervicibus altis.* Their task fulfilled, they glide off to shelter, *at gemini lapsu . . . effugiunt,* and hide beneath the feet of the statue of Pallas, *sub pedibusque deae . . . teguntur.*

This terrifying picture, as verbal echo and parallel event and situation recall it to the memory throughout the rest of the book, is seen in retrospect to contain all the violence of the sack of Troy. These lines foreshadow not only the arrival of the Greek fleet, but the attack, the Trojan resistance, the deaths of Polites and Priam, and the flames which tower over the burning city. They present the fall of Troy as the action of the serpent.[4]

The next forty lines (228-68) apply the metaphor to the particular agents and events of the city's fall. The process begins at once. The two lines which follow immediately (228-29) describe the reaction of the Trojan bystanders to Laocoon's death:

> Tum vero tremefacta novus per pectora cunctis
> insinuat pavor.
>
> (Then indeed a new fear wound its way into our trembling hearts.)

"A new fear winds into our breast" (Mackail). *Insinuat pavor* is a reminiscence of Lucretius' *Divom metus insinuarit pectora,* "fear of the gods has wound its way into our breasts" (5.73), but in Virgil's line the word *insinuat* stands out sharply, for though it is one of Lucretius' favorite words Virgil uses it only here. *Sinuare,* which it brings to mind, is one of the stock words used of the serpent, and *insinuat* is a striking echo of *sinuat,* which has been used only twenty lines previously—*sinuatque immensa volumine terga* (208). This terror, which causes the Trojans to accept Laocoon's fate and disregard his advice, helps to prepare for the fall of Troy; it is one of the agents of the disaster, and it is here suggested, lightly but none the less impressively, that it is itself a serpent.

The narrative proceeds to the description of the entry of the horse into the city (234ff.), and here the same suggestion is made, this time more emphatically. The Trojans attach wheels[5] to the horses'

---

[4] The twin serpents appear three more times in the *Aeneid.* (On their dramatic function for the poem as a whole see G. E. Duckworth, *Foreshadowing and Suspense in the Epics of Homer, Apollonius and Vergil* [Princeton: Princeton University Press 1933], p. 57, and references there.) They are in all three cases portents of destruction. Allecto (7.450) rouses the hesitating Turnus by rearing two snakes from her tresses, *geminos erexit crinibus angues,* Hercules (8.289) strangles the twin serpents sent by Juno, *geminosque premens eliserit anguis,* and on the shield of Aeneas Cleopatra calls on her army and does not see the twin snakes behind her (8.697), *necdum etiam geminos a tergo respicit anguis.*

[5] J. W. Mackail, *Aeneid* (Oxford: Clarendon Press, 1930), *ad loc.,* notes, "Here, however, *rotae* strictly means rollers." The other two passages in which Virgil uses *labi* and *rotae* together suggest otherwise, and in any case this technical

feet, and Virgil describes this action in the words *pedibusque ro-tarum subiciunt lapsus,* "under the feet they throw the gliding of wheels" (235-6). *Rotarum lapsus,* "the gliding of the wheels," is an arresting phrase, a Grecism, as Mackail points out, and probably a specific imitation of τρόχων βάσεις in Sophocles' *Electra* 718, as Conington suggests. In that case it is a typically Virgilian imitation, for the phrase has undergone a transformation, the metaphor has changed. βάσεις (βαίνω) suggests the "strides" made by the chariots overtaking one another in the race, but *lapsus,* though it can be used to convey the same impression of speed, suggests methods of moving which have nothing to do with strides. Virgil uses forms of *labi* together with *rotae* in two other places, and in both passages the combination is used to describe the speed of a chariot; a racing chariot in *Georgics,* 3.180, *aut Alphaea rotis praelabi flumina Pisae,* "or to glide with your wheels past Pisa's stream, the Alpheus," and a divine (and amphibious) chariot in *Aeneid,* 1.147, *atque rotis summas levibus perlabitur undas,* "and with light wheels he skims over the tops of the waves." But this impression of speed, in the case of Neptune's chariot of effortless, frictionless speed, is violently incongruous in a description of the movement of the wooden horse. The other phrases of Virgil's description suggest, not speed, but the laborious effort involved in moving the horse into the city. *Dividimus muros,* "we make an opening in the walls," says Aeneas; the horse, as Conington says, was "heaved over broken walls." *Accingunt operi, scandit fatalis machina muros,* "they make themselves ready for the task, and the fateful machine climbs the walls." Far from gliding swiftly, the horse sticks four times at the entry, *substitit;* the word recreates the sudden friction-bound halt of the vast mass. The incongruous suggestion of speed is emphasized by a repetition of the disturbing word, *inlabitur urbi,* "it glides in upon the city." The emphatic repetition increases the strain to which this word is being subjected, and an unusually elaborate echo makes it clear that this word, like *insinuat* in line 229, recalls the figure of the serpent. The closing lines of the description of the serpents, only ten lines back, are recalled by three verbal echoes, and the reappearance of *lapsus,* the emphatic word, in the same position in

---

meaning is inappropriate, for it adds a concrete detail to a picture which seems to be deliberately vague. Virgil's reference to the horse in 6.515, *cum fatalis equus saltu super ardua venit Pergama,* "when with a leap the fatal horse overcame the lofty citadel," indicates a vision of the wooden horse as something with a will of its own, almost alive, something magical; the same impression is produced by the words *scandit . . . subit . . . inlabitur . . .* and *monstrum* in our passage. (Cf. G. E. Duckworth, *C.J.,* 1944, pp. 99ff.) To insist on the connotations of *rota* as a technical engineering term destroys this fine effect.

the line. The serpents (225-27)—at gemini *lapsu* . . . effugiunt . . . *sub pedibusque* deae . . . teguntur. The horse (235-36)—*pedibusque rotarum subiciunt lapsus.* The echo suggests the likeness of the horse to the serpents; *lapsus* and *inlabitur* intensify the suggestion, for *labi* and its compounds are words that occur sooner or later in almost any passage which describes the movement of the serpent; indeed, were it not that *serpere* claims the honor, *labi* might be described as the *vox propria* of the serpent. *LAPSU,* remarks Servius on line 225, *labi proprie serpentum est.*

The metaphor is surprising, if not grotesque; a horse is not much like a serpent, and a wooden horse less so than a live one. But that this image, the Trojan horse moving like a serpent upon its prey (*inlabitur urbi*), was possible for a Latin poet, is indicated by Propertius' description of the same event (3.13, 63-64). "Cassandra alone," he says, "proclaimed the horse a trick, as it crept upon her fatherland":

> sola
> fallacem patriae serpere dixit equum.

In the Virgilian *lapsus* and *inlabitur* the metaphor is latent; but Propertius' *serpere* can hardly suggest anything else but the horse as a serpent. This is recognized by Rothstein, who comments as follows: "The threatening danger of the wooden horse is presented in the image of a serpent, which creeps unnoticed upon its prey; in this sense Propertius can . . . use *serpere* of a horse." [6]

Virgil emphasizes his comparison of the horse to a serpent later in Book 2, by another significant echo. The line which describes the snake to which Pyrrhus is compared (475) *arduus ad solem et linguis micat ore trisulcis,* "he rears up toward the sun, and his forked tongue flickers in his jaws," repeats the salient word of Panthus' description of the wooden horse (328) *arduus armatos mediis in moenibus adstans,* "towering within the walls [the horse pours forth] armed men." This repetition of *arduus* (not used elsewhere in Book 2) would be negligible were it not for the fact that Virgil often associated this word with both horses and serpents; he applies it elsewhere four times to horses, and three times to serpents.

The lines which follow the account of the triumphal entry of the horse (250ff.) contain a description of the night approach and arrival of the Greek fleet. The verbal parallels between these lines and those which describe the approach and arrival of the serpents from Tenedos have already been mentioned; they were pointed out

[6] *Die Elegien des Sextus Propertius,* erklärt von Max Rothstein (Berlin, 1898) *ad loc.*

by Henry. The most striking correspondences are: *gemini a Tenedo,* of the serpents, *a Tenedo,* of the fleet (203 and 255); *tranquilla per alta,* "through the quiet deeps," of the serpents, *tacitae per amica silentia lunae,* "under the benign silence of the quiet moon," of the fleet (203 and 255); *pariter* of the serpents, *instructis navibus,* of the fleet (205 and 254); *ad litora tendunt,* "they head for the shore," of the serpents, *litora nota petens,* "making for the familiar shore," of the fleet (205 and 256). To Henry's full discussion may be added the fact that *pariter,* used of the serpents in 205, is used in *Aeneid,* 5.830 to describe the coordination of naval manoeuvres, and the remark that he sees in the correspondences between the two passages only the "prefiguring" of the fleet in the serpents, and does not examine the complementary effect, that the fleet, like the Trojan fear after Laocoon's death and the wooden horse, is implicitly compared to the serpents.

One of the essential factors in the fall of Troy is the deep sleep of the Trojans on that fatal night. *Invadunt urbem somno vinoque sepultam,* "they rush upon the city as it lies buried in drunken sleep." This sleep is mentioned in line 253, in the passage which describes the approach of the Greek fleet. *Sopor fessos complectitur artus,* "sleep winds itself about our weary limbs." The image of the serpent appears again, for this phrase is a complex echo of the words which described the death of Laocoon's children, thirty-five lines before (214-15):

> serpens amplexus uterque
> implicat et miseros morsu depascitur artus.

The metaphor *sopor complectitur artus,* which Virgil uses nowhere else, is revealed as another manifestation of the dominant image by the elaboration of the echo. The verbal echo *amplexus . . . artus, complectitur artus,* is strengthened by the metrical repetition, *depascitur artus, complectitur artus;* even the onomatopoeic sibilance of *miseros morsu depascitur artus* reappears in *sopor fessos complectitur artus.*

The word *complectitur* is full of a tension which is typical of Virgil's language. Its associations of friendly or loving embrace are appropriate for the Trojans' feeling as they yield to the sleep that ends their first day of peace, and by its evocation of the serpent the word represents Aeneas' horror at the recollection of that sleep as he tells his tale some seven years later. This tension is even more striking in the passage which follows immediately, Aeneas' preface to his account of his dream (268-69):

Tempus erat quo prima quies mortalibus aegris
incipit et dono divum gratissima serpit.

(It was the time when the first slumber begins for weary
mortals, which creeps in, most welcome, by the gift of the
gods.)

In the melody of the first line we feel again the Trojans' welcome
acceptance of sleep, but there is a touch of foreboding in the sadness of *mortalibus aegris*. The second line is filled with foreboding.
Dono divum is a hint of discord, for *donum*, which has been used
five times already in Book 2, has always appeared in a menacing
context, it has referred each time to the horse. Aeneas' statement
is couched in general terms—rest is a gift of the gods—but the associations of *donum* remind us that his general statement has a
precise and terrible application. This rest is indeed a gift from the
gods; it is part of the divine plan for Troy's overthrow. *Inimicaque
Troiae numina magna deum*, "and the mighty will of the gods,
hostile to Troy." And the last word of the line brings back the
familiar metaphor; *serpit*, this rest creeps like a serpent. *Serpere*
is a word that could hardly become a dead metaphor in Latin as
long as the word *serpens* remained in use to keep it alive. This is
the *vox propria* of the serpent, and Servius seems to have felt something of its force in this famous passage, for he glosses it with
latenter membris infunditur, "it pours itself secretly into our limbs."
The metaphor *quies . . . serpit* is a violent one, and I have not
been able to find any parallel to it in the Latin poets.

There is, of course, a word often used with *quies, sopor,* etc. to
convey precisely the effect of Servius' *latenter membris infunditur*,
a word which has no serpentine connotations, *repere*. It is used in
contexts similar to Virgil's *quies . . . serpit* by Catullus (76.21:
surrepens imos ut torpor in artus, "creeping like languor deep into
my limbs"), Ovid (*Heroides*, 18.46: *sed movet obrepens somnus
anile caput*, "but sleep creeps up and makes her aged head nod,"
Fasti, 3.19: *blanda quies furtim victis obrepsit ocellis*, "seductive
sleep creeps up and overcomes their eyes"), and Statius (*Silvae*, 1.4,
56: *fessos penitus subrepsit in artus/insidiosa quies*, "insidious slumber crept deep into their weary limbs"). These instances, from one
of Virgil's predecessors, a contemporary, and one of his successors,
show that Virgil, as so often, is varying a stock expression, and the
variant he employs calls attention to the dominant metaphor.
Seneca, who imitates this passage in Virgil very carefully in his

Troades, avoids Virgil's *serpit* and substitutes the more usual word. Andromache is describing her dream (Seneca, *Troades* 440ff.):

> Ignota tandem venit afflictae quies
> brevisque fessis somnus obrepsit genis . . .
> cum subito nostros Hector ante oculos stetit
> non qualis . . .

> (Rest, so long a stranger, came to me in my distress, and a short sleep crept on my weary self . . . when suddenly Hector stood before my eyes, not as he was . . .)

Seneca's indebtedness is clear, and his avoidance of *serpit* striking. His restoration of the usual *repere* is a reminder that Virgil's suggestive word is not the consequence of the paucity of the Latin poetic vocabulary, nor even a case of submission to the much-invoked goddess Metri Gratia. *Dono divum gratissima serpit* strengthens and develops the metaphor of the Trojan sleep as a serpent which first appeared in *sopor fessos complectitur artus.*

Aeneas awakes from his dream to see all Troy in flames. The spectacle is compared to a crop-fire and a flood (304-7). Deiphobus' house collapses in flames, and the fire towers over it, *Volcano superante.* This phrase recalls the serpents again, the serpents whose crests tower over the waves, *superant undas,* and who tower over Laocoon, *superant capite et cervicibus altis.* The reminiscence is repeated much later, when Aeneas sees his own house in flames, *exsuperant flammae* (759).

The principal instruments of the Trojan downfall, the Trojan fear, the horse, the Greek fleet, the deep sleep, the fire, have all now been linked with the image of the serpent. All except one, Sinon, the personification of Greek treachery. The actions of Sinon are described before the arrival of the serpents from Tenedos, so that in his case there can be no question of verbal reminiscence; yet the same metaphor is implied, in at least one place strongly, in the language which Virgil puts into his mouth. His name itself, with its resemblance to *sinus, sinuo,* etc. helps to bring out the suggestion; it is contained in his lying story of his escape from sacrifice at the hands of the Greeks (134-36):

> . . . vincula rupi,
> limosoque lacu per noctem obscurus in ulva
> delitui . . .

> (I broke my bonds, and lay hidden all night in a muddy
> swamp, concealed in the sedge . . .)

Delitescere is an uncommon word, and one which is used with
peculiar appropriateness of the serpent; "iam ista serpens" says
Cicero, "quae tum hic delitescit," "Now this snake, which was then
lying hidden here . . ." (*De Haruspicum Responsis,* 25), and Virgil,
in the only other place where he uses this word, applies it to the
viper (*Georgics,* 3.416-17):

> Saepe sub immotis praesepibus aut mala tactu
> vipera delituit . . .
>
> (Or often the viper, foul to the touch, lies hidden in
> neglected stables . . .)

Sinon's *delitui* is no more than a suggestion, but seen in the context
of the imagery of Book 2 as a whole, it is a significant one.

  When Aeneas sees Troy in flames, and hears the explanation
given him by Panthus, he loses his head, and forgets his duty. His
duty is to run away; he is ordered to do so three times, in almost
identical words: by Hector, Venus, and Anchises. Hector's command, the first, is ignored. Aeneas turns instead to violence. It is
mad violence, and he admits it, *arma amens capio* (314).

  Aeneas' first victim is the Greek Androgeos, who appears in a
line which almost exactly reproduces the line which introduced the
first Trojan victim, Laocoon (40 and 370):

> Primus ibi ante omnis magna comitante caterva
> Laocoon . . .
>
> (First then before all the others, with a great throng accom-
> panying, Laocoon . . .)
>
> Primus se Danaum magna comitante caterva
> Androgeos . . .
>
> (First of the Danaans, with a great throng accompanying,
> Androgeos . . .)

Virgil does not use the Homeric formulaic line, and this close correspondence is unique. Its significance is clear. Laocoon and Androgeos are somehow alike; the likeness is revealed by the simile
which follows. The first Trojan victim was destroyed by serpents,

and so is the first Greek victim. Androgeos is killed by Aeneas and his companions, and it is at this point that Androgeos is compared to a man who has come unaware upon a snake (378-81):

> Obstipuit, retroque pedem cum voce repressit.
> improvisum aspris veluti qui sentibus anguem
> pressit humi nitens, trepidusque repente refugit
> attolentem iras et caerula colla tumentem.

> (He stopped short, and stepped backward with a cry: like a man who treads upon a snake unforeseen among the thorns, and at once leaps back in terror, as it lifts its head in anger and puffs out its dark neck.)

Improvisum, unforeseen, because concealed; the word reminds us of Sinon's ironical prophecy *improvisi aderunt* (182). But now the rôles are reversed. Aeneas and his Trojans now deal in the violence of the serpent to which they are compared, and they proceed at once to assume another characteristic of the serpent, concealment. At the suggestion of Coroebus, they disguise themselves in the armor and insignia of the Greeks they have killed. *Dolus an virtus, quis in hoste requirat?* ("Treachery or courage? who asks, when it is against an enemy?") says Coroebus (390). The Trojans adopt the Greek weapon, *dolus,* as their own; it is the mark of the serpent, they fight now from concealment, *haud numine nostro,* "under alien auspices," as Aeneas says (396).

This appearance of the serpent, for the moment identified with Aeneas and his Trojans, interprets the events. Aeneas himself admits that his action is madness; this is emphasized by the melodramatic despair of his speech to his men (348ff.)[7] and his comparison of his Trojans to a band of ravening wolves (355-58). But the suggestion, implicit in the simile and its immediate sequel, that Aeneas has usurped the attributes of the serpent that has so far stood for violence and deceit deepens immeasurably the sense of his wrongness and folly, and reminds us how far Aeneas has strayed from his duty, which is not to fight, but to yield to a greater purpose, as he does yield in the end. *Cessi,* runs his concluding line, *et sublato montis genitore petivi,* "I yielded and, carrying my father, I sought the mountains."

By the time the violence of Book 2 reaches its climax in the assault on Priam's palace, Aeneas' impulsive counter-attack has

---

[7] For some stimulating remarks on this whole passage see D. L. Drew, *The Allegory of the Aeneid* (London: Basil Blackwell & Mott, Ltd., 1927), pp. 62-63.

failed. He is betrayed by his own deceit; the Greek crests on the borrowed helmets draw fire from the Trojans. This fatal confusion is expressed in the phrase *Graiarum errore iubarum,* "by mistaking the Greek crests" (412), a reminiscence of the crests, *sanguineae iubae* (206), of the serpents that killed Laocoon and his sons. At this moment the Greeks too attack him; his men are cut down, and he escapes from the slaughter with only two companions, one an old, the other a wounded, man. Aeneas' violence has ended in failure, and his brief assumption of the characteristics of the serpent is revealed, in the succeeding lines, as a pathetic masquerade; the real serpent is at the gates of Priam's palace.

This is Pyrrhus, son of Achilles. The verbs alone of lines 480ff. are enough to make it clear that he is violence personified—*perrumpit vellit cavavit instat insequitur premit.* This is the man who, as Aeneas says later, "cuts down the son before the face of his father, the father at the altar," *natum ante ora patris, patrem qui obtruncat ad aras* (663). The time for concealment is past; Pyrrhus' violence is open, like that of the serpents which killed Laocoon and his sons; like them he kills the son first, and then the father who attempts to intervene; like them, he kills his victim at the altars. When Pyrrhus twists his left hand in Priam's hair to hold the king's body firm for the final stroke, *implicuitque comam laeva* (552), the words recall the serpents that twisted their coils round Laocoon's sons, *corpora natorum serpens amplexus uterque implicat* (214-15).

This parallel is emphasized by the simile which, at the very beginning of this magnificent passage, compares Pyrrhus to a snake (471-75):

> Qualis ubi in lucem coluber mala gramina pastus
> frigida sub terra tumidum quem bruma tegebat
> nunc positis novus exuviis nitidusque iuventa
> lubrica convolvit sublato pectore terga
> arduus ad solem et linguis micat ore trisulcis.

> (As when a snake swollen with foul grasses, whom winter's cold has kept hidden underground, and who now has shed his old skin and gleams with renewed youth; he rolls his slippery coils, and lifting his neck he rears up toward the sun and his forked tongue flickers in his mouth.)

This simile illustrates the general transition, now complete, from concealment to open violence; from the lies of Sinon and the subterfuge of the horse to the ferocity of the assault on the palace; for

Pyrrhus in particular, the transition from concealment in the dark belly of the horse to violence in the glare of the burning city. The caverns of the horse's belly are twice (38 and 55) called *latebrae,* a word suggestive of the serpent's hiding-place; Pyrrhus is the serpent that has emerged.

This is the third overt appearance of the serpent in Book 2, and it is different from those that precede it. The simile presents the serpent as the symbol of rebirth and this new connotation of the serpent is appropriate for the immediate object of the comparison, Pyrrhus. The snake, in contrast to the darkness from which it came (*sub terra . . . quem bruma tegebat*), is bright and shiny, *nitidus,* and this corresponds with the real Pyrrhus, *luce coruscus aena,* "blazing with a brazen light," and with his name, Pyrrhus, Πυρρός, "flame-colored." The snake is new, *positis novus exuviis,* and this reminds us of Pyrrhus' other name, Neoptolemus, new war, new warrior. He is the renewal of the old war, the rebirth of the old warrior; Pyrrhus is Achilles reborn in his son. Just as Achilles killed and mutilated Hector before the eyes of Hecuba and Priam, Neoptolemus now kills Polites before the same unhappy pair who witnessed his father's cruelty. *Instat vi patria,* "he presses on with the might of his father," says Virgil (491), and Neoptolemus is followed by his father's constant companion, *equorum agitator Achillis armiger Automedon,* "Achilles' squire, the charioteer Automedon."

The terms of the simile at the same time subtly qualify the identification of father and son which they suggest. If on the one hand they make a comparison between Achilles and his son, they none the less suggest a contrast between them. The serpent in this book of the *Aeneid* has come to stand for the merciless and unthinking violence which was typical of Achilles at his worst; but we remember, even before Priam reminds us of it, that he had a better side. Achilles killed the son, but revered, in the person of Priam, old age; Neoptolemus kills father and son alike. This Achilles reborn is not the true Achilles; the comparison of Neoptolemus to a serpent (his father was a lion) anticipates Priam's taunt *satum quo te mentiris Achilles,* "you lie when you claim Achilles as father" (540). Only the worst of the father is reborn in the son; his sarcastic words to Priam, *degeneremque Neoptolemum* (549), are the truth.

The simile is complex in application and rich in meaning, for it is loaded with the cumulative significance of the dominant image. There is more to it still. For this new association of the serpent, the cycle of winter hibernation and spring renewal, death and rebirth, though applied specifically to the reappearance of Achilles in his son, is not so limited in the reader's imagination. It is a familiar and universal symbol, suggesting the process which is common to all nature, the process of life, death, and rebirth. Troy too is to be reborn; that is the implication of Hector's neglected command to Aeneas, *his moenia quaere magna* (294-95). At the climax of Troy's destruction, just before the most terrible incident of the city's last night, the image of the serpent appears again, not only to portray the invincible ferocity of the attackers, but also to suggest the promise of salvation for the defeated. In this image is a hint that the fate of Priam is more than the cruel murder of an old man; this death is part of a birth.

This simile is the turning-point in the development of the dominant metaphor; it prepares for the final appearance of the serpent, which is unequivocal, an unmistakable portent of Troy's eventual rebirth. But meanwhile there is a last glimpse of the old serpent, with its connotations of concealment and destruction unmodified. It is contained in the famous lines that describe Helen (567-74). Aeneas comes upon her in hiding:

> limina Vestae
> servantem et tacitam secreta in sede latentem

> (keeping close to the door of the temple of Vesta, and lurking silently in her hiding-place).

Secreta in sede latentem is a familiar suggestion, and it is repeated a few lines later, *abdiderat sese* (574). *Limina servantem* sounds like a reminiscence of Virgil's description of the serpent that killed Eurydice, *servantem ripas,* "keeping close to the river bank" (*Georgics,* 4.459); there are other reminiscences of the Eurydice passage in this book of the *Aeneid*.

The final appearance of the dominant metaphor is a celebrated passage. Aeneas, now intent on his duty, prepares to leave Troy with all his family, but his plans are hindered by old Anchises' refusal to leave. Aeneas returns to counsels of despair, *rursus in arma feror,* "I rush back to arms" (655), but Anchises' mind is changed by a portent, the flame which appears on the head of Iulus (682-87):

> ecce levis summo de vertice visus Iuli
> fundere lumen apex, tactuque innoxia mollis
> lambere flamma comas et circum tempora pasci.
> nos pavidi trepidare metu crinemque flagrantem
> excutere et sanctos restinguere fontibus ignis.

(Behold, from the top of Iulus' head a gentle tongue of fire
was seen to pour forth light, and a gentle flame, harmless to
the touch, licked his hair and played about his temples. We
trembled with fear, and tried to beat out the flames in his
hair and extinguish the divine fire with water.)

These words are full of reminiscences and suggestions of the serpent.
Lambere brings to mind the serpents which attacked Laocoon,
sibila lambebant linguis vibrantibus ora, and *pasci* recalls the snake,
mala gramina pastus, to which Pyrrhus was compared and the serpents that fed on Laocoon's children, *miseros morsu depascitur
artus. Tactuque innoxia* refers by contrast to the proverbial un-
touchableness of serpents, *mala tactu* Virgil calls the viper in
Georgics, 3.416; and *innoxia,* in the only other place where Virgil
uses it, *Aeneid,* 5.3.92 (a passage which echoes and clearly refers to
the one under consideration), describes the serpent which came out
of Anchises' tomb:

> libavitque dapes, rursusque *innoxius* imo
> successit tumulo, et depasta altaria liquit.

> (It tasted the offerings, and retreated harmlessly back
> into the recesses of the tomb, leaving the altars where it
> had fed.)

These indications that the famous flame is described in terms of
the now familiar image are strengthened by a consideration of the
retractatio of this passage written by one of Virgil's most sedulous
imitators. Silius Italicus follows the Virgilian description closely
when he comes to describe the flame which at an equally critical
moment appeared on the head of Masinissa (*Punica,* 16.119ff.):

> carpenti somnos subitus rutilante coruscum
> vertice fulsit apex, crispamque involvere visa est
> mitis flamma comam atque hirta se spargere fronte.

> (As he was asleep, suddenly a reddish gleam flashed from his
> head, and a gentle flame was seen to wind through his curly
> hair and play over his shaggy forehead.)

The deliberate nature of Silius' imitation is clear; apart from the
verbal repetitions, the word-groups are rhythmically identical in *fundere lumen apex* and *vertice fulsit apex,* and very similar in *lambere
flamma comas* and *mitis flamma comam; mitis* in Silius corresponds

to *innoxia* and possibly to *mollis* as well in Virgil, and *atque hirta se spargere fronte* to *et circum tempora pasci*. Silius goes on to imitate the next two lines, and his words suggest strongly that he saw the image of the serpent in his Virgilian model:

> concurrunt famuli et *serpentes* tempora circum
> festinant gelidis restinguere fontibus ignes.

(The servants rush to him and hasten to extinguish with cold water the flames winding about his temples.)

The separation of *serpentes* from its noun by almost a line and a half makes the metaphor almost unmistakable here, and its appearance in so close an imitation of the Virgilian passage confirms the suggestion that Virgil's flame is another appearance of the metaphor which dominates the imagery of Book 2 of the *Aeneid*.

It is the last. In this flame the pattern of the dominant metaphor is complete. The development of the image, the increasing complication of meaning which constitutes its plot, comes to an end. The serpent has cast its old skin. All previous significances of the serpent are here by implication summed up and rejected in favor of the new. In the shape of Sinon, Helen, and the wooden horse, the serpent stood for concealment; here all is light, and abundance of it, *fundere lumen*. In the form of Pyrrhus, the serpents from Tenedos, and even Aeneas himself in his madness, it stood for violence; here it is *tactu innoxia*, harmless to the touch, and *mollis*, though grammatically it may qualify *comas*, adds to the contrast. The serpent stood also for the destructive flames of Troy's fall; here it is still a flame, but a sacred one, *sanctos ignis*, a harmless one, *innoxia*, more, a beneficent flame. The fourth connotation of the serpent image, rebirth, a significance held in reserve in the earlier part of the book and first faintly suggested at the climax of the violence, the lowest depth of Troy's fortunes, is here its proclaimed and only meaning. The flame, which Virgil's allusive language presents as the final manifestation of the serpent metaphor, is a portent of Troy's rebirth. Anchises does not realize its full significance, but he is joyful (*laetus* 687), and prays that the omen be confirmed (691). The confirmation comes in the form of thunder on the left, a falling star, and finally Creusa's prophecy to Aeneas of a new kingdom in the West.

This analysis is an attempt to examine some of the rich complexities of one of Virgil's many sustained images. To support it by an appeal to Virgil's intentions would be barren and irrelevant.

But in this particular case there is some ground, apart from the analysis itself, for suggesting that Virgil, as he composed the second book of his *Aeneid,* did have serpents in mind throughout, for the book is full of echoes of some earlier lines of his which constitute a short "catalogue of serpents." The short passage in the third *Georgic* (414-39) which describes the snakes the horse-breeder must beware of contains the phrase *mala tactu vipera delituit* (416-17) which is echoed in Sinon's *delitui* (2.136) and in *tactuque innoxia* (2.683), the description of the flame; the same passage contains also the line (421) *tollentemque minas et sibila colla tumentem,* "lifting its head threatening, and swelling its hissing neck," which is the basis of a line in the Androgeos simile, *attolentem iras et caerula colla tumentem* (381); finally it contains three separate lines (*Georgics,* 3.426, 437, and 439),

> Squamea convolvens sublato pectore terga
>
> (he rolls his scaly coils with lifted neck)
>
> cum positis novus exuviis nitidusque iuventa
>
> (when he has shed his old skin and gleams with renewed youth)
>
> arduus ad solem et linguis micat ore trisulcis
>
> (he rears up toward the sun and his forked tongue flickers in his jaws)

which all reappear, with little or no change, in the Pyrrhus simile (*Aeneid,* 2.473-75). Further, this early passage contains an account of a savage serpent, the terror of the country-side in the dry season,

> exsilit in siccum, et flammantia lumina torquens
> saevit agris
>
> (he leaps forth onto the ground, and rolling his flaming eyes he rages through the fields)

(*Georgics,* 3.433-34), which sounds like the basis of the description of the serpents that came from Tenedos.

This is clearly a passage which was often present in Virgil's mind as he wrote the second Book of the *Aeneid;* its presence there may be connected with the dominance which the image of the serpent assumed. More than this can hardly be suggested, for in the complexity of a great poet's imagery we must recognize a mystery which lies beyond the frontiers of conscious art. Οὐκ ἐκ τέχνης, says Plato, ἀλλ' ἔνθεοι ὄντες καὶ κατεχόμενοι, "Not from art, but divinely inspired and possessed," and although here, as always, he is grinding his antipoetic axe, he is more right than wrong. To probe Virgil's mind at work is beyond any powers of analysis, though analysis may occasionally reveal fresh treasures in the poetry which his mind produced. There is no fear, in Virgil's case, that the process may dissipate the poetry; its riches are inexhaustible. In his use of the sustained metaphor, a power which he shares with Aeschylus and Shakespeare, Virgil defies any final analysis; a glimpse such as this into the "chambers of his imagery" reveals only further chambers beyond: *Apparet domus intus et atria longa patescunt.*

Discolor Aura:
Reflections on the Golden Bough

by Robert A. Brooks

Virgil's golden bough is one of the crucial images of the *Aeneid*. In it the poet catches up plot and hero into one of those knots of meaning which unify the poem. The importance of the bough is universally allowed; its significance is not. The depth and multiplicity of meaning which it provides have served too often to lead away from the image, and the poem, instead of toward them. Commentators have followed the threads of reference rather than the threads of suggestion. What they have found relates to the more or less distant environment of the *Aeneid,* to tradition, belief, and ritual, which must be considered in the interpretation of the poem, but which cannot constitute that interpretation, or even begin it. The oak-spirit and the King of the Wood, the mistletoe and the Queen of the Dead are all impressive concepts. But if the "real meaning" of the golden bough lies in these or near them, then Virgil must be considered an artist after the fashion of the late David Belasco, who painted the back of his stage sets as well as the front. What is actually happening on the stage or in the poem we may suspect to be illusory or subsidiary; the real action may be taking place in the carefully prepared but invisible recesses of the scene, approachable only by those who have a pass backstage. This is not Virgil's method, and least of all could it be his at this point in the development of the *Aeneid*.

The sixth Book is the center of the poem, symbolically as well as literally. The journey to Italy is over; the war has not yet begun. It is the still point between the two fields of action postulated for the hero in the first words of the poem, between the predominantly

"Discolor Aura: Reflections on the Golden Bough." From the *American Journal of Philology*, LXXIV (1953), 260-280. Reprinted by permission of the *American Journal of Philology*. A number of the footnotes in the original version have been omitted.

individual experience of the man, and the predominantly social experience of arms. In this pause, the destiny which frames the hero in both his worlds, as son and as city-ancestor, is supernaturally consummated. But to encounter both father and race, past and future, is an experience of terror, in fact, of death. It can only take place in another world whose perceptions envelop, confuse, and sometimes deny the validity of the life-experience on earth. The underworld and all the images that go with it are demanded by the necessities of the poem. They are neither intruded upon Virgil by convention nor lightly used by him for mystification and "atmosphere." Every passage in the book is a new and integral perception of what has gone before, and an ineluctable framing of what is to come. There is not place here for tricks of staging, for external matter half-hidden, in one scholar's phrase, by "a haze of poetry." It is not only possible, but necessary, to view the golden bough as part of the *Aeneid*'s structure, to evolve its meaning primarily from its context and from what Virgil says about it, not from what we know or he may have known about its origins.

Sic fatur lacrimans. The fifth Book passes instantly into the sixth, from Aeneas' words to the tears which accompany them. No other passage from book to book in the *Aeneid* provides so little pause. Throughout the earlier books Aeneas has been prepared to confront the underworld; now he is almost hurried to the encounter. After a moment's pause before the Daedalian doors of the temple at Cumae, the prologue begins. Spatially it has an elaborate development in the penetration of one recess after another.[1] The hero passes from chamber to chamber, to the temple, the Sibyl's cave, the grove of the bough, and finally the underworld itself. His progress is cast by Virgil into the rhythmic structure of ritual. It opens

---

[1] The theories of W. F. Jackson Knight, *Cumaean Gates* (Oxford: Basil Blackwell & Mott, Ltd., 1936), and of R. W. Cruttwell, *Virgil's Mind at Work* (Oxford: Basil Blackwell & Mott, Ltd., 1946), concerning the symbolism of the temple doors need attention here. Knight's work was not available to me (except indirectly through reviews), but both authors apparently see a symbolic reference to the rites of initiation and the tortuous passage to the underworld in the labyrinth carved by Daedalus upon the doors. This view seems particularly appropriate to the formal ritual pattern and to the progress from level to level which forms the rest of the prologue. Unfortunately I feel that the labyrinth image is not intrinsically important to Virgil. It is one of a series which passes in quick review the whole Cretan episode; it bears no more weight than Pasiphae or the Minotaur and considerably less than Icarus. The enormous breadth of parallels adduced by Knight and Cruttwell may possibly convince one of an archetypal image working below Virgil's consciousness, but Virgil's mind at work is not necessarily at work upon his poetry. Their interpretation is cabalistic, not symbolic; it involves too many secret keys to be applicable as criticism.

with a sacrifice to Apollo, and proceeds to the two prayers of Aeneas, which are answered in turn by the priestess as god and the priestess as mortal. Both exchanges are balanced again by the two tasks which they impose upon Aeneas, the finding of the bough and the burial of Misenus. The great sacrifice to the gods of the dead closes the prologue as it began, and hastens the hero into the kingdom of Dis.

The prologue-rite, like others, conveys meaning beyond and through its formal structure. The movement, words, and action of Aeneas not only bring him from the doors of Daedalus to the jaws of hell, but convey him from one level of existence to another. Objectively he passes from life to death, subjectively from the impotent and chaotic perceptions of mortality to a power over himself and the world which barely falls short of being ultimate knowledge as well. The book opens with Aeneas' futile and ignorant lament for Palinurus; at the end of the prologue he has come to command, at least temporarily, his own fate, both social and personal. Within the frame of ritual, Aeneas' experience of the past and his will for the future, "memory and desire," meet and are unified. For the first time in the poem there is a total realization of the central character. It is this inner progress which is really necessary for the mysterious journey.

An external agent, the Sibyl, guides the hero throughout. Far more than any person so far introduced in the poem, even Aeneas himself, she would be to the Roman a figure of history and authenticity. With the coming of Aeneas to Italy the heroic world, Greek and Trojan, begins to be absorbed into the Roman-historical sphere, and this process continues throughout the latter half of the poem. The Sibyl is the first agent and representative of the change. But she is more than a type of Roman religious authority; Virgil portrays her as a personality, after a popular tradition which is far wider than Rome. Like the witch-concealed divinity familiar in folktale, in fact like the mysterious woman who bargained the Sibylline books away to Tarquin, she accosts the hero abruptly, even abusively, but proves his helper and guide: "This is no time for sightseeing." Equipped with the pragmatic folk-wisdom of such figures, as well as with the prestige of Rome, she acts as foil to Aeneas, historical against heroic, social against individual, and consequently "real" and skeptical in the face of the inner experience of the hero.

She demands his prayers, and he asks first for his people—*Latio considere Teucros*, "that the Trojans be allowed to settle in Latium." This is the collective destiny, to be followed in the second prayer by individual experience, relations, and will. They are not to remain as *Teucri,* however. After a cento of reminiscences from the previous wanderings, with a suggestion of divine responsibility for his erratic course as well as for his safety, Aeneas asks for an end (62): "Thus far, and no further, may the future of Troy have followed us." The society of the heroic past must be wholly removed, for Troy survives only as a curse that drives him on. He prays for a consummation of that death announced by Pantheus in the second Book (325-26):

> fuimus Troes, fuit Ilium et ingens
> gloria Teucrorum,

> (We Trojans are no more; Troy has come to an
> end, and our former great glory)

using the same utterance of finality (6.64-65):

> dique deaeque omnes, quibus obstitit Ilium et ingens
> gloria Dardaniae . . .

> (gods and goddesses all, who hated Troy and the great glory
> of the Trojans . . .)

For the new birth of his people, new temples and new oracles are vowed. Aeneas speaks here as the leader, the fore-shadow of Augustus. But he is answered with the agony of the Roman Sibyl, and finally with the mouth of the god. His journey will end as it began, in the convulsion of war. Only on the other side of that cycle is peace and *salus.*

Of course this answer is not enough, for us or for the poet. It is a crisis in that peculiar dualism which is the essence of the *Aeneid.* Virgil spares us no hindsight throughout; Rome and the ancestor-hero of Rome are brought forth at every turn in the proper attitudes of piety and consummation. But opposed to these axioms of success is a complex series of incongruities in speech, character, and action, which are fully as important to the structure of the poem. It seems that the poet has no intention of fulfilling the comfortable expectations which he himself creates. The story of the *Aeneid* is a continual evasion of necessities. The chain of history is already forged. Success is foreordained. But its nature, and the struggle which achieves it, are not, and this indeterminate quality presses continually upon the accepted order of things, forcing it into new and strange aspects. We are compelled to ask whether Aeneas is really achieving anything, whether Rome is really the crown of his destiny. At this point in the poem the incongruity between fact and attitude, history and the individual, emerges in the plainest manner. Now of all times the destiny which lies beyond peace and *salus* demands expression, and does not receive it. It is not only the narrative which creates this impression—a request for settlement and a new society is answered with a prophecy of war—but the undercurrent of images reinforces the denial. Upon the conclusive and orderly phrases of Aeneas' speech, the prophetic certainty of the Palatine temple and the Sibylline priests, follow the animal frenzy and ominous obscurity of the Sibyl. The result of the contrast is an acute tension between the poet-observer and the hero, between the historical order which is the fact and frame of our existence, and the individual who struggles painfully and fallibly toward its realization.

Relief follows, but again not in the expected pattern. The second prayer of Aeneas and its consequences bring him to a fulfilment, and eventually to the revelation which we demand. But the route is devious; the corporate destiny lies deeper than the Sibyl's cave, and before it is uncovered the individual soul must be prepared. This inner attainment is the function of his second request to the Sibyl. Significantly, before he makes it, she becomes again the human *vates,* instead of the mouthpiece of the god (102): "As soon as her frenzy ceased and her raving mouth grew quiet."

He puts aside the *horrida bella* which he as leader of his people must direct and suffer (105-6): "I have foreseen all of this, and have gone over it in my mind already. One thing I ask—" and his prayer is not for further revelation of some divine purpose which lies behind them. Instead (108-9): "May I be allowed to go speak to my father face to face." He asks for and at the same time reveals a completion of his own nature. *Pius Aeneas,* until now, has been another of those apparent norms of the poem which are formally insisted upon and substantially evaded. Aeneas has been dutifully subordinate to his father while alive—and continually frustrated in knowledge and action by this pious position. In Troy it is the vision of doom and terror, *dirae facies,* which is given to him; Anchises and Iulus, the generations on either side of him are vouchsafed the divine signs of safety (the flame) and hope (the shooting star). His father's panic loses him Creusa; his father's misreading of the oracle leads him to the false home in Crete. In all this the son of course says nothing of blame, or, more important, of love; he merely follows and suffers. It is Virgil's presentation of the relationship which creates the tension, and quietly corrodes the traditional formalities of *pietas.* The poet comes closest to being explicit, through the mouth of Aeneas, in the central episode of the third Book. After meeting Helenus and Andromache, Aeneas, privately speaking to his seer-cousin, shows himself for once pragmatic and hopeful (3.362-68): "Tell me—for every omen has been favorable to my course and all the gods have urged me to seek Italy and to make a trial of the land that awaits me—what dangers shall I first avoid? What should I follow in order to overcome such great obstacles?" But after the colloquy Anchises and Iulus reenter the scene. His divinely certified family closes in upon him, receives further encouragement for the future, and Aeneas sinks to the contrary mood of despair (3.493-96): "May you be happy, you whose destiny is fulfilled; we are called from fate to fate. Your rest is won: you have no sea to plow, no ever-receding Ausonian fields to seek." Nothing that Helenus has said would change Italy from a land hidden but accessible to the obedient hero, to a phantom receding before his search. The alteration is subjective, and by it Virgil associates Anchises with a feeling of futility and oppression. Aeneas is the fate-driven man; but in the presence of his family he realizes that it is not his own fate which is driving him. After death, in the fourth Book, Anchises continues to oppress his son. Throughout the idyll at Carthage, not once, like Mercury, but every night (351-53): "As often as night covers the earth with dewy shadows, as often as the fiery stars rise, the troubled ghost of my father arises to terrify me and warns me in my sleep."

Here, then, in the sixth Book, *pietas* is still ambiguous at best. Anchises' shade has already commanded Aeneas to descend to the lower world, and we can expect no more than the dutiful response. But to respond so at this point and in these words connotes much more than duty:

> ire ad conspectum cari genitoris et ora.

> (to go to speak to my father face to face.)

The vision of Anchises is substituted for the vision of Rome. Expression and cadence recall the first mention of his father in the second Book: impelled by the blood of Priam and the fires of Troy (560):

> subiit cari genitoris imago.

> (Suddenly the thought of my dear father came to me.)

This first rush of love and anxiety, the reaction of the natural un-fated man, is at last fulfilled here. The intervening frustrations, springing from the double pressures of fate and parental authority, are erased. Anchises in Aeneas' eyes is no longer *sancte parens,* the dominant and divine old man, but helpless and pitiable, his journey viewed here for the first time in purely human terms (112-14): "He was my companion in my travels; infirm as he was, he endured all my voyages with me, and all the threats of sea and sky, beyond either the strength or the deserts of old age." The revela-tion of destiny follows, not because he asks for it, but because by this act of the personal will he has shown himself worthy.

This is not a complete resolution (there is none in the *Aeneid*): the tension between knowledge and ignorance, history and the in-dividual, is not so easily discharged. But Aeneas' speech, catching up together the levels of his experience, gives him a power found nowhere else in the poem. His particular excellence, the heroism of obligation, reaches its summit here, in the act of going down to death.

The Sibyl's second reply, like the first, runs counter to the tone of Aeneas' request. She speaks here above all as the folk-seer, the primitive skeptic who finds reality only in the tangible, the ap-parent world. She says little of Anchises, and observes the inner consummation of Aeneas with a cold eye, seeing only, from the out-side, the antithesis of life and death which he presents. Her speech parodies, somewhat cruelly, the solemn words of the hero. He has addressed her as the guardian of hell's gate, which indeed she is (106-9):

> quando hic inferni ianua regis
> dicitur . . .
> . . . . doceas iter et sacra ostia pandas.

> (since this is said to be the portal of the king of the underworld . . . do you show the path, and open the consecrated doors.)

But she answers, with an intentional misunderstanding which is almost mockery, that the gates of hell are not guarded at all (126-7):

> facilis descensus Averno:
> noctes atque dies patet atri ianua Ditis.

> (the descent to Avernus is easy: night and day the portal to the dark underworld stands open.)

Anyone may die; there is no need to ask her for permission. But to pass through the kingdom of death and still remain alive, that is a fearful task even for those who boast of their divine descent. She forces us and the hero to recognize the enormity of his request. His κατάβασις is not to be an Odyssean adventure, but an equivalent performance of the real death-journey.

Later in her speech, the paradox is put as sharply as possible (133-35):

> quod si tantus amor menti, si tanta cupido est
> bis Stygios innare lacus, bis nigra videre
> Tartara . . .

> (but if your love is so great, if you have such a great desire to venture twice upon the waters of the Styx, twice to look on the black regions of Tartarus . . .)

The first line recognizes the subjective experience of Aeneas. *Amor* is the transcendent condition of *pietas* at which he has finally arrived. By one of Virgil's continual echoes, the phrase immediately recalls *sed si tantus amor* in the second Book. The connection is deep and illuminating. This is another yielding of the self to share with another an extraordinary and terrible experience. In the earlier book Dido was to share with Aeneas the disaster of his city, the death of his race. Here Aeneas is to share with Anchises an end even beyond this, the death of the individual.

But the object of *amor* which the Sibyl perceives is neither the one stated by Aeneas (the union with Anchises), nor the enlargement of personality implied by this line. She emphasizes the cold and fearful fact of death, not the attitude which leads Aeneas to accept the experience. The two crossings of the Styx come of course from the *Odyssey* (12.21-22): Virgil's line, though, is more concrete, and significantly different in its position. Circe speaks thus to Odysseus and his crew *after* they return from the underworld. They realize their action in retrospect. Here Aeneas must know that his mission will be the death-journey *before* he undertakes it. It is the immediate condition of his love and life.

The Sibyl, always the folk-wise observer, gives this union of opposites no encouragement. The line which follows expresses a curious contempt (135):

> et insano iuvat indulgere labori.

> (if it pleases you to indulge in this mad undertaking.)

The verbs suggest laxness and pleasure; joined with *insano* the phrase makes of Aeneas' request something almost indecent, to the Sibyl's pragmatism, and certainly unnatural. It is *amor* perverted. If it is to succeed, there must be a sign.

So, suddenly, we come upon the golden bough (136-48; 200-211):

> latet arbore opaca
> aureus et foliis et lento vimine ramus
> Iunoni infernae dictus sacer; hunc tegit omnis
> lucus et obscuris claudunt convallibus umbrae.
> sed non ante datur telluris operta subire
> auricomos quam qui decerpserit arbore fetus.
> hoc sibi pulchra suum ferri Proserpina munus
> instituit. primo avulso non deficit alter
> aureus, et simili frondescit virga metallo.
> ergo alte vestiga oculis et rite repertum
> carpe manu; namque ipse volens facilisque sequetur,
> si te fata vocant; aliter non viribus ullis
> vincere nec duro poteris convellere ferro.

(There lies hidden in the dense wood a golden bough, leaves and tough branch both of gold, said to be sacred to Juno of the underworld; this the whole grove shelters, and shadows enclose it in dark confines. But it is not given to anyone to descend into the depths of the earth until he has plucked the gold-tressed branch from the tree: fair Proserpina has set it as the tribute to be brought to her. When one bough is torn off, another one of gold grows in its place, and the branch bears leaves of like metal. Therefore watch well for it, and when you have found it, duly pluck it with your hand: for it will come willingly and easily of itself, if the fates summon you; otherwise with no amount of strength could you overcome it, nor could you rip it off with hard iron.)

* * *

> inde ubi venere ad fauces grave olentis Averni
> tollunt se celeres liquidumque per aera lapsae
> sedibus optatis geminae super arbore sidunt,
> discolor unde auri per ramos aura refulsit.
> quale solet silvis brumali frigore viscum
> fronde virere nova, quod non sua seminat arbos,
> et croceo fetu teretis circumdare truncos,
> talis erat species auri frondentis opaca

ilice, sic leni crepitabat brattea vento.
corripit Aeneas extemplo avidusque refringit
cunctantem, et vatis portat sub tecta Sibyllae.

(Then, when they [the doves] came to the jaws of foul-
smelling Avernus, they rose, and gliding swiftly through the
clear air they alighted side by side in their chosen resting
place, on a tree through whose branches shone the rare
hues of gold. Just as in the cold of winter the mistletoe in
the forests, which never is found save on other trees, bright-
ens with new growth and girdles the smooth trunks with yel-
low shoots, such was the appearance of the gold blooming
on the dark ilex, thus the metal leaves rattled in the light
wind. Aeneas seized it at once and eagerly pulled it off
resisting, and carried it into the cave of the priestess, the
Sibyl.)

Within the frame which I have tried to outline, we approach
this extraordinary image. Clearly, there is in it an element of the
external. Virgil reached beyond the world of his poem for a fact or
belief or tradition which existed independent of his own imagination. Despite many conjectures it appears equally clear that we shall
never trace down the referent in specific terms. Servius suggested
the rites of Proserpina, and interjected that famous *publica opinio*
about the grove of Nemi which was to lead Frazer forth on his
massive pursuit of the tree-spirit and the sacrificial king. Heyne suggested, among other origins, the golden apples of Juno and the
Hesperides, the pomegranate of Proserpina, the branch of the sup-
pliant, the *aurea virga* of Mercury as psychagogue, and the Golden
Fleece.[2] Conington thought of the mysteries of Isis.[3] Frazer ended
with the derivation of the bough from folk beliefs concerning the
properties of the mistletoe.[4] Norden too approached the image
through the mistletoe simile, but added the concept of the bough
of myrtle or olive brought as a gift to the goddess Proserpina/Kore
and as a symbol of life and rebirth in the mystery rituals.[5]

The diversity of conclusions does not result from any lack of

[2] C. G. Heyne and G. P. E. Wagner, eds., *Publius Vergilius Maro*, 4th ed.
(Leipzig, 1833), II, 1014-15.

[3] J. Conington, ed., *P. Vergili Maronis Opera* (London, Whittaker & Co., 1884),
II, 426.

[4] J. G. Frazer, *The Golden Bough*, 3rd ed. (London, Macmillan, 1913), II, Part
VII, *Balder the Beautiful*, 279-303.

[5] E. Norden, *Aeneis* VI (Stuttgart, 1927), 163-75.

diligence. No amount of searching, in literature or anthropology, will ever arrive at a single incontrovertible "answer," and this does not greatly matter. For whatever lies behind the bough-image lies also behind and outside the *Aeneid*. The golden bough of the *Aeneid* means exactly what Virgil, in his enormously complex and allusive way, says that it means, no less and no more; in other words, it means what it is in the poem. None of the conjectures, therefore, which relate ultimately to the circumstances of the poem, and of the poet, should be entertained until the internal progress, the organic coherence of Virgil's imagination, has been examined. The point is universal. The creative product is never a logical and predictable result of its environment. The necessities and sequences of poetry are its own; if they are considered as fully explicable in terms of external statement—historical, philosophical, religious, or critical—poetry is destroyed. Because this image has received such a vast burden of attention from this external point of view, it is one of the critical points at which the nature of poetry must be maintained.

The poet has presented life and death, both as opposites, in the wisdom of the Sibyl, and as union, in the will of Aeneas. The human actors have reached the impasse of inner experience and outward observation, two irreconcilable aspects of reality. The golden bough is the necessary and external sign demanded to resolve the antinomy, and bears a fundamental relation to it. Let us take, for the present, the bough in its simplest aspect as a thing of gold. It grows in a dense tree, like the mistletoe, on an oak. It exists on a living thing, the last outpost in fact of the live world before the stinking jaws of Death. But the bough is made of gold—therefore it is not alive itself. It does have the semblance of a living branch; it grows leaves—*frondescit*—but always *simili metallo,* "of like metal." This flowering is denied the accustomed tissues of the kingdom of life. When the breeze catches the bough, *crepitabat brattea vento,* "the metal leaves rattled in the wind." The line obviously represents sound, and by no stretch of the auditory imagination could it be the sound or motion of any living thing. The gold takes its meaning from the tree on which it grows, and the essential purpose of the image, resolving symbolically the conflict between Aeneas and the Sibyl, is to create a contrast between living and dead which is at the same time a vital union. The idea is grandly developed again by Aeneas (195-96):

> derigite in lucos ubi pinguem dives opacat
> ramus humum.

(direct your steps into the grove where the rich bough
shades the fertile soil.)

The epithets both signify wealth, but one connotes the abundance
of the life-giving earth, while the other casts upon it the shadow
of a different splendor. This, too, the sense of alien things in union,
is the first significance of the mistletoe simile, and the contrasts in
the simile itself, winter and growth, tree and parasite, emphasize
the division.

Aeneas, in fulfilling his own life, must pass into death. He is not
merely to see the underworld, but to undergo an analogue, dan-
gerously close to reality, of his ultimate death-journey. The Sibyl,
essential and external seer, observes this paradox with some dis-
belief. Life-in-death contravenes the natural order of mortality.
If Aeneas' will is to become the exceptional reality, a sign of success
is demanded. That sign is the golden bough; death-in-life. The
magic is allopathic; the two strange unions complement each
other and together complete an invulnerable circle which transcends nature. The bough becomes a guarantee both of Aeneas'
ability to enter the underworld and of his protection while passing
through it. Not only Aeneas and the bough, then, but his action
upon the bough and the consequent journey are reciprocal symbols.
As he plucks the bough from the tree, death from life, so he de-
parts from the underworld unharmed, life from death.

The bough appears again at the crossing of the Styx (405-10),
where the contrast of living and dead is most explicitly marked
and the anomalous position of Aeneas is challenged (by Charon's
recognition of a live soul, by the boat sinking under his weight).
Finally he leaves the *munus* at the palace of Dis and Proserpina
(628-36). This is the center of the triple scheme of the underworld.
First Aeneas encounters the traditional Hades, then the vision of
hell and heaven, Tartarus and Elysium, and finally the prophetic
cycle of the souls and ages. Between the two elements of the central
vision is the palace of the infernal king and queen, and the end
of the bough's journey. It is no longer needed; the dangerous
death-passage is ended (through the hopelessness of Aeneas' own
mortal experience, through the eternity of evil), and the journey
into life, indeed to something beyond life, is about to begin. *Lar-
gior hic aether*, "here the pure air is more abundant"; Elysium
is a different world.

The essence of the golden bough is the contrast between its lifeless nature and its organic environment. But we cannot stop here.

Obviously the image of gold must express other relevant associations; otherwise lead or iron or stone would have done equally well. These are not, however, the associations which have generally been conjectured for it—those of Pindar, for instance, for whom gold is a constantly recurrent symbol of glory and power. We look in vain in Virgil's lines for an unequivocal expression of brilliance, glory, or life as inherent in the golden bough. Rather, the first words give the key: *latet arbore opaca,* "it is hidden by a dense-leaved tree." The bough is hidden by tree and forest; the hero cannot find it without supernatural guidance. Once it is plucked it is hidden again in the garments of the Sibyl (406). It enables Aeneas to descend to the "hidden places of the earth." This is not like the worked gold which is displayed as the emblem of wealth and splendor, but rather suggests the rare metal which must be sought in the depths of darkness and the earth. The *aureus ramus* is a secret, symbolically buried as well as lifeless. It belongs physically below the earth, in the dead world, and so is a peculiarly appropriatae *munus* for the queen of that world, the consort of Dis/Πλούτων who is lord of the riches under the earth. In fact, the bough is not so much given to Proserpina as returned to her. When the Sibyl carries it down to Hades, it is recognized by Charon as something *longo post tempore visum,* "seen again after a long time." I suggest that this does not refer to any previous heroic journey with the bough, but rather to the fact that it *belongs* in Charon's world underground. Its existence in the upper air is considered here to be temporary and unnatural.

The only suggestion of shining or brightness develops at the moment of the bough's discovery, and it is presented in a curious and baffling expression (204):

> discolor unde auri per ramos aura refulsit.

The brightness is *discolor,* not pure light, but rather another and strange color in the dark and green of the wood. *Aura* is even stranger. Virgil is playing of course on the sound of *aurum,* but this cannot be the whole explanation. Normally the word has no visual sense; it means a quality of the atmosphere, an emanation, an "air." The poet may have been thinking of *superasque evadere ad auras,* "to escape back into the atmosphere of the upper world," in the Sibyl's speech above (128); if so, the *aura* of the bough would again connote the underworld, and would be truly *discolor* to the living green of the tree. In any case, if Virgil is trying to describe the brilliance of gold, this is a strangely hesitant and unsatisfactory

way to do it. Of course he is not. The hidden thing is found, but
in revealing itself it maintains a secret and enigmatic quality. It
appears to the hero's eye; it is his to gather. But even at the moment
of action and success Virgil is unwilling to give himself up to one
perception alone. Everything implies its opposite; the bough is seen,
but by some faculty which is not exactly visual. Aeneas plucks it,
but not with the necessary ease (210-11):

> avidusque refringit
> cunctantem.

> (eagerly he tears it off despite its
> resistance.)

Another antithesis is already beginning to take form.

The significance of the bough as death, or rather as the tension
between life and death in a single unit of being, does not exhaust
the image. It certainly does not preclude the traditional interpretations, but at this point requires them, and determines their application to the poem. The studies of Norden and Frazer have explored
the wide importance of vegetation as related in primitive thought
to life and death, and the survival in ritual or quasi-ritual pro-
cedures of these modes of thinking.[6] In relation to the grave and the
underworld, vegetation universally appears to have the significance
and power of life. It is impossible to transfer this significance sum-
marily to Virgil's bough, which is not vegetation, and whose symbolism is far too complex to represent life alone. But the investiga-
tors, although they have misinterpreted the image as a whole, have
uncovered one point at least of supreme importance to the pattern
which I have attempted to trace.

Virgil compares the bough to the mistletoe (205-8):

> quale solet silvis brumali frigore viscum
> fronde virere nova, quod non sua seminat arbos,
> et crocea fetu teretis circumdare truncos,
> talis erat species . . .

> (just as in the woods in winter new growth appears on the
> mistletoe that grows from other trees, and it surrounds
> their smooth trunks with yellow tendrils: such was the
> appearance . . .)

---

[6] Norden, *Aeneis* VI, pp. 164-68; compare Frazer's discussion of the mistletoe
and the "external soul"; *Balder the Beautiful*, pp. 76-278.

We have already seen how the contrasts of color, texture, and growth between mistletoe and oak reinforce those between bough and tree. But the mistletoe, as Norden and Frazer point out, also possesses, in popular and mythical thought, extraordinary qualities of magic and sometimes of divinity. The simile then forms an overt point of contact, at which power is released from that deep reservoir of primitive belief and practice lying beyond Virgil's image. Norden remarks of the mistletoe that it seems to have a double aspect, as a power of fertility, protection, and life, and as a power of death. It can heal disease and avert demons, but can also kill the tree on which it grows. Loki opens the doors of hell with a sprig of mistletoe, and kills Baldur with the same. "Death and life in mythical thought are not always opposites, but can form a single unity." [7] This is crucial. When an object has enough magical power to represent life, in a sense to *be* life, this power can be expressed and used negatively as well, to cause death, to *be* death. The power of life and death is a single reality. The golden bough, generically as vegetation-magic and specifically as assimilated to the mistletoe, has such a power. Like the lesser oppositions of color, texture, alienness, the primary paradox of life/death, immanent in the healing and parasitic plant, reinforces the created image of the poet. Again I do not mean that Virgil simply took over some primitive "idea" and proceeded to put it into verse. It seems rather doubtful that in such cases there is anything which can be called an idea, a formulation of phenomena, already existing in the folk mind. We may make abstractions like the one above which cover observed beliefs or customs, and the poet may draw his paradox from the same source, but both are products of a "sophisticated state of language and feeling." [8] It was Virgil who perceived or felt an ambiguity underlying the whole mass of observance, belief, and legend concerned with the relation of the vegetative power to life and death, and expressed it through his own imagery. The mistletoe-simile is the dark and environmental aspect of his meaning, connecting it with the secrecies of the primitive mind. But the union of life and death implied by the simile could not have the same power—could not, in fact, convey its meaning at all—if the same meaning had not already been pre-

---

[7] Norden, *Aeneis* VI, p. 166. He discards this paradoxical unity in his interpretation, however, for the *progress* of nature from death to life, which is a different matter.

[8] W. Empson, *Seven Types of Ambiguity*, 2nd ed. (New York: New Directions, 1947), p. 195. His discussion of the union of opposites in a single word is extremely valuable.

sented by the primary and immediate image of the gold, hidden and lifeless in the living tree. One mode of thought enlarges the other, and works the whole into a complex and sinister unity.

Interlocked with the task of the bough and obviously parallel to it is the mission to find and bury Misenus (149-83; 212-35). The two signs complete and guarantee the two requests of the hero. As the first answers Aeneas' personal will, so the other follows upon his prayer for his people's settlement. Misenus is not for Virgil merely an awkward doublet of Palinurus. Each does correspond partially to Elpenor in the *Odyssey*, the fore-runner who goes down to the shades in advance of the hero. But beyond this each episode has something to express peculiar to itself and organic to the poem. The resolution in Misenus' case is relatively simple. He has been the trumpeter of Hector and Aeneas, giving the signal for the battles of the past. Virgil used him thus deliberately, to make him the embodiment of the *Troiana fortuna,* the unfortunate destiny of the race, for whose end Aeneas has prayed. Like Troy, he is dead but not buried and, laid in that state, pollutes the whole company of *Aeneadae.* Once he is laid to his final rest, they are made *casti* at last, free from the curse of the dead city, and can participate vicariously with their new leader in the journey of purification and rebirth to a new land.

Underneath its stoical surface the *Aeneid* is a web of antithetic symbols, of tensions and oppositions never finally resolved. The golden bough is one of the most critical and complex events in this internal structure. For Aeneas it is a symbol of power to match and complete his own. But the completion is produced on the level of magic, of the wonderful conjunction of external things. It is the Sibyl as folk-woman who demands it, makes it possible, and limits it to this sphere. The bough then is a testament of power, but not of resolution. As in the prayer for settlement, the poet has brought his other self, the hero, to a point of expression which demands revelation, and again the sign which is given does not answer the demand.

Aeneas in praying to see his father has come as close as may be to a divine sensibility, to an ultimate inclusiveness and reconciliation with experience. He realizes in himself at last the inner meaning of that Tree of Life to which he is compared in the fourth Book (441-46):

> ipsa haeret scopulis, et quantum vertice ad auras
> aetherias, tantum radice in Tartara tendit.

(the tree itself grows on crags, and stretches its top as far
into the sky as its roots extend underground to the infernal
regions.)

The whole simile, of which this is the conclusion, compares Aeneas'
stubbornness in the face of Dido's passion and Anna's pleading to
that of an oak wrenched but still undestroyed by the winds.[9] In
the context of the fourth Book, the image seems rather too large
for its setting. Aeneas is obeying the *fatum*, but there is not yet an
adequate reason why in doing so he should encompass both hell
and heaven. Virgil has suddenly passed beyond the immediate comparison and into a prophetic insight of something far deeper in
the significance of Aeneas, which is not to be made plain until the
descent to the underworld in the sixth Book. The quest for the
bough recalls images of tree, heaven, and hell in a pattern which
completes the likeness. Aeneas is led to the bough by twin doves,
creatures of the air and messengers of his divine mother. As they
approach the goal (201-3): "When they come to the jaws of foul-
smelling Avernus, they fly upward swiftly, and gliding through
the clear air they both come to rest on the spot they sought." There
is a symbolic upward movement here, both in the connotation of
the birds and in their action. But the flight of the birds is not only
a reaching to heaven; it is also an escape from hell. The tree is
rooted in the jaws of Avernus, and the breath of the place is deadly
(239-41): "No birds could fly over it with impunity, such were the
fumes that poured forth from the black jaws and rose to the vault
of heaven." The doves can lead him to the tree which is in this case
his magical counterpart, but no further. The creatures of heaven

---

[9] The image comes directly from the *Georgics*, 2.291. There it refers to the
aesculus, and is part of a practical discussion of how trees should be planted.
The passage continues:

> ergo non hiemes illam, non flabra neque imbres
> convellunt. . . .

One could reason from this that the isolation of the image in the fourth Book
simply derives from the fact that it is copied. Storm and immobility suggest the
tree-image from the *Georgics*, and the tree-image brings along heaven and hell
as superfluous baggage. In spite of this I should like to argue for relevance. The
image which joins tree with stress has a peculiar internal importance in the
Aeneid. The vision of Troy overthrown by the gods in the second Book culminates in the simile of the tree cut down by human hands. In the fourth Book
the man of Troy stands against a human storm. Certainly the *quantum vertice
ad auras aetherias* takes on a relevant meaning in this context, and the whole
sense is completed by the association with Aeneas, bough, and tree in the sixth
Book.

cannot enter hell. Only the hero himself, like the tree which carries both bough and doves, can unite the two in thought and actuality, the realms of his mother and of his father, *amor* and death.

In doing so, he strains the nature of mortality. Such a mode of experience is possible only beyond the bounds of the normal human faculties. When a sign is given to guarantee this inner experience, one must expect it to have a similarly transcendent quality, passing beyond the contrasts of nature to an ultimate harmony. The bough does not possess this quality. Like Aeneas himself, in the Sibyl's skeptical view, it is unnatural, embodying the contrasts of nature, rather than supernatural, transcending them. The scene of its finding is pure magical prescription. No words are spoken; everything is action and movement in a ritual silence. The rite is effective and the hero receives his power, but not the knowledge of what the power should mean. At the summit of his experience Aeneas looks for a sign, and finds it to be but a mirror-image of himself, life-in-death confronting death-in-life.[10] The *amor* which impels him to pass living into death receives no answer. This deeper antithesis of success in action/frustration in knowledge is the central and fundamental significance of the golden bough. Certainly it is this which effects that curious distortion of the language at the moment of the bough's discovery. *Discolor aura:* not the light of revelation, but the dubious and shifting colors of the magic forest.[11]

The golden bough is a moment in a larger progress. The relation which it expresses between the hero and the world is one which is repeated at various levels and in various forms throughout the poem. Aeneas is continually arriving at a kind of order, a limited state of grace, and as continually finding that this is not the whole condition of his destiny. Always he must go on to more knowledge and suffering. The actual excludes consummation.

His world in Troy is that of the epic hero, and he is ready to fulfill the last demands of this heroism. In the last night of the city, the gods have departed from their worshippers. The hopeless struggle, however, must still remain as the hero's necessity (2.351-53):

[10] The mirror-image of the bough even has a quality of distortion and mockery; the dead-parent/living-child relationship, the substance of Aeneas' fulfilment, is reflected and inverted in it too, but like the mistletoe the bough is something *quod non sua seminat arbos.*

[11] See M. Bodkin, *Archetypal Patterns in Poetry* (London: Oxford Univ. Press, 1934), pp. 129-36. I am deeply indebted to Miss Bodkin's discussion of the bough. She is concerned, however, with seeking a universal archetype of the imagination which will include not only the bough but Dante's angel at the gates of Dis, and so tends to ignore some aspects of Virgil's own context.

excessere omnes, aris adytisque relictis
di quibus imperium hoc steterat; sucurritis urbi
incensae: moriamur et in media arma ruamus.

(they have all departed, leaving their altars and shrines deserted, the gods under whom this empire existed; you go
to the aid of a city in flames: let us die rushing into the
midst of the fighting.)

He expects his heroism to be futile; he does not expect it to be
falsely construed. For he will see that the gods have not departed.
They are still there, laboring at the destruction of their city. His
vision of them at once denies him epic heroism and sends him forth
in search of another means through which order may be found.

In Rome he attempts the opposite, the pastoral construction of
the world, taking on the humility and communion of the Arcadian
kingdom (8.364-65):

aude, hospes, contemnere opes et te quoque dignum
finge deo.

(dare, o guest, to spurn riches and make yourself also worthy
of the god.)

But his assumption of the mantle of Hercules plunges this same
kingdom into war, kills its heir, and destroys the *aurea aetas* to
which he has just been admitted. Even before the event he realizes
that this effort at order is not the end (8.520-22):

vix ea fatus erat, defixique ora tenebant
Aeneas Anchisiades et fidus Achates
multaque dura suo tristi cum corde putabant.

(scarcely had he finished speaking, and Aeneas son of
Anchises and trusty Achates kept their eyes fixed on him,
and were bitterly thinking many harsh thoughts to themselves.)

The end of the poem brings no finality of knowledge. The Fury,
for all her terror, is the angel of Jupiter, bringing the decision and
the peace Aeneas has looked for so long. But he is blind to her, and
sees only, in his private rage, the belt of Pallas. Dido's curse is

already coming true, in a sense deeper than its original intention
(4.618-19):

> nec, cum se sub leges pacis iniquae
> tradiderit, regno aut optata luce fruatur.

> (nor, when he has yielded to the terms of an
> unfair peace, may he enjoy his kingdom or the day he
> has hoped for.)

Aeneas never fully possesses either the light or the kingdom that
is ordained for him. Clearly the kingdom—Rome or Lavinium—is
a historical fact, and Aeneas' failure to realize it is evolved circum-
stantially from the myth. It is far stranger, and more moving, that
he never fully possesses that divine order of which he is the literal
and symbolic carrier. Virgil seeks justification for Aeneas, not only
by time, as Ancestor of the City, but in experience, as the individual
who is driven by forces and looks for a personal fulfilment outside
and beyond himself. The justification is never found. The failure
is what we have already taken to be the central thread of the
Aeneid, and the episodes quoted above, above all that of the bough,
lie very close to it. The *Aeneid* is an attack on the part of the
indeterminate, the various and fallible nature of man, upon the
necessities both of history and of fate. The attack begins by assuming conquest; it ends by implying defeat and destruction. Man does
not fit in history. Neither the hero nor the poet ever comes to terms
with the ends which are so easily postulated and so desperately
sought throughout the poem.

The *Aeneid* is a work in limbo. Virgil had left behind the satisfactory order informing his previous work—*fortunatus et ille.* He
was in passage to the end of his own life-journey, never to be
achieved:

> felix qui potuit rerum cognoscere causas.

> (happy the man who knows the causes of things.)

The world of the *Aeneid* lies between the two, and hints at failure
of the capacity to go further. The causes of things are never to be
known with the same ecstatic certainty as Lucretius'. Neither causes
nor things are the same, in Virgil's world. They are revealed, not
deduced, and conceal themselves again in the act of revelation. In
the fourth Canto of the *Inferno* Dante has his master say of the
sphere which he inhabits for eternity:

semo perduti, e sol di tanto offesi
che senza speme vivemo in disio.

At the center of Virgil's poem, the golden bough, in all its density of suggestion, is the primary symbol of this splendid despair.

Basic Themes

by Viktor Pöschl

The First Sequence of Scenes (*1.8-296*)
as Symbolic Anticipation of the Whole Poem

The first climactic point in the *Aeneid*—the event that sets
the tone, arousing and preparing the reader's mind for the extraordinary actions about to take place—is the storm which drives
Aeneas to the shores of Carthage. Its introductory position in the
poem indicates that it is more than just another episode in the destiny of the homeless Trojans. The pulsating breath of tragedy and
the atmosphere of wild pathos embody with the greatest compres-
sion the nature of the emotion which permeates the whole poem.
It is, as it were, the "musical" motif that from the start marks the
events with passionate grandeur and the demonic power of fate.[1]
Only the image of the strongest, wildest movement in Nature—
which had, of course, been transmitted through Homer, where it was
first raised to the level of art—seemed to Virgil sufficiently grave and
imposing for the opening of his Roman epic.

This kind of beginning was not borrowed from the *Odyssey*,
certainly, for that epic opens much more peacefully. If there is
any parallel in Homer, it is in the plague which opens the *Iliad*.
Indeed, the entire *Aeneid* in its dramatic impetus is more to be
compared with the *Iliad* than with the *Odyssey*. But even in the
Iliad Homer swiftly progresses to the quarrel between Achilles and
Agamemnon as the starting point of the real action, without uti-
lizing the mood established by the plague motif. As for Apollonius

[1] Statius has imitated the motif in the beginning of the *Thebais* in the night
storm which drives Tydeus and Polyneices into Adrastus' house. It would be
interesting to follow the history of "storms" as an element in tragedy and as an
opening symbol in Shakespeare and the moderns. It is very important in opera.

hodius of Hellenistic times, who in the casual manner of a story-
teller began his epic with an almost comical anecdote—the oracle of
the man with one shoe—he achieves nothing of the *Aeneid*'s symbolic power. Contrary to common assumption, he is much farther
from Virgil's artistic conception than is Homer.

The scene sequence dominated by the storm at sea (1.8-296) anticipates the whole poem in thought as well as mood. It is the prelude
of the work, announcing the basic motifs after the manner of an
overture.[2] Let us examine it.

As for the motif of Juno's hatred, the poet, after the proem,
expounds upon her counterplan for Carthage's control of the world.
The opposition of the two world powers is announced immediately
upon the introduction of Rome's historic rival: *Carthago Italiam
contra* (1.13), in which *"contra"* is meant much more symbolically
than geographically. With a slight change it returns in Dido's curse:

> Let your shores oppose their shores, your waves their waves, your arms
> their arms. That is my imprecation.

4.628:

> Litora litoribus contraria, fluctibus undas
> Imprecor, arma armis, pugnent ipsique nepotesque . . .

Thus, the contest between Rome and Carthage for world dominion
appears as a main theme from the very beginning, and Juno's stub-
born fight against the hero's *fata* symbolically anticipates it, as do
the battles in the last half of the poem—as stated in Jupiter's
speech (10.11).

This historically decisive contest is itself only a representative symbol of all the hard wars in Roman history. The last half of the
poem is symbolic also of the Italo-Roman struggle and the civil
wars. Moreover, it contains a searching examination of the nature
and uncanny duality of politics; the image of the dark demon of
passion in Turnus confronts the shining spiritual and moral power
in Aeneas. Roman history is presented as a struggle between two
principles, and Rome's victory is seen as the victory of the higher
one. Thus, the first and the last halves of the *Aeneid* are symbolic in
different ways. (Here I remind the reader how important to our

---

[2] Virgil often makes one think of opera because of the great sweep and pathos,
the skillful arrangement of the proceeding action, and the striving for impressive
images and gestures. Modern, especially German, criticism too often tends to
take a negative view of this necessary "theater." Virgil directly as well as indirectly exercised considerable influence on the evolution of opera in Italy. See
Romain Rolland, "L'Origine de l'opéra," in *Musiciens d'autrefois*.

subject it is to realize that a symbol by its very nature admits of
—and demands—more than one interpretation. The essence of a
symbolic relation is that the correspondence between the symbol and
the thing symbolized is not precise, but flexible, opening up an
infinite perspective.)

In a letter to Schiller (August 17, 1797) Goethe[3] wrote: "Symbolic
objects are outstanding cases representing in their variety many
others. They are characterized by a certain inclusiveness; they demand a certain sequence. They evoke in my mind pertinent and
similar as well as foreign ideas. Consequently, from within as well
as from without, they claim a certain oneness and universality."
And in *Maximen und Reflexionen:*[3a] "The symbol transforms the
visible into an idea and the idea into an image in such manner that
the idea in the image stays infinitely potent and unattainable, remaining unutterable even if spoken of in all languages." Similarly,
in his *Tagebücher* (ed. Bamberger, I, 236), Hebbel says: "Every
genuine work of art is a mysterious symbol with many meanings,
to a certain degree incomprehensible." Juno, then, is first the mythical personification of the historical power of Carthage, and in this
role she causes the storm at sea and the shipwrecked landing on
Carthaginian soil. It is most significant that her passionate hatred
really stems from love. The *Aeneid* has been called the "epic of
grief." It could as well be called the "epic of love," for its deepest
tragedy is that its people "loved too much." This is true of Euryalus,
of whom the poet says (9.430): *"Infelicem nimium dilexit ami-
cum"* (He loved too much his wretched friend);[4] it is just as true
of Juno, Venus, Turnus, Dido, and Latinus (12.29: *Victus amore
tui . . . vincla omnia rupi:* conquered by love of you . . . I burst
all bonds), and of Amata, Laocoön, and Evander. Love is the mo-
tivating force in all that Aeneas does. Even the fall of the monster
Mezentius is transfigured by grief over the death of his son Lausus
in what is basically a suicide for love.

On the human level Aeneas, as the personification of things Roman, meets this very real blow of fate with the firm resolve to strive
on through all dangers (1.204ff.), while on the divine level Jupiter
reveals the solution of the conflict to Venus:

[8] I am indebted to Richard Meister for pointing out these quotations from
Goethe. A further discussion of the symbol occurs in Goethe's essay on "Philos-
tratus' Painting" (Weimar ed., 1889 f.), v, 49, 141.

[3a] *Iubiläumsausgabe,* 35, p. 326.

[4] Wjatscheslaw Iwanow, *Vergil, Aufsaetze zur Geschichte der Antike und des
Christentums* (Berlin, 1937), p. 66, notes the coincidence with *quoniam dilexit
multum* in the gospel of Luke 7:47.

She (Juno) will change her plans for the better and together with me she will protect the Romans, the masters of the world, the people in the toga . . .

4.281:

> Consilia in melius referet mecumque fovebit
> Romanos rerum dominos gentemque togatam.

As the action is in the highest sense carried out between Jupiter and Juno, the first unit of the *Aeneid* is framed by the appearances of the two major divinities. The composition is expression of a fact, the balance of scenes is image and symbol of an equivalence of forces. Human action is embedded in divine action, not only as an artistic means but also as a statement of fact. To understand this is to hold one of the keys to the secret of classical composition. Besides being subject to the autonomous law of beauty, the form is founded on the subject itself, which through its organization in clear antitheses appears in its very essence. "Formal perfection is just another aspect of mental penetration" (Ernst Robert Curtius).

The contrast between Jupiter's quiet serenity (1.255) and Juno's angry passion underscores the inner tension of the poem. The passion-consumed goddess is confronted by Virgil's sublime Jupiter, the majestic master of the world, enthroned above suffering and passion.[5] This aspect of highest divinity becomes even more evident in the verses preceding Jupiter's decision in the quarrel between the two goddesses:

> But then the Father Almighty, who holds first authority over the world, began to speak; and as he spoke, the gods' high hall fell silent, the earth deep down was set trembling, the steep sky was soundless, and then too the west winds sank and the ocean hushed its surface.

10.100:

> Tum pater omnipotens, rerum cui prima potestas,
> Infit, eo dicente deum domus alta silescit
> Et tremefacta solo tellus, arduus aether,
> Tum Zephyri posuere, premit placida aequora pontus.

[5] For this formal reason alone—a formal criterion always has *primum gradum certitudinis* in a classical work—Friedrich, "Exkurse zur Aeneis," *Philologus*, 1940, is wrong when he suggests that Virgil had planned to discard Jupiter's speech in the final draft and to introduce Jupiter himself for the first time in the assembly of the gods in Book 10. The reconciliation in Book 12.791ff. demands their presence in the first. This does not diminish the correctness of Friedrich's suggestions on the temporary prop character of the verses introducing and ending the conversation.

Heaven and earth, the winds, and the sea are silent; the wild forces of nature, all elements bow to him.[6] Compared to the other gods he represents not only a higher power but a higher level of existence. And in this he differs from the Homeric Zeus. Zeus is stronger than the other gods, Jupiter more sublime.[7] We do not see Jupiter shaking the universe with his scowl as Zeus does, but as imposing reverence on it. (Only at the close of the scene is the famous verse from the *Iliad* imitated: 10.115; also 9.106.)

In Jupiter is most clearly manifest the divine power that binds the demonic forces and the basic strength of Latinity, *serenitas*—which includes in one untranslatable word, mental clarity, cheerfulness of soul, and the light of the southern sky. From the image of the Virgilian Jupiter the concept of *serenitas* has remained alive in the intellectual history of the successor states of the Roman Empire into our own time; for example, in the words with which Romain Rolland late in life described the human task: *"la liberté de l'esprit qui sereine l'anarchie chaotique du coeur."*

Virgil's Jupiter is the symbol of what Rome as an idea embodied. While Juno as the divine symbol of the demonic forces of violence and destruction does not hesitate to call up the spirits of the nether world: *"Flectere si nequeo superos, Acheronta movebo,"* Jupiter is the organizing power that restrains those forces. Thus, on a deeper level, the contrast between the two highest divinities is symbolic of the ambivalence in history and human nature. It is a symbol, too, of the struggle between light and darkness, mind and emotion, order and chaos, which incessantly pervades the cosmos, the soul, and politics. A spiritual path leads from this level of contrast directly to the historical concepts of the Christian Middle Ages as stated by St. Augustine.

The struggle and final victory of order—this subduing of the demonic which is the basic theme of the poem, appears and reappears in many variations. The demonic appears in history as civil or foreign war, in the soul as passion, and in nature as death and destruction. Jupiter, Aeneas, and Augustus are its conquerors, while Juno, Dido, Turnus, and Antony are its conquered representatives. The contrast between Jupiter's powerful composure and Juno's confused passion reappears in the contrast between Aeneas and Dido and between Aeneas and Turnus. The Roman god, the Roman

---

[6] The Stoics had the idea of a lord of the universe. See Cleanthes' hymn to Zeus: "And the universe obeys trembling, where it is hit by the force of the lightning" (Wilamowitz).

[7] Zeus, too, has sublime traits. But Virgil's Jupiter would never argue from physical strength, as the primitive god of the *Iliad* does (especially 8.5ff.).

hero, and the Roman emperor are incarnations of the same idea.

Therefore, as the result of inner necessity, Jupiter, in the concluding speech of the initial sequence of scenes, announces that the idea of Augustus' *pax Romana* rests upon the conquest of *furor impius*. At this strongly emphatic place the basic idea of the whole poem becomes visible in a symbolic picture:

> And the terrible iron-constricted Gates of War shall shut; and safe within them shall stay the godless and ghastly Lust of Blood, propped on his pitiless piled armory, and still roaring from gory mouth, but held fast by a hundred chains of bronze knotted behind his back.

IV.294:

> Claudentur Belli portae. Furor impius intus
> Saeva sedens super arma et centum vinctus aenis
> Post tergum nodis fremit horridus ore cruento.

This is the best example in the *Aeneid* of a symbol which condenses a historic event into a single image.[8] This image, still trembling with the bloody events of the civil wars, climaxes and ends the speech of the god, thus channeling the wild motions of human life into the quiet order of the divine *fata*. After the *"altae moenia Romae"* which significantly concludes the proem and the *"tantae molis erat Romanam condere gentem"* which ends the section beginning with *"musa mihi causas memora,"* a view opens for the third time on the real object of the poem—the destiny of Rome. Moreover, the symbolic meaning of Roman history reveals itself here as a divinely inspired order—the result of hard fighting and bitter suffering.

Jupiter and Juno surround the storm at sea and into this larger frame is fitted the smaller one of Aeolus and Neptune. The contrast between Aeolus' ominous calm and Neptune's buoyant ocean voyage corresponds to that of Juno's uncontrolled temper and Jupiter's serenity. The wind-king reins his wild forces with the hand of a Roman master—a gesture without parallel in Homer:

> But Aeolus, the king who rules them, confines them in their prison, disciplined and curbed. They race from door to bolted door, and all the mountain reverberates with the noise of their resentment. But Aeolus, throned securely above them, scepter in hand tempers their arrogance and controls their fury.

---

[8] The image itself is Greek. I mention the painting of Apelles, showing Alexander with the lightning, the Dioscurs, and Nike on a triumphal chariot, followed by War with hands tied behind his back. Servius says that there was such a representation of Furor Bound in the forum of Augustus.

1.52:

> Hic vasto res Aeolus antro
> Luctantis ventos tempestatesque sonoras
> Imperio premit ac vinclis et carcere frenat.
> Illi indignantes magno cum murmure montis
> Circum claustra fremunt, celsa sedet Aeolus arce
> Sceptra tenens mollitque animos et temperat iras.

Here, political history may be sensed in the nature myth. The relation of Aeolus' mastery of the winds to Augustus' conquest of *furor impius* is easily seen. And it becomes even clearer in the Neptune scene.

The sea god, great Neptune, both in his actions and appearance of contained power, in allaying the raging storm is like Jupiter, a contradiction of brute force.[9] Moreover, the taming itself, in a simile emphasized by being the first in the poem and not taken from Homer, is compared to a political act:

> It had been like a sudden riot in some great assembly, when, as they will, the meaner folk forget themselves and grow violent, so that firebrands and stones are soon flying, for savage passion quickly finds weapons. But then they may chance to see some man whose character and record command their respect. If so, they will wait in silence, listening keenly. He will speak to them, calming their passions and guiding their energies. So, now, all the uproar of the ocean subsided.

1.148:

> Ac veluti magno in populo cum saepe coorta est
> Seditio saevitque animis ignobile volgus

[9] 1.126:   graviter commotus et alto
> Prospiciens summa placidum caput extulit unda.

Also 154ff. On the "contradiction" between *graviter commotus* and *placidum caput extulit unda* Sainte-Beuve remarks: "Il n'y a pas là de contradiction pas plus que dans le *mens immota manet, lacrimae volvuntur inanes.* Si un homme ferme et qui a pris un parti pénible, peut verser des larmes sans que son coeur soit ébranlé, un dieu peut bien être ému au dedans, sans que cette émotion ôte le charactère de haute placidité à son front." One might go further and say that Aeneas, Neptune, and Jupiter all represent the taming of passion. Man does this with much pain, God with sublime serenity. Winckelmann in the famous passage on "noble simplicity and quiet grandeur as outstanding characteristics of the Greek masterworks" quotes the lines:

> tum pietate gravem ac meritis si forte virum quem
> conspexere, silent arrectisque auribus adstant

to illustrate the placid quiet of the majestic figures in Raphael's "Attila and Leo the Great."

Iamque faces et saxa volant, furor arma ministrat,
Tum pietate gravem ac meritis si forte virum quem
Conspexere, silent arrectisque auribus adstant,
Ille regit dictis animos et pectora mulcet:
Sic cunctus pelagi cecidit fragor.

The above has been interpreted as alluding to a political event of the year 54 B.C., when in a similar manner Cato calmed the raging populace (Plutarch, *Cato Minor*).[9a] Such an allusion is not impossible. The republican Cato was the ideal Roman in Virgil's eyes and appears as such on Aeneas' shield in contrast to Catiline, who is shown doing penance for his crime (8.760).

Sallust had already idealized Cato by introducing him in his *Coniuratio Catilinae* as the incarnation of the principles of Roman grandeur[10] and probably had conceived of the Cato-Catiline contrast as a simile of the conflict (seen in the *Aeneid*) between Octavian and Antony. There is also an ideal image of Cato in Horace's Roman ode, *Iustum et tenacem propositi virum*. The heralds of the Augustan renaissance, Sallust and Cicero (especially in his lost *Cato*), and the poets of the renaissance, Virgil and Horace, each in his own way pays homage to the most uncompromising representative of the Roman mind and attitude. For the Augustan Age, too, Cato embodied the ideal of a true Roman—which is indicative of the spirit of reconciliation toward Caesar's opponents and of the seriousness of the intent to restore the Republic.

However, for the very reason that I am willing to accept the possibility of a connection between an event in the political career of Cato Uticensis[11] and the first simile of the *Aeneid*, I must emphatically declare that it means very little. Even to Sallust, disciple of Thucydides, Cato was no more than an ideal type of Roman statesman, just as the conspiracy of Catiline was no more than a symptom of Rome's decay. The poet's mind, then, is not intent upon Cato nor on any historical individual, but definitely on the *idea* that the individual personifies—in this case, the idea of the statesman whose authority dominates the crowd. He gives to the idea the form of a poetic symbol—of transfigured reality.

The champions of the allegorical interpretation of the *Aeneid* obscure the fact that equations purporting to balance historic and

[9a] R. S. Conway, "Poesia ed impero," *Conference Vergiliane* (Milano, 1931).
[10] Cp. Pöschl, *Grundwerte roemischer Staatsgesinnung in den Geschichtswerken des Sallust* (Berlin, 1940), p. 10.
[11] As in Horace, it can be no more than a vague memory. *Pietas*, although it may be ascribed to Cato, is not the first virtue by which he is distinguished.

poetic personalities are not only unverifiable but are a priori false—
at least as postulated. The mistake is in confusing symbol and
Allegorie: a symbol may exist even without reference to what takes
shape within it, while the *Allegorie*[12] exists only through that reference. The symbol permits, even demands, more than one interpretation, the *Allegorie* allows only one.[13] The nobility and style of
the *Aeneid* exclude the *Allegorie* that can be completely unlocked
with a political or historical key. To resolve the heroic epic into
Allegorie, then, is to misunderstand both its validity as an ideal
and its artistic character. Its scenes may from time to time recall or
point symbolically to real events and persons, as with Cato or the
monster Cacus (8.185ff.), whose actions, as Conway believes, perhaps
unveil the atrocities of Antony's proscriptions.

The true relation between these scenes and historic fact is more
mysterious and less simple. The metamorphosis takes place on a
higher plane.[14] Historic events and the poet's inner experience are
stripped of everything accidental and actual. They are removed
from time and transported into the large and distant land of Myth.
There, on a higher plane of life, they are developed in symbolic
and poetic shapes having a right to an existence of their own. The
fact, therefore, that the subjection of the storm is described in a
simile for a moment highlighting a very important sphere of the
poem (namely that of the historical world) is more decisive than a
possible allusion to the younger Cato. In the *princeps rei publicae,*
where Cato calms the riotous populace, we meet political reality in
a situation representing the defeated antithesis of Augustan order.
Then, the historical background of the mythical events becomes
momentarily visible.

The idea of regulation is expressed five times in the first sequences
of scenes in the *Aeneid:* where Aeolus holds the winds in subjection,
where Neptune calms them, in Aeneas' reaction to fortune's blow,
where Augustus chains *Furor impius* in Jupiter's prophecy, and
finally in the power of the god himself, who firmly controls the *fata.*
To find no more than commonplace Roman metaphors in the
Roman gesture of Aeolus and in the simile of Neptune and the

[12] Translator's note: There is no English counterpart for the German *Allegorie,* which by definition admits of only one meaning, something in the
nature of a large parable.

[13] Cp. also Friedrich Gundolf, *Shakespeare und der deutsche Geist* (Bonn,
1911), p. 1: "Symbol is essence, coincides with the thing, represents its being.
Allegorie points to something which it is not."

[14] This shows the way in which the results of Conway and of D. L. Drew, *The
Allegory of the Aeneid* (Oxford, Basil Blackwell & Mott, Ltd., 1927), have to be
modified.

princeps rei publicae is to destroy the poem's unity of form and content as well as to fail to understand that it has a deeper unity than is commonly assumed. In the Neptune episode, for example, a natural event explained by means of a political event serves to show that nature is a symbol of political organization. The connecting simile becomes an expression of the symbolic relation between nature and politics, myth and history, which is at the heart of the *Aeneid*. As in the *Georgics* the relation between the two orders is not only a matter of poetical metaphors but of ontological realities. Jupiter, the master of the world, controls them both. Their unity finds its most sublime expression in the religious and philosophic revelation in the sixth Book.

It is more, then, than hyperbolic expression that Augustus sets the limits of empire with the ocean and those of his glory with the stars. Cosmic infinity is united with the majesty of *imperium Romanum*. The conviction that Roman order is founded in the same divine whole from which it derives its grandeur[15] is important to the Augustan view of the world. It is also basic to the interpretation of the Roman *res publica* in Cicero's *de Republica*. Virgil adheres to Cicero's philosophical views. He accepts the Platonic idea of the unity of Cosmos and Politeia from which came the Ciceronian idea of the unity of world order and true *res Romana*. He combined this with the Homeric belief that the unity of nature is incorporated in the human world. He thus created a new synthesis—the Augustan idea of Rome.

Even where it involves natural phenomena, the myth of Aeneas is a metaphor of Roman history and its Augustan fulfillment. But it does not stop there. The *Aeneid* is a poem of humanity, not a political manifesto. In it, myth and history acquire meaning and grandeur as expression of a higher level, the realization of a divine order, the symbol of the cosmic law of destiny revealed in the existence of the world of man. There are three levels of reality: (1) Cosmos, the sphere of divine order, the world of ideas and law; (2) Myth, the heroic world of poetic persons and destiny; (3) History, the world of historical and political phenomena. These are inlaid, one with another, and at the same time they are stratified. Myth, as the poetic intersymbol, partakes of both the upper and lower strata. In one direction it incorporates Roman history, and in the other, the eternally valid laws of the universe. Likewise, the tragedy in the *Aeneid* is a symbol not only of the tragedy in Roman history,

---

[15] Cp. Klingner, "Rom als Idee," *Die Antike*, 3 (1927), 3, and *Das neue Bild der Antike*, 234.

but in human life as well. Indeed, it is a symbol of the tragedy in all nature and is found in its most sublime expression in the *Georgics*.[16] Alone, neither of these interpretations would do justice to the poetic depth of the *Aeneid*. Virgil's epic must always be approached with both references, cosmic and Roman, human and historical, in mind. Each is justified and necessary, but only together do they make possible an understanding of the whole.

Here, then, is our result: the initial sequences of scenes in the *Aeneid* contain in essence all forces which constitute the whole. The opening storm is a wave breaking against Roman destiny. Many waves will follow and Augustus will subdue them all, thus limiting the *Imperium* with the ocean and its glory with the stars. The demand made by Goethe upon the drama, that each scene must symbolically represent the whole, is fulfilled in the exposition of the Virgilian epic in an ideal manner.

The Storm at Sea (1.8-296) and the Allecto Scenes (7.286-640) as Initial Symbols of the "Odyssey" and "Iliad" Halves of the Aeneid

In the two parts of the *Aeneid*, the *Odyssey* and the *Iliad* are fused to create a higher unity. As early in the work as the proem, a reference to the recreation of the *Odyssey* is made: *"Multum ille terris iactatus et alto,"* while *"multa quoque et bello passus"* refers to the *Iliad*. Possibly, as Servius believed, *arma* in the very first line refers to the *Iliad* and *virumque* to the *Odyssey*. The storm sequence (1.8-296) is significant, therefore, not only as an introduction to the whole but as the first great trial of Aeneas. It is the frontispiece, as it were, of the "Odyssey," half of the poem. The storm is followed by further trials: the Odysseus-like wanderings of Aeneas (3), his Dido adventure (4), the *Iliupersis* (2) and the games (5). (The *Iliupersis* probably stems from the Trojan War memoirs in the *Odyssey*, especially as contained in Nestor's and Menelaos' speeches in the *Telemachy* and Demodokos' song of the destruction of Troy.)

The storm at sea, the first motif from the *Odyssey*, and the other Homeric passages in the first Book adhere more closely to the model than do those of the following Books. This fact has been already recognized by Sainte-Beuve in *Étude sur Virgile* (2nd ed., p. 107): "This first eclogue, I mean the first chronologically, is scattered

[16] "The field of the epope, if it is worthy of its name, claims so to speak the co-operation of the whole nature, a complete view of the world between heaven and earth." Herder, *Adrastea*, X. Stueck, v.24.281 Suphan.

with Theocritus' most graceful images, just as the first book of the *Aeneid* is decked with Homer's most famous and conspicuous similes. He (Virgil) displays and presents them at the beginning and in the most obvious places. Far from being embarrassed by this, he takes pride in it."

Moreover, in the first Book it is not a question of appropriating individual motifs and using them in situations of different character, but rather of transposing situations of vital significance to the story. The following come from the *Odyssey:* the hostile divinity's planning of the catastrophe, the catastrophe itself, the hero's monologue of despair, the "Phorcys harbor," the exhortation *O socii* (1.198), Aeneas' encounter with Venus—transposed from that of Odysseus with Athena in Ithaca, invisible Aeneas' walk through Carthage—Odysseus' unseen arrival in the Phaeacian city, the meeting with Dido—the Nausicaa simile, Aeneas' appearance before Dido in the goddess-given guise of a dazzlingly beautiful godlike stranger, the conversation between Jupiter and Venus—after that of Zeus and Athene in the first Book—and the *cantus firmus* of Jupiter's speech —the theme of the poem.

The idea of giving the whole poem a higher meaning at the very beginning of the divine father's speech comes from the *Odyssey,* where Zeus, in referring to Orestes' destiny, points to the murder of the suitors as the climax of the story and establishes punishment of guilty mortals as the primary theme. Although Virgil in Aeneas' first two speeches (1.94 and 1.198) consciously emphasizes his debt to Homer through verbatim appropriation of the beginning words (1.94/*Ody.* 5.306; 1.198/*Ody.* 12.208), he subsequently develops his theme independently, going beyond Homer. Likewise, the drama of the Carthaginian queen begins with Homer's Nausicaa simile, but develops in the *Aeneid* into the tragedy of Dido—not another Nausicaa episode. The scene sequence at the beginning of the poem is simultaneously an indication of Virgil's deep respect for Homer and an example of his competition with him. The more openly he attests his dependence upon Homer, the more ambitiously he strives to surpass him in the perfection of the form and the interpretation and connection of motifs. For this reason the first Book offers the most favorable conditions for comparing the two poets and for understanding Virgil's artistic principles.

In contrast, the Odyssean motifs in the remaining books are handled much more independently. As concerns the *Iliupersis* (2), this is well known. In the Wanderings (3), where a close conformity to Homer might certainly be expected, Virgil is more concerned with the melancholy echoes of the past (Polydorus, Helenus, Andromache) and the gradual revelation of the future than with the adventures themselves. The main interest is not in the physical terrors of the journey, but rather in Aeneas' deepening spiritual sorrow as more and more he realizes the importance and greatness of his mission. Echoes of the *Odyssey* are scarce. The theme of feminine attraction, only hinted at in Homer's Calypso, Circe, and Nausicaa, is elevated into tragedy in the figure of the deserted woman, Dido, and Aeneas' concomitant trial (4). The games differ widely from those of Homer in the manner of the contests (5). Finally, Aeneas' journey to the underworld is much more than just one adventure among many. Like the encounter with Dido, it has become a trial of the hero, a test of his *pietas,* and a revelation of the symbolic meaning of the whole poem (6). Surpassing Jupiter's speech in the first Book, this contains the most comprehensive interpretation of the poem. Here the connection of the legend with the two spheres of which the poetical partakes—universal order and the Roman order of the world—is most patently visible. In the mythical form of a visit to the underworld from where it is singularly possible to observe the world and its otherwise mysterious machinations from a distance,[17] Aeneas realizes the connection of mortal life with world order and that of his own destiny with the history of Rome. Again, the existence of a firm relation between divine and Roman order is shown. The former is announced by Phlegyas: *"Discite iustitiam moniti et non temnere divos"* ("Take this warning, and learn justice, and not to neglect the gods"), and the latter is revealed by Anchises at the end of the book: *"Tu regere imperio populos Romane memento"* ("You, Roman, remember to rule peoples under your sway"). Justice is the foundation of both and is also the first principle of the Platonic-Ciceronian concept of *res Romana*. It is brought about in the underworld as in ours through the subjugation of demonic forces, great criminals, and lawbreakers.

Violators of world order—those who rebel against the rule of Jupiter (6.583ff.)—are confined behind a triple wall in Tartarus to pay forever for their crimes. There, too, are the instigators of ruthless war (*"qui arma secuti impia"*: 6.612f.). The inner connection of motifs is betrayed in the affinity of the triple wall (6.548ff.) with the mountain of winds and that of the gate of Tartarus with the gate of Janus. In the "Roman" Tartarus on Aeneas' shield, Catiline, chained to the rock, represents the enemies of the Roman state (8.668ff.—this was excluded from Book 6 for "chronological

---

[17] Cicero's *Somnium Scipionis* is another variation of the same form, as remarked by Norden.

reasons"). Thus, Dante's idea of having great political criminals do penance in purgatory is founded on Virgil.

Inasmuch as the first Book clings comparatively closely to the motifs of the *Odyssey,* and the other books stray farther from this model, it is noteworthy (and I believe it to be the result of conscious intention) that of all the books of the "Iliad" half of the *Aeneid,* the last contains the greatest number of transferred situations. Conversely, the seventh and eighth Books are the least *Iliad*-engenered, while the sixth Book may be considered the most Virgilian of the first or "Odyssey" half. (Book 6 shows the influence of Apollonius rather than of Homer.) Virgil with his wonderful sense of balance permeating the whole poem thus achieves perfection: he rises from the narrowly Homeric to his own zenith and returns again to Homer. Within the Homeric shell lies the Virgilian kernel.

The Allecto scenes symbolizing the tragic mood of the last half of the poem (7-12) correspond to the dramatic tempest introducing the disastrously fateful atmosphere of Aeneas' "Odyssey" in the first half (1-6). Heinze[18] has shown that these two groups of scenes balance each other perfectly, particularly in both beginning with Juno. This correspondence proves that the interpretation of the storm as a beginning symbol represents the poet's intention and is not an arbitrary assumption. As this symbolization is the obvious function of the Allecto scenes which have no Homeric model, the same must be true of the storm (according to the law of strict symmetry for classical composition). Therefore, the parallel function of the scenes as "symbolic" overture to both parts of the epic may be added to the correspondences noted by Heinze.

The demonic force of nature in the first Book, then, is paralleled by the demonic force of the historical world in the seventh. And inasmuch as the *Iliad* is more majestic than the *Odyssey,* the "Iliad," or second, half of the *Aeneid* is greater than the first:

A greater sequence of events opens before me, and I now begin a grander enterprise.

7.44:

Maiorum rerum mihi nascitur ordo,
Maius opus moveo.

Accordingly, in the last half, the power of the hostile fate that rises against the Trojans has grown considerably: Allecto's acts are incomparably wilder and more demoniac than those of Aeolus' winds.

---

[18] Richard Heinze, *Virgil's epische Technik,* 3rd ed. (Leipzig, 1915), p. 82.

And while the storm at sea develops an Odyssean motif, Virgil has become independent of Homer. He dares, as Homer did not, to introduce the powers of Hell into the action of the story. It appears to me highly improbable that Ennius would have had a comparable sequence of scenes, although (as Norden[19] has shown) he contributed some details and prefashioned some important traits of Allecto in his Discordia. There is, however, a considerable difference between Ennius' war demon, Discordia, and Virgil's fury, Allecto.

Allecto's hellish nature is revealed in three scenes: the increasing delusion of Amata,[20] the dramatic violence of Turnus' dream, and the fast-moving hunt for Silvia's stag. She first appears as a snake to invest Amata with her serpent's spirit (7.351), then as the torch thrust into Turnus' heart (456), and then as the sudden madness of Ascanius' dogs (479).

The first of these scenes, particularly, serves to translate the demonic character of Allecto into impassioned movement and thus contributes to the heightened action. Heinze, the first to inquire into its meaning, concluded that the motif was not fully utilized owing to a "lack of clarity in the treatment." [21] There is, however, no lack of clarity and the poet is not, as Heinze suggested, primarily interested in finding a new reason for the outbreak of war.[22] Fried-

---

[19] On *Virgil and Ennius,* Norden (Berlin, 1915) and S. Wiemer, *Ennianischer Einfluss auf Vergil's Aeneis VII-XII,* Greifswalder Beitraege zur Literatur-und Stilforschung (Greifswald, 1933).

[20] The intensification is mentioned more than once: 7.354ff., 374.

385: Quin etiam in silvas simulato numine Bacchi/majus adorta nefas major-emque orsa furorem/evolat.

This would explain that, as Heinze says, we hear at first of "simulated" madness (*"simulato numine Bacchi"*), and then of the real thing (*"reginam Allecto, stimulis agit undique Bacchi"*). There would then not necessarily be a contradiction. But *"simulato numine Bacchi"* does not signify "simulated" madness. *Numen* here, as in 1.8: *"quo numine laeso"* and 7.583: *"bellum perverso numine poscunt,"* is the will of the goddess. The phrase means that she pretends the will of the gods, as if Dionysos had ordered her to go to the woods, but not that her madness itself is pretended.

[21] Heinze, *op. cit.,* p. 187. The connection with the beginning of the war is sufficiently clearly stated through the verses:

7.580ff.: Tum, quorum attonitae Baccho nemora avia matres
         Insultant thiasis neque enim leve nomen Amatae
         Undique collecti coeunt Martemque fatigant.

The mothers who belong to Amata's *thiasos,* take Turnus' side against Aeneas; they are for war and they, of course, influence their sons.

[22] For the war was sufficiently motivated by the success of the new suitor who upsets the queen's and Turnus' plans and the hunting crime against the stag of Silvia.

rich has noted correctly that the *"impotentia"* of the Trojans' adversaries is symbolically expressed here. The object was to symbolize unleashed passion as well as the insanity of civil war. The war is a "civil war" because the Trojans and Italians, from the very beginning conceived of as belonging together, are destined for peace through assimilation. But the scene has a formal reason too: Virgil found it necessary to prepare the war events with a sequence of wildly moving scenes. High pathos and the spirit of tragedy fills the first of these. The Bacchic ecstasy of the Maenads, treated as tragic motif in several of Euripides' plays, may have seemed especially suitable for this purpose.[23] The Dido tragedy is similarly constructed.[24] In both places the image of furious movement in the form of the nocturnal *thiasos* marks a tragic development. The deeper justification and artistic sense of the scene are to be found, therefore, in the inner emotional sequence of the poem. Here at the start of a tragic development it demands the *élan terrible* of a furiously pressing movement, because the poet wished to create an introductory symbol for the "Iliad" half in the form of an *allegro furioso e appassionato* leading to war.[25] At the same time he wanted to give symbolic expression to his concept of war as a creation of Hell, a godless crime and sinful mania.[26] For such a presentation he could borrow nothing of value from Homer to whom this concept was alien.

[23] The raging of the Sibyl (6.77), is connected with the war prophecy through the motive of "divine madness."

[24] 4.68: Totaque vagatur urbe furens compared with

7.376: Ingentibus excita monstris
immensam sine more furit lymphata per urbem.

4.300: Saevit inops animi totamque incensa per urbem
Bacchatur, qualis commotis excita sacris
Thyias, ubi audito stimulant trieterica Baccho
Orgia nocturnusque vocat clamore Cithaeron.

[25] It would have been impossible to achieve a movement of similar force through the Turnus scene (7.406ff.) or the hunting scene (476ff.) alone.

[26] 7.461: scelerata insania belli

7.583: Ilicet infandum cuncti contra omina bellum
contra fata deum perverso numine poscunt.

Latinus calls the war a crime that must be expiated:

7.595: Ipsi has sacrilego pendetis sanguine poenas
O miseri. Te, Turne, nefas, te triste manebit
Supplicium votisque deos venerabere seris
Latinus 12.31: arma impia sumpsi
11.305: bellum importunum, cives, cum gente deorum
invictisque viris gerimus.

The Virgilian Diomede (11.255ff.) also considers the Trojan war a crime.

The three scenes are composed with a rising pitch, swelling mightily toward tempestuous movement. The first scene spins toward the whirling frenzy of the Maenads in the lonely woods, the second plunges toward Turnus' madness which is then compared to a cauldron boiling over (an image of growing movement in itself), and the third mounts to the uncontrollable commotion of war—to the tidal wave of the Italian army as it gathers in response to Allecto's call:

> Now they sought decisions by their two-edged [27] blades. War's standing crop stretched afar, iron-gray with the shudder of drawn steel. Bronze gleamed under the sun's reflection, and flashed light upwards against dark clouds; as when at a wind's first breath waves begin to whiten, and gradually the sea rises and builds them higher, until at last it leaps from all its depths to the sky.

7.525:

> Sed ferro ancipiti decernunt atraque late
> Horrescit strictis seges ensibus aeraque fulgent
> Sole lacessita et lucem sub nubila iactant,
> Fluctus uti primo coepit cum albescere ponto,
> Paulatim sese tollit mare et altius undas
> Erigit, inde imo consurgit ad aethera fundo.

The above is based on the Homeric simile (*Iliad* 7.63):

> The ranks were set close, and bristled with shields and helmets and spears, as the waves of the sea ripple and crinkle[28] when the west wind blows it black.

Inspired by other parts of the *Iliad* (2.457 and 13.338; cf. 4.422ff.; 13.795ff.; 14.394ff.; 15.381ff.) and perhaps by Ennius, Virgil added the brilliantly glancing reflection of the weapons, which, in an intensification based on Homer, he compares to the white crests on a dark sea (*Iliad* 14.696ff.). However, he was so caught up in the accelerating movement and the crescendo of the outbreak of war that he augmented the whole effect with the simile of the storm becoming a hurricane. This simile embodies the strong pressure and excitement of Juno's presence. It is part of the rhythm of the whole poem. Here, one of the most important principles of Virgil's art becomes effective—the striving for unity, or as Woelfflin called it in a lecture entitled "The Classical," "the principle of assimilation" (the forms

[27] Meant also symbolically in reference to the dark end of the war.

[28] Hermann Fränkel, *Die Homerischen Gleichnisse* (Goettingen, 1921), explains φρίξ as "shimmering blinking" (*blinkendes Flimmern*).

assimilate each other): "the work of art is organized into self-supporting parts, unified by homogeneous imagery and a moving rhythm common to every detail." [29] The tendency to compose whole scene sequences aimed at one goal serves the same purpose—dramatic development. A goal-directed movement is dramatic, while one seemingly without a goal is epic.[30] Virgil's art would be inconceivable without the Greek drama, for that is where the idea of unity first found a perfect poetic form by bringing all parts under the law of the whole. Although this idea is present in the Homeric epic, as emphasized by Goethe in his letter to Schiller of April 28, 1797 (in contrast to Schlegel and Wolf),[31] it is not completely executed. In the *Aeneid,* the unity is complete. It is symptomatic of the ignorance of Virgil among Germans that he does not play a role in the discussion between Goethe and Schiller concerning the nature of the epic, even though the epic "fulfills its nature" only in the *Aeneid.* Virgil was the first to give the epic that closed form for which, contrary to Schlegel's opinion, it had been destined from the beginning. He was the first to give it its "classic form."

Besides rising independently toward an image of increasing movement, the Allecto scenes combine into a larger unit. If the images climaxing each scene are compared, it is evident that they are suitably attuned to each other. Amata's orgiastic frenzy, the surge of boiling water, the whirling black steam of Turnus' cauldron, and the developing hurricane of the war host are increasingly emphatic symbols of uncontrollable elementary forces. And the last of these—the storm at sea, the most powerful manifestation of Nature in action—is the strongest symbol imaginable. Points of comparable function in the framework of composition are accentuated by related symbols and so we see that such a storm occurs at the beginning of both the "Iliad" and "Odyssey" halves of the *Aeneid.* When Latinus, broken and full of disastrous foreboding, finally yields to fate, and when Juno breaks open the iron gates of the temple of Janus, the feeling of unleashed movement is so vivid, the

---

[29] Sainte-Beuve has stressed this principle: "Cette qualité souveraine qui embrasse en elle et unit toutes les autres et que de nos jours on est trop tenté d'oublier et de méconnaître: je veux parler de l'unité de ton et de couleur, de l'harmonie et de la convenance des parties entre elles, de la proportion de ce goût soutenu, qui est ici un des signes du génie, parce qu'il tient au fond comme à la fleur de l'âme et qu'on me laissera appeler une suprême délicatesse."

[30] But this boundary is fluid. Homer shows the beginning of unifying "dramatic" presentation and Aristotle demands drama from the epic (*Poetics* c. 23).

[31] As proved especially by Schadewaldt, *Iliasstudien* (1938). Emil Staiger, *Grundbegriffe der Poetik* (Zurich, 1946), points out that in Homer the stress is on the episode, not on the unity (p. 124f.).

principle of harmonious forms so efficient, and the rhythm, carrying and sweeping away the events like a swollen torrent, so strong, that Latinus is compared to a rock amid the breakers (7.586ff.; cf. *Iliad* 15.618ff.). He perceives the fatal outbreak as a hurricane, in the face of which human power cannot prevail (7.594: *"Frangimur heu fatis, inquit, ferimurque procella"*: " 'We are wrecked, alas, by the fates,' he said, 'and driven by the storm' "). Once again the image of the storm and shipwreck serves as the symbol of destiny.

As a unit, the Allecto scenes clearly show the poet's artistic skill in creating ascending, accelerating movement. From the measured gesture of the hopeful line, *"Sublimes in equis redeunt pacemque reportant"*: "High on their horses' backs they return, and bring back news of peace"),[32] which inaugurates Juno's interference, the story becomes increasingly dark and tense as it heightens for the outbreak of war. Yet to appreciate fully this gradual intensification of plot, it is necessary to return to the book's beginning, for the story grows from the blessed morning peace of the Tiber landscape to the tempestuous movement of the resplendent, armored host. The poet strives for external contrast throughout the Book. In order to enhance the power of the movement, he begins with a tranquil and distant scene. Thus, we see that the inner development of the seventh Book is the reverse of that of the first; the latter develops out of storm and tension through the quasi-serious meeting with Venus[33] to the pleasantly joyful Dido audience and the solemn banquet at the end. Conversely, as we have seen, the seventh Book opens in tranquillity which is subsequently replaced by increasingly turbulent movement rising toward the roaring finale of the Italian war hosts, a pageant crammed with violent *élan* and wild power, like a triumphant glorification of all the tribes of Italy.

[32] The poet intentionally put the word *pacem* at the end of the first passage of the seventh Book. Juno's interference which leads to war, follows immediately.

[33] The scene opens with the serene verses 1.314ff., and it closes with the bright glamor of Paphos (1.415f.), but the tragic tone is not absent. It is heard in Aeneas' speech (1.371) in *crudelis tu quoque mater* and in the tale of Dido's life.

Chronology of Important Dates

B.C. 70   Birth of Virgil at Andes near Mantua

60   First Triumvirate (Caesar, Pompey, Crassus)

49-45   Civil war between Caesar and Pompey; defeat of Pompey at Pharsalus (48); death of Pompey in Egypt and subjugation of his followers

44   Ides of March, death of Caesar

43-42   Civil war between Caesar's heirs (Octavian and Antony) and his murderers (Brutus and Cassius)

42   Battle of Philippi, defeat and death of Brutus and Cassius

41   Civil war between Octavian and Antony

40   Reconciliation of Octavian and Antony, Peace of Brindisi

37   Publication of the *Eclogues*

32   Civil war breaks out again between Octavian and Antony

31   Battle of Actium, defeat of Antony and Cleopatra

29   Publication of the *Georgics*

27   Octavian takes the title Augustus

23   Publication of Horace's *Odes,* Books 1-3

19   Death of Virgil at Brindisi

   Publication of the *Aeneid*

Notes on the Editor and Authors

STEELE COMMAGER, editor of this volume, is the author of a critical study of Horace's *Odes,* and is Associate Professor of Greek and Latin at Columbia University.

SIR MAURICE BOWRA, Warden of Wadham College, Oxford, has edited the Oxford text of Pindar, and is the author of numerous works, ranging in subject from early Greek elegy to Edith Sitwell.

R. A. BROOKS was formerly a member of the Classics faculty at Harvard University, and is now a business consultant in Boston.

WENDELL CLAUSEN, editor of the Oxford texts of Juvenal and Persius, is Professor of Classics at Harvard University, and preparing a book on Hellenistic influences on Latin literature.

The late THEODORE HAECKER, German metaphysician and theologian, was best known for his studies of Kierkegaard.

BERNARD KNOX, formerly Professor of Classics at Yale University, is now Director of the Center for Hellenic Studies in Washington, D.C. He is the author of two studies of Sophocles, *Oedipus at Thebes,* and *The Heroic Temper.*

The late C. S. LEWIS, poet and novelist, author of studies on the Middle Ages and the Renaissance, is best known for his *The Allegory of Love.*

R. W. B. LEWIS, who is well known for his studies of Melville, Hawthorne, and Edith Wharton, is Professor of English and participant in the American Studies Program at Yale University.

BROOKS OTIS, Chairman of the Classics Department at Stanford University, is the author of numerous articles on Classical and Medieval literature, as well as of the recently published *Ovid as an Epic Poet.*

ADAM PARRY, Associate Professor of Classics at Yale University, has written articles on Plato and Homer and is preparing a book on the history of Greek literature.

JACQUES PERRET is Professor at the Sorbonne, and author of a recent book on Horace.

VIKTOR PÖSCHL is Professor of Latin at Heidelberg. He is the author of studies on Cicero and, most recently, on the *Eclogues* of Virgil.

BRUNO SNELL, editor of Pindar and Bacchylides, is the author of *Poetry and Society* and *Scenes from Greek Drama.*

Selected Bibliography

Comparetti, Domenico. *Virgil in the Middle Ages,* trans. E. F. Benecke. New York: The Macmillan Company, 1895. A study of Virgil's influence.

Cruttwell, R. W. *Virgil's Mind at Work.* Oxford: Basil Blackwell & Mott, Ltd., 1946. An intricate analysis of certain symbols in the *Aeneid.*

Drew, D. L. *The Allegory of the Aeneid.* Oxford: Basil Blackwell & Mott, Ltd., 1927. A study of the relationship between Aeneas and Augustus.

Duckworth, George E. *Structural Patterns and Proportions in Vergil's Aeneid.* Ann Arbor: University of Michigan Press, 1962. A mathematical analysis of the structure of the *Aeneid,* emphasizing its closeness to the proportions of the "golden section."

Eliot, T. S. "Vergil and the Christian World," in *On Poets and Poetry.* New York: Farrar, Straus & Co., Inc., 1957.

Eliot, T. S. "What Is a Classic," in *On Poets and Poetry.* New York: Farrar, Straus & Co., Inc., 1957.

Graves, Robert. "The Virgil Cult," *Virginia Quarterly Review,* XXXVIII (1962), 13ff. An attack upon Virgil and his admirers, T. S. Eliot in particular.

Greene, Thomas. *The Descent from Heaven.* New Haven: Yale University Press, 1963. A comparative study of the epic, with one chapter on the *Aeneid.*

Havelock, E. A. "Virgil's Road to Xanadu," *Phoenix,* I (1946), 3-8; II, 2-7; III, 9-18. A study of the *Georgics,* particularly the fourth, and of the influences upon them.

Highet, Gilbert. *Poets in a Landscape.* London: Hamish Hamilton, 1957. Contains a chapter on Virgil and his background.

Jackson Knight, W. F. *Roman Vergil.* London: Faber and Faber, 1944. A comprehensive study of Virgil, particularly interesting on language and style.

Lewis, R. W. B. "Homer and Virgil: The Double Themes," in *Furioso* V (1950), 47ff. A comparison of the *Aeneid* and the *Odyssey.*

MacKay, L. A. "Hero and Theme in the Aeneid," in *Transactions and*

Proceedings of the American Philological Association XCIV (1963), 157ff. A study of Aeneas as an epic hero.

Myers, F. W. H. *Essays Classical,* London: The Macmillan Company, 1883. Contains a brief general section on the *Aeneid.*

Nelson, Lowry, Jr. "Beaudelaire and Virgil," *Comparative Literature,* XIII (1961), 332ff.

Pöschl, Viktor. "The Poetic Achievement of Virgil." *Classical Journal,* LVI (1961), 290ff. A short general appreciation of Virgil.

Putnam, M. C. J. *The Poetry of the Aeneid.* Cambridge, Mass.: Harvard University Press, 1965. A close study of Books 2, 5, 8, and 12 of the *Aeneid.*

Quinn, Kenneth. *Latin Explorations.* London: Routledge and Kegan Paul, 1963. Contains an essay on Dido and on Virgil's narrative technique.

Rand, E. K. *The Magical Art of Virgil.* Cambridge, Mass.: Harvard University Press, 1931. A comprehensive study of Virgil.

Ridley, M. R. *Studies in Three Literatures.* London: J. M. Dent & Sons, Ltd., 1962. An examination of the possibilities of the Greek, Latin, and English languages for poetry.

Rose, H. J. *The Eclogues of Virgil.* Berkeley and Los Angeles: University of California Press, 1942.

Van Doren, Mark. *The Noble Voice.* New York: Henry Holt & Co., 1946. Includes a markedly unsympathetic essay on Aeneas.

Wilkinson, L. P. "The Intention of Virgil's *Georgics,*" in *Greece and Rome,* XIX (1950), 19ff.